Suzy Bowler is a professional chef and hotelier turned freelance food writer. She spent many years cooking on an island where food supplies were limited and unreliable and became an expert in adapting, using and making something out of nothing. Now she shares her know-how of ingredient-inspired cooking with hundreds of suggestions for using every conceivable leftover.

D0242155

Other titles

Creative Ways to Use Up Leftovers

Suzy Bowler

A How To Book

ROBINSON

Leabharlanna Poibli Chathair Baile Átha Cliath
Dublin City Public Libraries

ROBINSON

First published in Great Britain in 2018 by Robinson

Previous edition first published in Great Britain in 2013 by Spring Hill, an imprint of How To Books Ltd., as *The Leftovers Handbook*

10 9 8 7 6 5 4 3 2 1

Copyright © Suzy Bowler, 2013, 2018

The moral right of the author has been asserted.

All rights reserved.
No part of this publication may be reproduced, stored in a retrieval system, or transmitted, in any form, or by any means, without the prior permission in writing of the publisher, nor be otherwise circulated in any form of binding or cover other than that in which it is published and without a similar condition including this condition being imposed on the subsequent purchaser.

A CIP catalogue record for this book is available from the British Library.

ISBN: 978-1-47214-054-8

Typeset in Great Britain by Mousemat Design Limited
Printed and bound in Great Britain by Clays Ltd, St Ives plc

Papers used by Robinson are from well-managed forests and other sustainable sources

Robinson
An imprint of
Little, Brown Book Group
Carmelite House
50 Victoria Embankment
London EC4Y 0DZ

An Hachette UK Company
www.hachette.co.uk

www.littlebrown.co.uk

How To Books are published by Robinson, an imprint of Little, Brown Book Group. We welcome proposals from authors who have first-hand experience of their subjects. Please set out the aims of your book, its target market and its suggested contents in an email to Nikki.Read@howtobooks.co.uk

Contents

Introduction

Whole libraries of books have been written on frugality and being green – this isn't one of them!

Creative Ways to Use Up Leftovers is about getting the utmost pleasure out of every single scrap of food available to you. The waste it tackles is not so much about money or resources but of good eating opportunities. As a bonus, of course, this will save you money and may even help the planet.

Of all the foods in the world, leftovers are my favourite ingredient and using them my favourite way to cook. Whenever I find myself with random bits and pieces to use up, I am delighted and frequently inspired. I enjoy the challenge of making a good meal out of something that would otherwise be thrown away, and then I enjoy eating it! It's an imaginative, fun and economical way of discovering new ideas and new dishes, some of which are so successful that they become family favourites.

So what do I mean by 'leftovers'? In this book, I use it fairly loosely to include:

- **Genuine leftovers** Either the tail end of a made-up dish or the last few scraps of ingredients which are surplus to the requirements of a recipe.
- **By-products of cooking** Things like Parmesan rind or potato skins, for example.
- **Excess** Too much of something, having been over-enthusiastic when picking blackberries or taking advantage of two-for-one offers.
- **Storecupboard scraps** Things that have been forgotten that were lurking at the back of the cupboard, such as 1 tbsp marmalade or half a packet of peanuts.
- **Snippets** Small quantities of things you wish you had more of, like two squares of chocolate when there are four friends.
- **Accidents** Such as what to do with the packet of biscuits you sat on.
- **Collections** It is a good idea, when you have just a little of something left, to group together similar scraps and leftovers

(e.g. meats, seafood, bread) in the fridge or freezer, as appropriate, and add to them till you have enough to make something delicious.

By their very nature, leftovers are random and unpredictable, so almost all the ideas and many of the recipes in this book are flexible and open to interpretation. In some cases, I haven't even given directions, I have just mentioned a possibility. Additionally as I am dealing with leftovers I may not adhere strictly to traditional recipes and apologise if I have left out 2g of butter here and a touch of wild hyssop there! And while I do touch on the obvious at times, I have assumed that most people who cook realise that if they have leftover bananas, then banana bread is an option and that spare egg whites often lead to meringues. My main intention is to suggest ideas that you may not have thought of.

When I started writing the book, I began with perhaps 200 food items, which I had divided into the usual chapters on meat, fish, vegetables and so on. But as I kept coming up with more and more ideas, it soon became obvious that listing them alphabetically was the only way to go. Once I realised that, the rest of the book was easy (pause for laughter!). There have been many, many recipes that I wanted to include but I couldn't honestly get them to fit even under my broad definition of leftovers.

The main body of the book therefore comprises an A to Z of foods that fit into the leftovers categories described above. But don't expect neat sections all the same length. U, X and Z, for example, have few, if any, entries, while C is massive!

Whilst I have tried to make this handbook as all-encompassing as possible, I had to stop somewhere, so I decided not to include long-keeping storecupboard items such as vinegar, oil, flour, sugar, dried spices or condiments; they can't really be called genuine leftovers.

To save space and avoid repeating myself, I put some foods into groups:

- Beans and pulses
- Beer
- Cheese
- Fish
- Herbs

- Nuts
- Offal
- Seeds
- Shellfish
- Spirits and liqueurs
- Wine and fortified wine

Each entry is organised in the same way so that you can quickly find your way around. Here's how it works.

Food heading
Most entries start with complementary flavours and affinities. There's quite a lot of information out there on food pairing but I have relied on my own palate and experience when listing what goes with what. Do feel free to disagree!

❄ Under this icon, the next paragraph tells you how to store and freeze the leftovers.

- **Ideas** Followed by all my ideas for what to do with leftovers.
- **Quick tips** Plus all kinds of ways to make the best of what you have.

HANDY HINT or COOK'S TREAT
Every now and then you'll find Handy Hints and Cook's Treats.

The A to Z is followed by two further chapters: Basic Recipes and Guidelines, which is referred to throughout the A to Z, and Your Storecupboard, a list of all the ingredients I think are essential, very useful, nice-to-have extras with notes on my personal peccadilloes. It is not much use having delicious leftovers and a good idea if you need to go shopping to complete the dish.

I am so very lucky to have been a chef for over 30 years and I have loved almost every minute of it. And I am even luckier that 16 of those years have been spent living and working (resting and playing) on the beautiful little island of Tortola in the British Virgin Islands, where the climate is fabulous, food supplies limited, deliveries unreliable and customers as pernickety as they are anywhere, so the best use of everything available was important to me. Back in Britain and seeing so much good food being thrown away, I have decided to tell people what to do with it, so to speak.

The A-Z of Leftovers

A

Aïoli – see also Mayonnaise

This rich garlic mayonnaise, traditionally served in Provence with salt cod and all sorts of veggies, is also good with roasted meats, pretty well all fish dishes, raw and steamed vegetables and fried potatoes.

❄ Keep well covered in the fridge for a few days.

- **Dip** Serve with a selection of crudités or with chips (English or American!).
- **Fish** Top crab cakes or other fried fish with a spoonful of aïoli.
- **Garlic bread** Spread the cut sides of a split baguette or thick slices of bread with aïoli, sprinkle with freshly grated Parmesan and bake in a preheated oven at 180°C/gas 4 until crusty on the outside and soft and delicious in the middle.
- **Meat** Aïoli is good with roasted meats – spread some in a chicken or roast beef sarnie, for instance.
- **Soups and stews** Stir into fish soups and stews in general and bouillabaisse-type dishes in particular, or try with a dish of mussels.

Alfalfa

Alfalfa tastes good with avocado, mild creamy cheeses, hummus, sesame seeds, and good bread and butter.

❄ Wrap cut alfalfa loosely in damp kitchen paper and then in an open plastic bag and it will be okay in the fridge for a couple of days. Don't even think about freezing it.
- **Sandwiches and salads** I can't think of a lot to say about alfalfa (which is a shame this being so early in the book!) other than add to sandwiches, salads or use as a pretty garnish.

A

Almond paste – see Marzipan

Although not exactly the same – marzipan being higher in sugar content
and more pliable – all my ideas in this respect are under Marzipan.

Almonds – see Nuts

Amaretti – see also Biscuits

The almond flavour of amaretti enhances and is enhanced by apricots,
cherries, peaches, nectarines and raspberries; brandy, coffee, vanilla and,
surprisingly, butternut squash and pumpkin.

❄ Store in an airtight container.

- **Breadcrumbs** Either replace or extend the breadcrumbs in
  treacle tart with crushed amaretti.
- **Creamy desserts** Sprinkle crumbled amaretti onto creamy
  desserts and ice cream or, even better, on Affogato (p150) or
  use as a crunchy layer in fools, mousses and sundaes.
- **Crumble** Add crumbled amaretti to fruit crumble topping
  (p290).
- **Peach and amaretti mess** For each serving, coarsely chop 1
  ripe peach and toss with 1 tbsp soft light brown sugar and 1 tsp
  brandy, if you wish. Macerate for an hour or so, then fold the
  peaches and their juices into a small dish of whipped cream
  together with a handful of broken amaretti.
- **Simple amaretti-stuffed peaches** Halve 4 fruit and remove
  the stones. Crush 2 handfuls of amaretti and work into 2 tbsp
  softened butter together with 1 tbsp soft light brown sugar,
  then spoon it into the hollows of the peach halves. Bake in a
  preheated oven at 180°C/gas 4 until crisp and serve, if
  possible, with clotted cream.
- **Squash** At the last minute, so as to retain their crunch,
  crumble amaretti and sprinkle onto squash dishes such as
  soup, pasta and risotto.
- **Truffles** Use to coat ice cream truffles (p150).

Anchovies – salt-packed or in oil

The strong flavour of anchovy goes well with capers, olives, lemon, garlic, potatoes, lamb, white fish, eggs, Parmesan-type cheeses and Mediterranean-style tomato dishes.

❋ Make sure anchovies in oil are completely covered with oil and salt-packed anchovies in salt and store them in a sealed container in the fridge. Anchovies can be frozen in a freezer bag with all the air squeezed out.

- **Anchoïade** A dip or spread from Provence, this can be made by pulverising garlic and anchovies together in a mortar or mini food processor and then gradually working in olive oil to your desired consistency. The ratios are about 1 garlic clove per 30g anchovy with 40ml olive oil. It's common to add 1 tbsp red wine vinegar, as well as some chopped parsley, black pepper and chopped almonds.

> **HANDY HINT**
> For a milder taste, soak oil-packed anchovies in cold milk for 10 minutes, pat dry, and if you know a cat give them the milk to drink. Salt-packed anchovies can be desalinated in the same way (apart from the bit about cats) using white wine vinegar instead of milk.

- **Anchovy butter** Mix soaked, drained and dried anchovies (see Handy hint above) together with twice their weight in unsalted butter, mashing well (p316). Add other seasonings such as capers, crushed garlic, black pepper, chopped fresh herbs, grated lemon zest but probably not salt. Serve slices atop steak, lamb or fish.

- **Anchovy croûtons** Mash an anchovy into 2–3 tbsp olive oil and season with grated lemon zest, black pepper, chilli flakes or crushed garlic and use to make croûtons (p45).

> **COOK'S TREAT**
> Crush an anchovy onto hot toast and then top with ... a spoonful of clotted cream!

- **Anchovy crumbs** Stir 2–3 coarsely chopped anchovies and 50ml olive oil together over a medium heat until the anchovies appear to have melted. Add 2 handfuls of fresh breadcrumbs and continue to cook, stirring, until they are crisp and golden. Drain on kitchen paper and sprinkle over pasta or fish dishes, cauliflower or egg mayonnaise. In some cases, the addition of a little grated Parmesan cheese is a boon.

- **Anchovy puffs** Spread some pastry scraps with anchovy butter (see above). Fold in half, enclosing the butter, and cut into shapes – little fish are fun. Glaze with beaten egg and bake in a preheated medium hot oven at 180°C/gas 4 for 12–15 minutes until puffed and golden.

- **Bread** Make anchovy or Caesar bread (see Compound butters p288).

- **Caesar butter** Mix some freshly grated Parmesan and crushed garlic into anchovy butter (above).

- **Classic Caesar dressing** Blend together 2 anchovies, 2 garlic cloves, 1 tbsp lemon juice, ½ tsp Dijon mustard, 60g grated Parmesan and 2 egg yolks. When completely blended, slowly add 120ml olive oil, whisking or blending, until emulsified. Taste and season, it probably won't need much salt but Worcestershire sauce and a generous amount of black pepper are good. Use to dress a salad of romaine lettuce and crunchy croûtons, then sprinkle with more Parmesan. For a convincing cheat, leave out the egg yolks and olive oil and instead fold the mixture into about 300ml ready-made mayonnaise.

- **Egg dishes** Cook finely chopped anchovy in with scrambled eggs (p298).

- **Fish** Add a little crushed anchovy to fishcakes or to mashed potato topping for a fish pie (p112).

- **Fish sauce** Make a quick sauce for pan-fried fish. Melt together 1 tbsp each of butter and olive oil and stir in 1 tbsp chopped capers, a couple of chopped anchovy fillets, a handful of chopped parsley, and 2 tbsp lemon juice.

- **Italian salsa verde** Anchovies are usually included in this fresh herb sauce (p142).

- **Light anchovy vinaigrette** Blend together 2 anchovies, 2 garlic cloves, 1 tbsp lemon juice and whisk in 3 tbsp olive oil.

- **Mayonnaise** Mash anchovy into mayonnaise for seafood salads or egg mayonnaise.

- **Mozzarella in Carrozza** Heat a chopped anchovy in a little olive oil with a squeeze of garlic and pour over Mozzarella in Carrozza (p69).

- **Pizza** Coarsely chop and scatter on top of pizza or make a pretty pattern with thin strips.
- **Potatoes** Tuck a few anchovies in with the potatoes in scalloped potatoes (p305) for a simple take on Janssen's Temptation, a traditional Swedish dish.
- **Tapenade** Anchovies are often included in this olive and caper sauce (p188).
- **Tomato sauce** Perk up tomato sauce with a little anchovy (I mean a little; just an eighth of an anchovy or so) cooked with the garlic and onion at the start of a recipe. It will dissolve in the sauce, adding a certain something without being intrusive.
- **Tuna** Add to Salade Niçoise or Tuna Tonnato (p118).
- **Vinaigrette** Add a little of the oil from a can of anchovies to vinaigrette for a certain *je ne sais quoi*; taste and salt carefully, if at all.

Apples

Apples go with pork, bacon, ham, sage, cinnamon, lemon, onion, cheese — particularly Cheddar, blackberries, cranberries and other berries; walnuts and other nuts; celery, squash, cabbage and horseradish.

❆ Store in a cool place for four weeks or even longer but do remove any apples that are spoiling because, as you well know, 'one bad apple spoils the whole barrel'. If the apples are in a plastic bag, don't seal or tie it; they need to breathe. Cut apple can be kept in the fridge for three days, tossed with acidulated water (p281) to prevent browning and stored in a covered container or freezer bag. Raw apples don't freeze well.

Raw apple
- **Apple raita** Toss grated apple in lemon juice, then squeeze the juice over a glass (see **Cook's treat**). Use the apple instead of cucumber in raita (p279).
- **Apple Yorkshire pudding** Toss chopped apple in the hot fat and pour the batter over. Serve with pork (p284).
- **Cabbage** Shredded apple is great cooked in with red cabbage.
- **Cheese sandwiches** Add thinly sliced or grated fresh apple to cheese sandwiches — toasted or otherwise.

A

- **Coleslaw** Coarsely grate an apple, with its skin still on if you like, and toss with the juice of ½ lemon then and add it to coleslaw (p287).
- **Pumpkin soup** A little apple is a delicious addition (p216).
- **Roast apple and vegetables** Toss wedges of apple and parsnips or butternut squash together with a little olive oil, salt, pepper and sage, if you've got any. Roast until tender and starting to caramelise and serve with pork dishes or purée for a great-tasting soup.
- **Scalloped potatoes** Add a layer of thinly sliced apple to the potatoes (p305).
- **Sweet apple clafoutis** Serve for dessert (p285).
- **Waldorf salad** There are so many recipes for this classic, it's probably best to make up your own! Basically it consists of apple, celery and walnuts dressed with mayonnaise – but use your imagination. Popular additions include grapes, blue cheese, Cheddar, watercress, black pepper, chicken, shredded cabbage, raisins and cranberries ... but not necessarily all at the same time.

> **COOK'S TREAT**
>
> When you squeeze grated apple to extract the lemon juice (see Apple raita and Coleslaw), squeeze it over a glass. Add the apple to the recipe you are making, then add sparkling water to the lemony apple juice and enjoy a refreshing drink, because you're worth it!

Apple Cribbly

This is a great way to use up apples and leftover
bread simultaneously.

SERVES 2

1 medium apple (Granny Smith is good but use any leftover apple),
peeled, cored and diced
60g sugar
30g butter
2 slices of bread, cut into similar-sized dice as the apple

1. Toss the apple in the sugar to coat.
2. Melt half the butter in a frying pan until it foams, add the
   apples and cook, shaking and tossing, for 5 minutes or so until
   the apple is tender and beginning to brown and the juices are
   caramelising.
3. Remove the apple from the pan with a slotted spoon, add the
   rest of the butter to the pan and fry the bread, turning
   frequently, until crisp and golden.
4. Return the apples to the pan and toss all together until hot and
   the bread has absorbed some of the buttery juices.
5. Serve immediately with ice cream or clotted cream.

A

Using a Glut of Apples

apples, peeled, cored and sliced
sugar
1–2 tbsp water

1. Taste the apples and decide how much sugar you think you need. For 450g apples, you'll need somewhere between 2 tsp and 3 tbsp. Err on the mean side; you can always add more later.
2. Put the apples, sugar and water into a saucepan and toss together.
3. Cover and cook over a medium heat, stirring occasionally, until the apples are completely and utterly tender – 10–15 minutes.

> **HANDY HINT**
> If you use Bramley apples they are self puréeing.

4. Beat to a chunky purée with a wooden spoon, mash with a potato masher or liquidise for or a smooth finish. Taste and add more sugar as needed.

Cooked apple

❄ Cooked apple freezes well.

- **Apple crumble sundae** Layer up with ice cream and baked leftover crumble mix.
- **Breakfast** Top porridge, rice pudding or yoghurt with a spoonful of cooked apple.
- **Pork** Serve warm with roast pork or stir into pork gravy.
- **Potatoes** Add a dollop to potatoes when mashing (p304).
- **Salad dressing** Mix 50:50 with mayonnaise for an unusual dressing, which is good on coleslaw (p287).
- **Sandwiches** Spread onto bread when making cheese, pork, bacon or ham sandwiches or try a layer under the cheese when making cheese on toast.

> **COOK'S TREAT**
> If you have enough, make apple pie or crumble, if not, make little turnovers using pastry scraps and bake or fry in butter.

Apple juice

❄ Freeze cubes to add to sparkling water or other cold drinks.

● **Apple caramel sauce** Simmer 90ml apple juice until reduced by half, add 3 tbsp sugar and continue to simmer until the juice turns a good golden caramel colour.
Stir in a knob of butter, a spoonful of double cream and a pinch of salt. This is lush on ice cream, pancakes, waffles, and so on.

● **Apple sauce for pork** After cooking pork chops, deglaze the pan with apple juice, simmer until syrupy and add a little cream for a simple sauce.

● **Cabbage** Cook red cabbage in apple juice.

● **Mulled apple juice** Heat apple juice with a pinch of ground cinnamon, a strip of orange zest and a few cloves over a low heat for about 10 minutes. Strain and sweeten with sugar, honey or maple syrup to taste. Serve hot.

● **Pork** Add a splash of apple juice, or a few frozen cubes, to pork stews and gravies.

Apricots – see also Fruit

Apricot affinities include pork and ham, lamb, almonds, honey, brandy, dark chocolate, cinnamon, cardamom, ginger and vanilla.

❄ Keep under-ripe fresh apricots at room temperature until they ripen, then store in the fridge for four or five days. Toss cut apricot flesh with acidulated water (p281) and store well wrapped in the fridge for just two or three days. Freeze in syrup (p299).

● **Fruit salad** Include with your selection of fruits.

● **Sauce** Make a sauce or coulis and maybe thereafter a fool (p300).

Dried apricots – see also Dried fruit

❄ Dried apricots should be kept in a sealed bag or container in a cool dry place and will keep for up to a year in this state. They can also be frozen for a few months longer but there doesn't seem to be much point!

A

- **Breakfast** Mix into muesli, granola and other breakfast cereals.
- **Cakes** Add to your favourite cake or biscuit recipe.
- **Stuffing** Add chopped dried apricots to stuffing especially for pork or lamb (p45).

Artichokes, globe

This includes fresh, canned, bottled and frozen globe artichokes.
(For Artichokes, Jerusalem see Jerusalem Artichokes.)

Lemon, hot butter sauce, vinaigrette, ham – especially air-dried bacon, Dijon mustard, eggs, garlic, mayonnaise, mint, Parmesan and potatoes all go well with globe artichokes.

❋ Sprinkle raw artichokes with a little water and store in a sealed bag in the fridge where they will be happy for up to four days; pat dry before cooking. Raw artichokes do not freeze successfully. Refrigerate cooked artichokes and use within two days. Dip cooked artichokes in lemon juice or acidulated water (p281) before freezing.

- **Artichoke fritters** Add garlic and Parmesan to the basic recipe (p285).
- **Artichoke salad** Toss in a lemony vinaigrette (p312). Add mint, ham and/or Parmesan.
- **Artichoke sauce** Purée 1 artichoke with 2 tbsp soured cream, 1 tsp lemon juice, a sprinkling of chopped parsley, salt and pepper and use as a dip or sauce for fish.
- **Hot artichoke dip** Mix together equal quantities of coarsely chopped artichoke hearts, mayonnaise and grated Parmesan cheese with enough cream to make a dipping consistency. If you have any leftover spinach add it now! Taste and season, pour into an ovenproof dish and bake in a preheated oven at 180°C/gas 4 for 20 minutes until hot and turning golden. Serve with veggies and chunks of good bread for dipping.
- **Omelette** Add with leftover cooked potatoes and ham to frittata or omelette (p295– 97).
- **Pasta** Cooked artichoke hearts are good tossed with ham and pasta in Alfredo sauce (p281).

- **Pizza** Scatter over pizza before baking.
- **Potatoes** Toss chopped cooked artichoke hearts with Parmesan and a little garlic and layer with scalloped potatoes (p305).
- **Risotto** Coarsely chop and stir into risotto together with the last addition of stock plus appropriate flavourings such as garlic, Parmesan, mint, lemon, ham and so on (p306).
- **Salads** Potatoes, artichoke hearts, mayonnaise and chopped fresh mint make a deliciously different salad, or try leftover artichokes, spring onion, lemon, parsley and olive oil.
- **Tapenade** Crush or purée into tapenade (p188).

Asparagus

Asparagus is delicious with bacon and ham, especially air-dried, salmon, trout and white fish and with butter, eggs, black pepper, peas, lemon and Parmesan.

❄ Wrap the cut ends of asparagus in a damp piece of kitchen paper and keep in an unsealed bag in the fridge for a few days. Cooked asparagus will be fine in the fridge for three or four days. Freeze cooked asparagus tightly wrapped in a freezer bag, although it's not as good texture-wise when thawed; use in soup or pesto.

- **Asparagus pesto** Steam asparagus for about 7 minutes until tender but not at all mushy. Drain and purée with butter and Parmesan cheese for a simple sauce or with the classic pesto ingredients – garlic, Parmesan, olive oil and pine nuts – to be almost authentic (p137–38). Season, a squeeze of lemon may be to your liking, and stir through cooked peas or hot pasta, or serve as a dip.
- **Eggs** Asparagus is a natural in egg

> **HANDY HINT**
> Asparagus, helpfully, has a natural snapping point separating the tender spear and tip from the tough ends. I have tried making soup with the tough parts but they are too woody, however, they do make good stock. Just cover with water and simmer for about 30 minutes until very tender, then strain, pressing to extract as much juice as possible.

A

dishes (p294). Serve asparagus 'soldiers' with boiled eggs. Toss the raw soldiers in a little olive oil, salt and pepper and roast for just a few minutes in a preheated oven at 200°C/gas 6. You want to keep them crisp.

- **Pasta** Toss with cooked pasta and leftover ham in Alfredo sauce (p281).
- **Salads** Cut raw asparagus into very thin diagonal slices or shave into fine strips to add to salads or dress with a light vinaigrette.
- **Side dishes** Spread a dearth of asparagus around by making a pretty side dish of peas, sugar snap peas and asparagus tossed together in butter, or mix with buttery new potatoes.
- **Stir-fries** Asparagus is a great addition to stir-fries (p310).

Aubergine – aka eggplant, brinjal and baingan

Tomatoes, onions, sweet peppers, rice, lamb, yoghurt, Parmesan, curry spices, chilli and garlic all go well with aubergine.

❊ Keep fresh aubergine in the fridge for up to a week; cooked aubergine will be good for four or five days and can be frozen.

- **Goats' cheese melts** Sandwich two slices of aubergine around a slice of goats' cheese or other complementary ingredients and grill or fry until the aubergine is soft and charred and the cheese is gooey.
- **Grilled or fried** Brush 10mm thick slices of aubergine with olive oil, season (maybe with a pinch of cumin) and grill or fry until soft and charred. Eat with a dollop of yoghurt.
- **Roasted with veg** Toss diced aubergine with whatever you have from a selection of sliced or chopped onion, peppers and courgettes in a little olive oil, season with salt and pepper and add a crushed garlic clove. Roast in a preheated oven at 190°C/gas 5, stirring occasionally, for about 30 minutes until everything is tender and the onions and aubergines are beginning to char; they are delicious like that! Use as a side dish, a pizza topping, a sandwich filling or with pasta.

Avocado

Avocado goes well with seafood, with smoked meats such as chicken, turkey, salmon or bacon, with spicy food, fresh coriander, citrus fruits, mango, grapefruit, pineapple and even strawberry.

❊ Under-ripe avocados will not ripen in the fridge; keep them at room temperature and maybe pop into a brown paper bag with a ripe banana or other fruit to give them a bit of encouragement. Ripe, whole avocados will keep in the fridge for three or four days; cut, they will keep for just a couple of days and it is important to brush or rub any exposed flesh with lemon or lime juice to stop discolouration. Wrap tightly in clingfilm for the same reason. Discoloured avocado is perfectly edible, however, just not as pretty. Avocado flesh doesn't freeze well as it is but can be puréed with ½ tbsp citrus juice per fruit and frozen for three months or so.

> **COOK'S TREAT**
>
> For a quick snack, mash a ripe avocado, spread it onto hot toast and sprinkle with a little sea salt. Top with crispy bacon or add something spicy – Tabasco or fresh chilli perhaps.

- **Avocado salsa** Mix a finely diced avocado with 1 small chopped red onion, a handful of chopped coriander, a squeeze of fresh lime juice, a drizzle of olive oil and seasoning to taste.
- **Avocado vinaigrette** Purée ripe avocado with citrus vinaigrette and fresh coriander (p312).
- **BLT w A** Add sliced or mashed avocado to a BLT!
- **Breadcrumbed** Coat slices with flour, beaten egg and then breadcrumbs or panko and shallow-fry until crisp and golden. Serve with a vibrant, spicy tomato salsa.
- **Chilled avocado soup** Process ripe avocado with enough cold vegetable stock to give a good soup consistency. Add a squeeze of lime juice, 2 tbsp yoghurt, salt and pepper plus a dash of Tabasco, hot sauce or mint until perfect. Serve chilled.
- **Chunky guacamole** Crush together diced avocado, tomato and red onion, being heaviest on the avocado. Stir in a handful of chopped fresh coriander, a little fresh chilli, garlic and a squeeze of lime, taste and season. Purée, of course, for a smooth guacamole.

A

- **Face mask** To make a face mask for dry skin (or a quick disguise), mash a ripe avocado and spread it gently on the face, avoiding the eye sockets. Relax for 15 minutes, then wash off with warm water.

COOK'S TREAT

To make an avocado smoothie, blend ¹/₂ ripe avocado with a squeeze of lime juice, 150ml yoghurt and a sprinkling of chopped fresh mint.

- **Hot avocado and chicken broth** Add shredded chicken, diced avocado, diced tomato, coarsely chopped fresh coriander and a pinch of hot chilli powder to a good chicken broth. Bring to a simmer, taste and season with salt, pepper and a squeeze of lime. Remove from the heat, cover and leave to stand for 10 minutes or so for the flavours to meld. Return to temperature and serve with crisply fried strips of tortilla to garnish.
- **Salads** Toss into salads especially with seafood, bacon, chicken, grapefruit or mango.
- **Topping** Mix with chicken or seafood and mayonnaise to top bruschetta, crostini, etc (p45).

B

Bacon

Raw bacon

Bacon is good with tomatoes, avocado, cabbage, spinach, mushrooms, onions, potato, black pepper, most cheeses, beans and pulses, apple, bananas, liver, black pudding, chicken, seafood, maple syrup, peanut butter, eggs and breakfast.

❄ Raw bacon will keep, well wrapped, in the fridge for at least a week. It can be frozen for up to a month but after that it may start to go rancid so should be discarded.

- **Bacon salt** Just one rasher of bacon makes a useful amount of bacon salt. Cook the bacon in a preheated oven at 190°C/gas 5 until seriously overdone; not burnt exactly but unappetisingly dark and leathery-hard. Pat dry with kitchen paper, cool, then break into pieces and grind in a pestle and mortar with 1 tsp coarse sea salt per rasher. This keeps well in a sealed jar in the fridge and is lovely sprinkled on poached eggs, roast tomatoes, cheese on toast and any number of other things.
- **Haluski** Add to this Eastern European dish (p59).
- **Potatoes** Add diced bacon to scalloped potatoes perhaps with some tender cooked onion (p305) or make bacon fried potatoes. Fry coarsely chopped bacon until crisp, and set aside. Sauté some potatoes in the residual fat adding oil if necessary. When golden and crunchy, stir in the bacon bits and serve.
- **Soup** Add chopped bacon to the vegetables at the start of the basic recipe (p309). If the bacon is fatty you may need no other cooking oil.
- **Stuffing** Cook bacon scraps in with the onions when making stuffing (p45).

B

Caramelised Bacon

This is nicest with smoky bacon but all bacon is good when caramelised.

2 bacon slices
1 tbsp soft light brown sugar

1. Preheat the oven to 200°C/gas 6. Line a rimmed baking tray with baking parchment and grease well.
2. Dredge the bacon slices in the sugar.
3. Arrange them a little way apart on the tray and bake, turning the rashers now and then until caramelised, 10–15 minutes. The longer you cook it the crisper it will end up but it won't *actually* become crisp until it cools.
4. Cool to room temperature and serve within 3 to 4 hours.

Cooked bacon

❄ Cooked bacon will keep, well wrapped, in the fridge for three or four days and can be frozen tightly wrapped for up to two months.

● **Baking** Crumble rashers of cooked bacon and add to your mixture when cooking scones, pancake batter, bread and other baked goods. When fresh out of the oven, brush with warm maple syrup.

● **Chicken livers** Fold finely chopped bacon into chicken liver pâté or add to Bayou dirty rice (p77).

> **COOK'S TREAT**
> Crumble over vanilla ice cream and drizzle with maple syrup.

● **Eggs** Use in omelettes, frittata and scrambled eggs (p298).

● **Fish** Bacon is great in fishcakes (p114–15).

● **Gratin topping** Coarsely chop, mix with fresh breadcrumbs and grated cheese to sprinkle over gratin dishes before cooking. This is lovely on macaroni cheese.

- **Pastry** For an interesting pie crust, sprinkle crunchy bacon bits over rolled out pastry, fold and roll again.
- **Pizza** Add to pizza toppings, but remember it can be salty, so take care what you combine it with.
- **Popcorn** Toss freshly cooked popcorn with maple syrup and crunchy bacon pieces.
- **Potatoes** Add bacon to hash and potato cakes (p211–12).
- **Praline** When making praline, replace the nuts with dry and crunchy bacon pieces (p179).
- **Soups, salads and sarnies** Add to soups, salads and sarnies, such as BLT.

Bacon fat

It is said that Dyer's Hamburgers in Memphis deep-fry (which is surprising in itself) their burgers in the same batch of bacon fat that they started with in 1912, apparently they strain it, top it up and keep going. Bacon fat can be used pretty well wherever you might use butter or oil, but don't use it too often as it is a saturated fat.

❋ Bacon fat is of course, a by-product of cooking bacon. Strain warm, liquid fat into a clean glass jar, cover, chill and add more each time you cook bacon. It will keep for a very long time in the fridge.

- **Chicken** Pan-fry in bacon fat or use to brown the meat before making a soup, stew or casserole.
- **Croûtons** Give croûtons an added depth by cooking them in bacon fat (p45).
- **Eggs** Scrambled eggs are extra flavoursome cooked in bacon fat (p298).
- **Fish and seafood** These two are excellent cooked in bacon fat.
- **Greens** Especially delicious wilted in bacon fat. Try cabbage, kale and spinach, or shred Brussels sprouts and sauté until bright green and *al dente*.
- **Hot bacon bread** (p289). Use bacon fat instead of butter.
- **Liver** Cook in bacon fat – and it is extra delicious if you then

> **HANDY HINT**
> If you trim the fat from your bacon before you cook it, feed the trimmings to the birds, especially in winter – they love it!

sprinkle with any residual crunchy bacon bits. It's also a good fat to use when making chicken liver pâté (p78).

- **Pancakes** Savoury pancakes are especially delicious if cooked in bacon fat (p251).
- **Potatoes** Sauté potatoes or hash in bacon fat when making potato cakes (p212).
- **Red eye gravy** See page 90 for this unusual coffee-based sauce.
- **Refried beans** Use bacon fat instead of oil or other fat in this recipe (p32).
- **Risotto** Bacon fat makes an excellent base to start all kinds of risotto (p306).
- **Thickening sauces** Use to make a roux for a sauce or gravy, especially for pork.
- **Vegetables** Use to fry the base vegetables when making soup (p309).

Warm Bacon Dressing

This is particularly good for spinach salads and on grilled lettuce. If serving immediately, add a handful of crunchy bacon pieces.

120ml bacon fat
1 tsp honey or soft dark brown sugar
30ml balsamic vinegar
freshly ground black pepper

1. Warm the bacon fat if it's not already hot.
2. Whisk in the rest of the ingredients, peppering to taste.

Bagels – see also Bread

Leftover bagels can be used in any recipe that calls for leftover bread and, as they come in quite a variety of flavours, you can match the bagel to the dish. There is, however, one specifically bagel way to use them up.

- **Bagel crisps** Slice leftover bagels thinly and horizontally through the hole. Lay them on a baking tray, brush with oil and season to taste. Bake in a preheated oven at 180°C/gas 4 for 10–15 minutes until crisp.

Baguette – see also Bread
As with bread, baguettes go with anything within reason.

- **Crostini and similar** Baguettes are perfectly shaped to slice into rounds or diagonals to make crostini, croûtes, tartines and bruschetta.
- **Hot baguette sandwich** Split and fill with your chosen and possibly leftover ingredients; cheese is always good in these. Wrap in foil and bake in a preheated oven at 190°C/gas 5 for about 10 minutes until crusty on the outside and hot and maybe melty in the middle.

Pan Bagnat

This soggy sarnie from Nice is traditionally made using a round, flat country loaf but is pretty good using a chunk of baguette. It is often filled with Salade Niçoise (p118) but other delicious, moist, savoury ingredients work well too.

SERVES 2

1 baguette, cut in half lengthways
1 garlic clove
2 tbsp good-quality olive oil
filling such as Salade Niçoise, roasted vegetables, tapenade, ripe tomatoes and goats' cheese
sea salt and freshly ground black pepper

HANDY HINT
If you have an inordinate amount of filling, scoop out some of the crumb from the bread (and add to your leftover bread collection in the freezer) before bushing with oil!

1. Rub the cut surfaces of the bread with a little fresh garlic and brush with good olive oil.
2. Fill the sandwich with your chosen combination of ingredients that will moisten the bread and tickle your fancy. Season well with salt and pepper.
3. Put the top on the sandwich, press together firmly and wrap tightly in clingfilm.
4. Chill for several hours, preferably with a weight on top of it.
5. Unwrap and slice thickly to serve.

B

Baked beans – see also Beans and pulses

❄ Store unused baked beans in an airtight container in the fridge. They do freeze but are little mushy when thawed.

● **Soups and stews** Add to soups, stews and chilli. Rinse first so that they don't taste too baked beany.
● **Toast** Cheesy beans on toast, obviously.

Bamboo shoots

The big thing about bamboo shoots is their lovely texture rather than their mild, slightly sweet flavour, and they add great crunch to a variety of dishes.

❄ Drain, rinse and keep in water in the fridge, changing the water daily, and they will be okay for up to two weeks.

● **Salads** Toss bamboo shoots into salads.
● **Soups** Add a handful to noodle soups when serving.
● **Stir-fries** They add a lovely crunch when tossed in at the last minute (p310).
● **Vegetables** Add to Asian-style vegetable dishes.

Bananas

Bananas are complemented by warm, spicy flavours such as cinnamon and cloves, and also by coconut, brown sugar, rum, chocolate, toffee, coffee, nuts, peanut butter and, surprisingly, bacon.

❄ Bananas won't ripen in the fridge but, once ripe, they can be refrigerated for up to a week; the skin may turn brown but the fruit will be fine. To enjoy them at their best, bring to room temperature before eating. Banana flesh discolours quickly so if you want them to look pretty, toss in a little lemon juice to stop oxidation.

● **Facial** Make a facial to brighten the complexion. Mash an over-ripe banana with 1 tbsp honey, smooth onto the face and

leave for 20 minutes. Rinse off with warm water and
immediately look gorgeous.

Ripe bananas

- **Bananas and bacon** Wrap a peeled banana with bacon –
  streaky is best as it's fatty. Cook under a hot grill, turning after
  a couple minutes, until crisp. Serve as an unusual nibble or for
  breakfast.
- **Banana bread pudding** Make the
  Bread and No-butter Pudding (p50)
  adding some sliced banana with the
  diced bread. Use soft light brown
  sugar instead of caster sugar and add a
  tot of rum, if you have any, and/or a
  drop of vanilla extract and/or a little
  strong coffee to the egg mixture.
  Sprinkle with more brown sugar and
  cinnamon before baking.

> **COOK'S TREAT**
> Make a grilled or fried
> banana sandwich –
> add bacon, peanuts,
> peanut butter, jam, or
> whatever takes your
> fancy. Elvis Presley
> liked this sort of thing!

- **Banana Cue** A Filipino way of cooking firm bananas – don't
  use them if they are soft or they will be too mushy when
  cooked – and sweet potatoes (see Kamote Cue p254).
- **Banana fritters** Flavoured with brown sugar and a drop of
  vanilla or rum (p285).
- **Banana rum fizz** Blend together 2 scoops vanilla ice cream
  with $\frac{1}{2}$ chopped ripe banana. Divide between 2 glasses and add
  a good splash of both Kahlua and dark rum. Top up with chilled
  soda water.
- **Banoffee sundae** Layer up Caribbean banana thingy (p28)
  with ice cream and sticky toffee sauce.
- **Breakfast** Slice and add to breakfast cereal or mix into hot
  porridge and top with brown sugar – rum is optional.
- **Caramelised banana ice cream** Fold the Caramelised
  banana below or some Caribbean banana thingy (p28) into
  softened vanilla ice cream and freeze.
- **Caramelised bananas** Cut a peeled banana in half
  lengthways, brush the cut surface with melted butter, sprinkle
  with sugar and cook under a hot grill until caramelised. Serve
  with cream or ice cream.

B

- **Chocolate stuffed banana** Don't peel the banana but split open lengthways so you can fill it with coarsely chopped chocolate. Wrap the whole thing in foil and bake in a preheated oven at 200°C/gas 6 for 10 minutes or so. Unwrap carefully and spoon the melting chocolatey flesh directly from the skin into your mouth.
- **Desserts** Chop over ice cream sundaes and add to fruit salads.
- **Famous one-ingredient ice cream** Freeze ripe bananas, then purée in a food processor, scraping down the sides frequently. Suddenly it will turn into ice cream! Fold in nuts, chocolate, maple syrup or whatever you fancy after the ice cream has formed. Eat immediately or freeze for later.
- **Scones** Fill scones with Caribbean banana thingy plus a spoonful of clotted cream.
- **Smoothies** Many smoothie recipes use crushed ice, which dilutes the smoothie and is hard on your liquidiser. It's far better to just use a frozen banana (p26).

> **COOK'S TREAT**
>
> Frozen banana is surprisingly good to eat – peel a ripe banana, place it on a non-stick liner and freeze. Eat straight out of the freezer, maybe dunked in melted chocolate.

Caribbean Banana Thingy

This is what my sister and I called this dish in our first restaurant, during the 80s. When I went to the Caribbean and became familiar with their 'thingies', I found that they call this Bananas Foster, as they do in America.

SERVES 2

30g butter
60g soft light brown sugar
2 bananas, sliced
a few drops of vanilla extract
1 tbsp dark rum

1. Melt together the butter and sugar.
2. Add the banana and cook gently until soft and beginning to caramelise, turning the slices now and then.
3. Stir in the vanilla then remove from the heat and add the rum. Return the pan to the heat and flame the dish if you are brave enough but it's not essential.
4. Serve hot with cream or ice cream.

Banana Brittle

This is delicious to nibble or use to garnish ice cream and other desserts.

SERVES 2

60g butter
1 tbsp oil
6 tbsp sugar
2 bananas, thinly sliced

1. Preheat the oven to 180°C/gas 4.
2. Melt together the butter and the oil and brush over a baking tray to coat completely. Sprinkle with the half the sugar.
3. Arrange the banana slices on the tray in a single layer.
4. Sprinkle the rest of the sugar onto the bananas.
5. Roast in the oven keeping a vigilant eye on them. Every time a banana slice goes golden and looks crisp, set it aside on a plate. I say 'looks crisp' because it won't actually become crisp until it cools. Continue cooking until the plate is full and the baking tray is empty. This takes about 30 minutes.
6. Cool the brittle and store in an airtight container for 4–5 days.

Over-ripe bananas

❄ Mash over-ripe bananas with 1 tbsp lemon juice per banana and freeze in sandwich bags with the air squeezed out.

● **Baking** Use in banana bread and cake recipes.

B

- **Pancakes** Make banana pancakes or, even better, Caribbean Banana Thingy Pancakes (p283).

Barley

Leftover barley can be treated in much the same way as leftover rice.

- **Breakfast** Warm leftover barley with a spoonful of cream and serve with fruit, maple syrup or butter and cinnamon sugar.
- **Pretend barley risotto** Fry a chopped onion until soft and caramelising, add a crushed garlic clove and maybe some sliced mushrooms and cook all together for 1–2 minutes. Stir in the leftover barley and a little hot stock and, when heated through, finish with grated Parmesan.
- **Soup** Add a handful of cooked barley to soup.
- **Stir-fry** (p310).

Bean curd – see Tofu

Beans and pulses – see also Chickpeas

Chickpeas have a separate entry because they are rather special! For green beans see Peas and Green beans.

This section deals with leftover cooked or canned dried beans and pulses. Whilst they each have their own characters and affinities, they have a lot of similarities and are often interchangeable, particularly when leftovers are involved.

Generally speaking beans go well with garlic, pork products – particularly fatty ones – olive oil, smoky flavours, and spices, especially cumin, chilli and smoked paprika.

- **Almost instant black bean soup** Black beans, a good dollop of spicy tomato sauce or salsa and a little cream or milk processed together makes a good soup.
- **Bean cakes** Mash beans and mix in chopped onion, crushed garlic, herbs

> **COOK'S TREAT**
> Warm the beans, pile onto hot toast, top with grated cheese and grill until bubbling.

and spices; if a wee bit wet, bind with breadcrumbs. Form into flat round patties and coat in flour or crumbs. Shallow-fry until hot and crisp.

- **Bean salad** Use as many different beans as you like – it doesn't have to be three bean salad! Toss the beans with chopped onion and fresh herbs in a good flavoursome vinaigrette. Stir in any other ingredients you like, taste and season with salt and pepper.

HANDY HINT

If you are able to think ahead, it is best to dress beans whilst still warm – this way they absorb some of the dressing and become even tastier.

- **Egg dishes** Add to omelettes, scrambled eggs or frittata (p294–98).
- **Mashed beans** Purée beans with a spoonful of cream, butter or oil, season and serve in place of mashed potato.
- **Pizza topping** Scatter over pizza, add bacon, sausages or pork and spices.
- **Soups** Add beans to soups like minestrone, or make bean soup by replacing some or all of the potato in the basic soup with cooked beans and flavouring appropriately (p309).
- **Tuna vinaigrette** Dress white beans with lemon vinaigrette together with tuna fish (canned or fresh) plus whatever you can muster of chopped red onion, black pepper and parsley or rocket. Serve with crusty garlic bread.
- **West Indian rice 'n' peas** Try this tasty dish (p224).

Dips, spreads and hummus-like concoctions

Hummus is Arabic for 'chickpeas', and similar recipes using other beans really have no right calling themselves hummus (my recipe p301). The technique, however, lends itself to all sorts of delicious bean pâtés and dips. Basically purée the beans and flavourings with enough oil or other liquid to make a softish mixture, then fold in anything chunky, maybe just some whole beans, for texture. Here are some flavour suggestions.

- Cannellini beans, garlic or roasted garlic, lemon juice, parsley and olive oil.
- Black beans, olive oil, garlic, lime juice, toasted cumin, chilli and fresh coriander, then fold in tomato, avocado, red onion.
- Butter beans, feta, oregano, garlic, olive oil, then fold in

coarsely chopped black olives.
- Lentils, curry paste and a little yoghurt plus fresh coriander.

Mrs Beeton's Potted Beans

MAKES ABOUT 225G

125g cooked or drained beans
30g Cheddar cheese, grated
30g soft butter, plus extra for finishing
30g fresh breadcrumbs
salt and freshly ground black pepper
cayenne pepper

1. Pound together the beans, cheese and butter until fairly smooth.
2. Mix in the breadcrumbs and season to taste.
3. Press into a pot and top with melted butter.
4. Chill until needed and eat with hot toast.
5. This is open to a lot of variation – different beans, different cheeses, all sorts of herbs and spices, garlic, lemon, and so on.

Refried Beans

These are usually made with pinto or black beans but any soft cooked beans work well.

SERVES 2

1 small onion, finely chopped
1–2 tbsp bacon fat or vegetable oil
1–2 garlic cloves, finely chopped
125g cooked or canned beans, drained
a little liquid from cooking the beans or vegetable stock

1. Cook the onion in the bacon fat or oil until soft and starting to brown, stirring occasionally.
2. Stir in the garlic and cook for a few seconds.
3. Add some of the beans and slowly mash into the oil so that they fry whilst being mashed. Keep adding beans, mashing and frying until they are all incorporated.
4. Stir in a little stock or cooking water until the beans are slightly runnier than you envisaged; they will firm up somewhat.
5. Taste and season, salt may be all that is necessary but a little chilli powder, cumin and oregano would all be in keeping with the dish.

Bean sprouts

These are popular more for their crisp texture than their mild flavour so add leftovers to:

- **Stir-fries** (p310).
- **Salads**
- **Soups** Add at last minute just to heat through.

Beef – see also Meat

The flavour of beef is good with blue cheese, black pepper, brown sugar, onion, horseradish, mustard, red wine, soy sauce, tomatoes, mushrooms, chilli, garlic, ginger and in certain situations coffee and chocolate (see Coffee and Chocolate).

Raw beef

❊ Raw beef should be stored, well wrapped, in the coldest part of the fridge for two or three days and can be frozen.

- **Beef stock** Collect trimmings and scraps in the freezer until there are enough to make an effort worthwhile: 500g at least. Fat, sinew and gore are all fine for this.
- **Stir-fries** Add to stir-fries (p310) or Bulgogi (p36).

B

Beef Stock

This may not be a classic stock but it has served me very well. I like to add a spoonful to sautéed mushrooms, to steak pans when deglazing, to creamy sauces, and to anything that could do with a beefy boost. The fat can be used to fry your next steak.

MAKES 500ML

2 tbsp oil
1 onion, quartered
500g beef scraps, defrosted if frozen
red wine

1. Heat the oil in a large pan and add the onion and all the beef bits. Cook over a high heat, stirring occasionally, until everything is well browned.
2. Add enough water to cover generously, bring to the boil, cover, turn down the heat and simmer for at least 2 hours until you have a rich brown stock.
3. Strain into a clean pan, discarding the solids.
4. Add half as much red wine as there is stock and boil until the liquid had reduced by 75 per cent.
5. Cool, pour into an airtight container, cover and chill.

❄ This keeps very well in the fridge. As it cools, the fat rises to the top and solidifies thus sealing the dish. It can be frozen; freeze in cubes as it is strong and you may only need a little at a time.

It's always worth freezing steak trimmings and using them to make both of these recipes, in whatever quantity you want.

Peppered Steak Salad

salad leaves
balsamic vinaigrette (p312)
steak trimmings, cut across the grain into strips about 5mm thick
salt and freshly ground black pepper
a little olive oil
1–2 tbsp brandy
a little double cream

1. Toss the salad leaves in a little vinaigrette to coat.
2. Season the steak with salt and a serious dose of black pepper as this will be the dominant flavour in the finished dish.
3. Heat the oil in a large pan and sear the steak, which will be enough to cook it. Set aside somewhere warm whilst finishing the sauce.
4. Add the brandy to the pan (carefully and if using gas do this away from the flame) and a goodly sloosh of cream and simmer for a minute or so until thick.
5. Arrange the steak on the salad and pour over the sauce.

Bulgogi

Also known as 'fire meat', this is a delicious Korean dish of marinated and seared beef. It is often eaten wrapped in lettuce leaves together with rice and kimchi (pickled cabbage) but I prefer it in a stir-fry. This is my simplified version.

1 tbsp soy sauce
½ tbsp soft dark brown sugar
½ tbsp sesame oil
½ tbsp toasted sesame seeds
1 spring onion, thinly sliced diagonally
1 garlic clove, crushed
a generous twist of black pepper
a little finely chopped hot red chilli (optional but I like it)
steak trimmings, cut across the grain into strips about 5mm thick

1. Mix together all the ingredients, cover and marinate in the fridge for several hours or overnight.
2. Grill or pan-sear the steak over a high heat until browned and cooked to your liking – it doesn't take long, about 30 seconds each side.

Cooked beef

❄ Cooked beef will be fine in the fridge for four days and freezes well.

● **Chilli** Turn leftover cooked minced beef into chilli by reheating in a tomato sauce together with beans, chilli and ground cumin.

● **Cottage pie** Coarsely chop your leftover roast beef. Cook a chopped onion in a little oil or butter (beef dripping would be ideal) until very tender. Stir in leftover gravy and dilute, if necessary, with water, beef stock or red wine. If there is no leftover gravy, mix a little flour into the cooked onions to make a roux and then add beef stock to make a sauce. Stir in the chopped beef

> **COOK'S TREAT**
> Leftover stew is good on toast. Even lovelier with a little cheese grated over it.

and put into an ovenproof dish. Try stirring 1– 2 tsp horse-radish sauce into some mashed potato, spoon over the pie and bake in a preheated oven at 200ºC/gas 6 for about 30 minutes until hot throughout and the potato is touched with gold. You can also try sprinkling grated cheese on top of the pie for the last few minutes of cooking, just to melt it.

- **Pasta** Sauce pasta with leftover stew and in this case I like to sprinkle with crunchy breadcrumbs (p44).
- **Pies** Top leftover stew with pastry, mashed potato or big buttery croûtons (p45).
- **Sandwiches and stir-fries** Add leftover steak to sandwiches, salads, pizza or stir-fry.
- **Sloppy Joe** This is simply sweetened minced beef (add a little tomato ketchup and/or brown sugar) served on soft burger buns, or make a Sloppy Joe grilled cheese sandwich.

Beer, lager and stout

'Beer – helping white people dance since 1868.' Sign in The Jolly Roger Bar in Tortola

Generally speaking, beer goes well with beef, cheese, sausages, bags of crisps, and so on, but it does very much depend on the beer in question; as one would expect, dark beers tend to be good with red meats and light beers with chicken, pork and seafood.

- ❋ Keep leftover beer, covered, in the fridge for a day or two, it will go flat but that's fine for our purposes. Beer freezes well; do so in small portions for ease of use or maybe try making manly ice lollies!

- **Beer batter** An excellent batter can be made by simply whisking together seasoned self-raising flour with enough beer to give a coating consistency, about 100g flour to 150ml beer. If time allows, chill before using for an even crispier result.
- **Bread** Try replacing some of the liquid in a bread recipe with beer to make a particularly cheese-friendly loaf.
- **Cheese** Add a spoonful of leftover beer to potted cheese (p65).

- **Soups and gravies** Add a splash to suitable soups, stews and gravies for the last few minutes of cooking.
- **Stews** Replace some of the stock or wine in a beef stew with dark beer or light beer if cooking chicken or pork.

Ale and dark beer

Welsh Rarebit

Traditionally, Rarebit – which is not, as many people believe, a fancy name for plain cheese on toast – is made with ale.

20g butter
100g Cheddar or other hard cheese, grated
½ tsp mustard powder
a dash of Worcestershire sauce
60ml ale
4 slices good bread

1. Melt the butter and then mix in the rest of the ingredients, except the bread.
2. Toast the bread, spread with the cheese mixture and pop back under the grill until bubbling.

Beer Marinade for Beef or Venison

120ml dark beer
60ml soy sauce
4 tbsp dark brown sugar
salt and freshly ground black pepper

1. Mix everything together, pour over a steak or two and set aside for between 30 minutes and several hours.
2. Remove the steaks and pour the marinade into a small pan, bring to the boil and simmer for 5 minutes.
3. Season the steaks and cook as you wish, basting with the marinade for the last few minutes.

Lager

- **Mussels** Replace white wine with lager when steaming mussels.
- **Pork** Lager also works in pork casserole.
- **Stews** Use lager as some or all of the liquid in a beef stew: the Belgians do.

Stout
One's thoughts naturally turn to Guinness but there are others.

- **Burgers** For extra tasty, extra juicy burgers add a spoonful of stout to the minced beef.
- **Chocolate** Dark chocolate and stout go well together so try replacing some of the liquid in chocolate cakes and brownies with a few spoonfuls of stout.
- **Steak sauce** After pan-frying steak, deglaze the pan with stout, boil to reduce by about half, stir in a little soft light brown sugar and season to taste. A splash of soy sauce or balsamic vinegar is good in this, as is a knob of butter.
- **Stews** Replace some or all of the liquid in a beef stew with stout.

Mulled Ale

This recipe is from my grandmother's 1908 edition of
Mrs Beeton's Cookery Book.

1 quart good ale (that's 1.2 litres)
1 tbsp caster sugar
pinch each of ground cloves, freshly grated nutmeg and ground ginger
1 glass of rum or brandy

1. Bring everything but the spirit almost, but not quite, to a boil.
2. Remove from the heat, add the spirit, adjust sweetening and spicing to taste and serve.

B

Beetroot

The flavour of beetroot goes well with brown sugar, dill, horseradish, cloves, orange, apple, vinegar, mustard, soured cream, onions, game, oily fish, walnuts and goats' cheese but NOT school dinners.

My niece, when she was little, having heard of someone going as red as a beetroot thought that this was a measure of extremity so in my family we tend to run as fast as a beetroot, for instance, or be as happy as a beetroot.

❄ Store unwashed in a cool place for a couple of weeks. Don't freeze raw but it's fine when cooked.

- **Beetroot mash** When boiling potatoes for mash, wait until the potatoes are almost tender, then add a few pieces of leftover cooked beetroot just to soften and warm through. Drain and mash together with cream and butter in the usual way.

> **HANDY HINT**
> If you get beetroot stains on your hands, remove by rubbing with a piece of (leftover) lemon.

- **Coleslaw** Coarsely grate raw beetroot and add to coleslaw (p287).
- **Pink purée** Add a little beetroot to a white bean purée (p31) or to smoked fish pâté (p117) for both flavour and colour.
- **Potato** Add a layer or two of sliced cooked beetroot to scalloped potatoes (p305).
- **Red flannel hash** A traditional New England dish which includes beetroot and often corned beef (that is, salt beef, not out of a can) or bacon (p211).
- **Roasted roots** Beetroot makes a good addition to a dish of roasted root vegetables.
- **Salad** Make a simple beetroot salad with finely shredded beetroot, shredded apple or pear, red onion and a mustardy vinaigrette (p312).

> **COOK'S TREAT**
> Slice warm beetroot onto fresh toast, top with goats' cheese and grill – or make a goats' cheese and beetroot pizza.

- **Soup** Add cooked beetroot to the basic soup recipe for 1– 2 minutes before puréeing (p309).

Berries – see also Fruit and individual berries

Berries go well with cream, meringues, cereals, sugar, brandy and sunshine.

❄ Freeze whole; spread on baking trays to freeze and then pour into a freezer bag for storage. This means they'll be 'free flow' and not frozen together in a clump, so you can take as many or as few as needed.

- **Berry butter** Use about half as much mashed fruit as soft butter and sweeten to taste with sugar or honey. Serve on hot toast, scones, waffles and pancakes (p283).
- **Breakfast** Scatter berries over breakfast cereals or yoghurt and granola for a boost to start the day.
- **Coulis and fools** Mix puréed berries to make a coulis then blend or layer with sweetened whipped cream for a delicious fool (p300).
- **Crumbles and pies** Add to other fruit and top with pastry, a crumble mix or buttery breadcrumbs.
- **Drinks** Add individual frozen berries to drinks to cool, flavour and look pretty all at the same time.
- **Meringues** Make a mess! (p172).
- **Rumtopf** Berries are perfect candidates for Rumtopf (p120).
- **Smoothies** Add colour and flavour to summer smoothies with a selection of berries (p308).
- **Sudden sorbet** Put frozen berries into the food processor together with caster sugar to taste and process all together. Refreeze, giving it a mash every now and then to stop large ice crystals forming.
- **Vinegar** See raspberry vinegar under Raspberries and do something similar with whatever berries you have.

B

Biscuits – aka Cookies
Store in an airtight container, possibly near the sofa.

- **Cheesecake base** This is generally made with crushed digestives, but any not too exciting biscuit will work. Crush 125g broken or leftover biscuits to crumbs, sweeten according to the biscuit and mix with 90g melted butter. Press onto the base of your cheesecake container. This same mixture can also be layered up with mousse in pretty glasses.
- **Desserts** Sprinkle broken biscuits over yoghurt and creamy desserts, ice cream in general and Affogato in particular (p150).
- **Ice cream** Stir into ice cream for a cookies and cream variation.

Recycled Biscuit Cake

150g dark chocolate
100g butter
2 generous tbsp golden syrup
200g broken biscuits

1. Over a low heat, melt together the chocolate, butter and syrup until completely smooth.
2. Stir in the biscuits.
3. Turn into a suitable container such as a silicone loaf 'pan' and chill until firm.
4. Slice and enjoy with a black coffee on the side.

Blackberries – aka brambles – see Berries and Fruit
As we are all aware, these go well with apples but also with vanilla, cream, white chocolate and game.

❊ Use fresh blackberries as soon as possible, they deteriorate quickly.

Blackcurrants – see Berries and Fruit
These are quite tart and pair well with cream, meringues and other fruits.

Black pudding – aka blood pudding or blood sausage
This goes well with bacon and all porky items, with apple, rhubarb, onions, potatoes, beans and pulses, fish and shellfish, especially scallops.

❄ Keep in the fridge and go by the use-by date. Black pudding freezes well.

- **Bubble and squeak** Add crumbled black pudding to potato cakes (p212) or bubble and squeak (p211); leftover apple would be a good addition, too.
- **Burgers** Mix with ground pork and cook a tasty pork burger.
- **Deep-fried** Dip diced or sliced black pudding in seasoned flour, beaten egg and finally breadcrumbs and shallow-fry to hot, crisp and golden or coat in flour and then batter (p282), and deep-fry.
- **Kedgeree** Add to this smoked fish and rice dish (p116).
- **Salads** Sauté crumbled or broken pieces in a little oil until crisp and black (I don't often say that!) and toss in a salad. Add a poached egg if you feel like it.
- **Scotch eggs** Add to sausage meat when making Scotch eggs (p105).
- **Stuffing** Add to stuffing (p45) especially for pork.
- **Throw it** Get yourself to The World Black Pudding Throwing Competition which is held in Ramsbottom, Lancashire every September and dates back to 1850. Contestants must lob three 'competition standard' (6oz) puddings underarm in an attempt to dislodge a pile of Yorkshire puddings that have been stacked on a 20 foot high (that's 6 metres) plinth! It is apparently a 'celebration' of the longstanding rivalry between Yorkshire and Lancashire.

B

Blueberries – see Berries and Fruit

Blueberries have an affinity with lemons, peaches and nectarines, soured cream, cinnamon and vanilla plus all the flavours normally associated with soft summer fruits.

● **Pancakes** They are excellent in pancakes (p283).

Bok choy – aka pak choi or Chinese cabbage – see Cabbage

Booze – see Beer, Cider, Spirits and Liqueurs or Wine

Brazil nuts – see Nuts

Bread

There is so much can be done with leftover bread it behoves one to keep every last bit – it goes well with almost everything if you put your mind to it!

❊ Keep a bread scraps box in the freezer to collect bits and pieces until you have a useable amount. Surprisingly keeping bread in the fridge is not a good idea as it stales faster.

● **Apple Cribbly** A quick and easy dessert (p13).
● **Breadcrumbs 3 ways**
   – Crunchy breadcrumbs
   Moisten fresh crumbs with a sprinkling of oil or butter and dry-fry, stirring almost constantly until crisp and golden and adding whatever seasonings are appropriate. A great way to use these crispy crumbs immediately is to push them to the side of the pan and fry an egg or two in the middle, sprinkling the crumbs over when the eggs are cooked – toast on eggs!

> **HANDY HINT**
> To refresh a stale loaf, wrap in a clean, damp cloth and put in a preheated oven at 200°C/gas 6 for a few minutes, watching carefully to make sure the cloth doesn't catch fire.

- **Dry breadcrumbs** Bake leftover bread in a single layer at 150°C/gas 2 until completely dry. Cool, process or crush to fine crumbs and season to taste with salt, pepper and ground spices. Freeze in airtight bags.
- **Fresh breadcrumbs** Tear up leftover bread and run through the food processor or hand grate to crumbs. Freeze in bags and use as needed.

- **Brown Betty** Fry 150g fresh breadcrumbs in 50g butter until crisp and golden. Mix in 50g sugar plus a pinch of ground cinnamon or mixed spice, or to taste. Serve sprinkled over or layered with warm, cooked fruit. Apples are traditional but not the only option.

- **Crostini, croûtes, tartines and bruschetta** or whatever you want to call a bit of toast with something tasty on it. Cut slices of bread into rounds or other attractive shapes and either toast or brush with oil and bake in a preheated oven at 200°C/gas 6 until crisp and golden.

- **Croûtons** Tear bread rather than cut it into dice; the pieces will then have lots of points and edges to go crunchy and will look prettier too. Spread them on a baking tray, drizzle with a little olive oil, melted butter, bacon fat or similar, season to taste and bake in a preheated oven at 200°C/gas 6 for about 10 minutes until crisp and golden.

- **Crunchy croûton pie topping** Tear bread into 2– 2 ½ cm pieces, toss in enough oil or butter to coat generously, and season according to your pie filling. Pile on top of hot filling and bake for a few minutes at 180°C/gas 4 until crisp and golden.

- **Sliced white bread cups** Remove the crusts, roll the slices out thinly and press into buttered muffin cups. Brush the insides with butter and bake in a preheated oven at 180°C/gas 4 until crisp and golden. Fill with something tasty, as if it were a vol au vent. Alternatively, de-crust and roll the bread as above. Put a spoonful of filling on each slice, fold in half diagonally and press the edges together to form a turnover. Brush with butter and bake in a preheated oven at 190°C/gas 5 until crisp and golden – best served hot.

- **Stuffing** Fry coarsely chopped onion together with your choice of chopped carrot, celery and garlic in a little oil until

Marino Branch
Brainse Marino
Tel: 8336297

45

starting to take colour. If adding raw bacon or sausage do so now. When that starts to colour, add 1– 2 handfuls of diced or torn dry bread and just enough hot stock to moisten it. Add a knob of butter, cover and set aside for about 20 minutes. Stir in the butter and make sure that the bread is thoroughly soaked through but not sitting in liquid. Taste, season and add any cooked meats, herbs and spices. Stuff into a bird, roll in a joint of meat or put in an ovenproof dish, drizzle with a little more butter and bake alongside the roast for the last 20 minutes or so of cooking. The top should be crisp and golden.

- **Toast**!

Panzanella – Tuscan Bread Salad

SERVES 1

1 tbsp olive oil
½ tbsp balsamic vinegar
salt and freshly ground black pepper
100g ripe tomatoes, coarsely chopped
½ small red onion
1 garlic clove, crushed
1 slice of good country bread

1. Mix together all the ingredients except the bread, mashing slightly so that the tomatoes release their juices.
2. Toast the bread until crisp, golden and maybe just starting to char a little!
3. Cool the bread, tear into pieces and stir into the tomato mixture.
4. Set aside for about 10 minutes. The aim is to have some of the bread soft and juicy and some of it still crisp.
5. Great additions to this are fresh basil, black olives and feta or goats' cheese.

Skordalia

A traditional garlicky sauce or dip from Greece.

80g dry bread
1 garlic clove, chopped
pinch of sea salt
1 tbsp red wine vinegar or lemon juice
4 tbsp olive oil

1. Soak the bread in cold water for a few minutes until saturated, then squeeze out as dry as possible.
2. Crush the garlic and the salt to a paste with a pestle and mortar.
3. Work in the damp bread and stir in the vinegar.
4. Gradually, a drop at a time, whisk in the olive oil to emulsify.
5. Alternatively liquidise everything but the olive oil and then gradually add it to the mixture.

B

A Luxurious Twist
on Traditional Bread Sauce

This is a new English recipe dating back to the 1980s when I first thought of it. Similar to the traditional sauce but with the ingredients rearranged, it is quite indulgent and everyone I know (except one) loves it.

1 onion, halved and thinly sliced
50g butter
125g hot vegetable stock, plus extra if needed
75ml double cream, plus extra if needed
100g dry bread, torn into pieces
salt and freshly ground black pepper
freshly grated nutmeg and ground cloves to taste
extra milk, stock or cream (optional)

1. Cook the onions in the butter (p303).
2. Add the stock and cream and bring to the boil.
3. Stir in the stale bread, cover and set aside for 30 minutes or until needed.
4. Taste, season and bring to a simmer. Dilute with milk, more cream or stock as necessary to reach the consistency you prefer.

❄ It freezes well.

● **Bread sauce stuffed mushrooms** And what do you do with leftover bread sauce? Remove the stems from large open mushrooms and brush inside and out with oil. Fill with the bread sauce, sprinkle with soft fresh breadcrumbs and bake in a preheated oven at 200°C/gas 6 for 15–20 minutes until hot through and the top is crisp and golden. These are extra good drizzled with balsamic glaze.

Manly Bread Pudding

Not the creamy, custardy bread pudding overleaf; this is the solid, filling stuff! Here is a flexible recipe.

225g mixed dried fruit
3 tbsp brandy, rum or whisky
225g leftover bread, diced or torn into pieces
240ml milk
60g butter, melted and cooled
2 eggs
90g sugar, plus more for sprinkling
pinch of ground cinnamon or mixed spice
1 tsp grated orange or lemon zest
any other suitable leftovers (optional)

1. Soak the fruit in the spirit for 30 minutes or use pre-soaked fruit (see p100).
2. Mix together the bread, milk, butter and eggs, stir well and set aside for 30 minutes or longer.
3. Preheat the oven to 180°C/gas 4 and butter an ovenproof dish.
4. Beat the mixture with a fork until the bread has completely broken down.
5. Stir in the sugar, dried fruit and any remaining alcohol (if using pre-soaked, add a spoonful of liquor) spice, zest plus any extra leftovers.
6. Pour into the dish, level the surface and sprinkle with a little extra sugar.
7. Bake for 1–1½ hours until firm.
8. Cool and serve with a mug of tea.

B

Bread and No-butter Pudding

Traditionally, this comprises slices of buttered bread layered up and baked in a custard but I don't think there is much to be gained by the butter and, if you don't have to butter it, random pieces of leftover bread are easier to use. If the bread isn't stale, dice or tear into pieces and either leave it around the place for an hour or so or put it on a baking tray and pop in the oven for a few minutes. It usually has about 75g of dried fruit, possibly alcohol-soaked, stirred in with the bread before the custard is poured over and this is delicious if you aren't using up any other specific leftovers.

SERVES 4

100–150g stale bread, torn into small chunks
200ml milk
100ml double cream
2 eggs
80g sugar, plus a little for sprinkling
½ tsp vanilla extract

1. Put the bread into a lightly greased ovenproof dish or divide between ramekins.
2. Whisk together all the other ingredients and pour over the top, pushing the bread under the surface to soak it. Set aside for 30 minutes or more – even overnight will do.
3. Preheat the oven to 180°C/gas 4.
4. Sprinkle the pudding with the extra sugar and bake for about 40 minutes until risen, golden and slightly wobbly when nudged.
5. Serve hot, warm or cold, but warm is best.

- **Savoury strata** As the name indicates, this means layers (so arguably this version should be a stratum as that's the singular). It is a savoury bread and (no) butter pudding usually containing layers of cheese and various other bits and pieces which are traditionally layered up. Use the recipe above but leave out the sugar and vanilla and season the egg mixture with salt and pepper and anything else appropriate to the ingredients you are using. Mix in grated cheese and other ingredients before pouring over the custard. Savoury strata are usually nicest served hot. Try soaking overnight and baking in the morning for a special breakfast.

French Toast

This is best made with softer breads rather than chewy artisan stuff. For a custardy middle, cut the bread a little on the thick side and give it a good long soak for 10 minutes or so before cooking. For a bready interior, briefly dip the bread in the mixture and fry immediately.

SERVES 1

1 egg
½ tbsp sugar
50ml milk, cream or a mixture of the two
a few drops of vanilla extract
pinch of salt
2 slices of bread
a knob of butter, for frying

1. Whisk together all the ingredients except the bread.
2. Soak the bread in the mixture.
3. Fry in butter until crisp and golden on both sides.

- **French toast pancakes** If you don't have whole slices of bread but still fancy French toast, don't worry – make French toast pancakes! Stir about 40g pieces of stale bread into the egg mixture in the recipe above and leave for a few minutes until completely soaked. Heat a lightly greased non-stick frying pan and, using a slotted spoon, carefully transfer the bread to the pan, forming it into two cakes. Cook until the bottoms are firm and brown, turn carefully and cook the other side.

B

Brioche – see also Bread and Cake

- **Crispy fingers** Cut into fingers, dip in beaten egg, fry in a little butter until golden and sprinkle with sugar.
- **Fruity toast** Top toasted brioche with fruit, sprinkle with sugar and pop under the grill until melted and starting to caramelise.
- **Sweet panzanella** Use fruit salad and follow the recipe (p46).
- **Sweet toasted cheese sandwich** Make with cream cheese and raspberry jam or similar.

COOK'S TREAT
Dunk into hot chocolate!

Broad beans – aka fava beans – see also Peas and Green beans

These summery beans taste well with bacon and ham, feta and goats' cheese, in particular, but other cheeses too, butter, olive oil, garlic and black pepper. I am sorry to say that in almost all cases broad beans are nicer if you remove not only the pod but, after cooking, the grey-green skin too. I cannot think of anything to do with these skins other than discard or compost them.

❋ Keep in the fridge in an open or perforated bag for up to five days, blanch to freeze.

- **Broad bean pasta sauce** Mash together cooked broad beans, garlic, lemon zest and juice, olive oil, grated Parmesan, a little goats' or cream cheese, salt and pepper. Toss with freshly cooked pasta, 1–2 spoonfuls of the pasta cooking water, some chopped fried or grilled bacon and a few more broad beans if you have them.
- **Bubble and squeak** Add tender beans (p211).
- **Crispy bean pods** Tender pods can be dipped in seasoned flour, then milk or egg and then the flour again and deep-fried until crisp. Drain and sprinkle with crunchy sea salt.
- **Dip or bruschetta topping** Mash together cooked broad beans, garlic, lemon zest and juice, olive oil, fresh mint, salt and pepper and maybe a little goats' or cream cheese. Serve cold as a dip or on bruschetta.
- **Egg dishes** Add beans to egg dishes such as frittata or omelette (p296–97).

- **Risotto** Stir beans into risotto with some bacon or ham and cheese (p306).
- **Soup** Young, un-stringy pods can also be used to make soup; add for the last few minutes of cooking and when tender, continue with the basic recipe (p309). Maybe stir in a few cooked beans to serve.

Broccoli

The slightly sulphurous, but pleasantly so, flavour of broccoli is comple-mented by butter, most cheeses, crunchy breadcrumbs, garlic, bacon, anchovy, chilli and nuts.

❄ Keep raw broccoli in an open plastic bag in the fridge for up to four days, cooked should be used within a couple of days. Blanch to freeze.

- **Broccoli and blue cheese pasta** Make an Alfredo sauce (p281) replacing some or all of the Parmesan with blue cheese. Toss just-tender, cooked broccoli and hot pasta with the sauce and, if possible, sprinkle with coarsely chopped toasted walnuts.
- **Broccoli cheese** Replace the cauliflower with broccoli (p62).
- **Broccoli soup** Peel and chop some tender stalks. Follow the recipe for my normal soup (p309) and add the stalks when the potatoes are almost cooked, then continue cooking until tender. Meanwhile blanch (see p286) and refresh the broccoli florets. Stir them in at the last minute so that they retain their bright colour and just crunchy texture. Stir leftover blue cheese or Cheddar into the finished soup or sprinkle on top.
- **Egg dishes** Add cooked florets to omelette or frittata (p296– 97).
- **Garlic buttered** Reheat cooked broccoli in a little butter and then stir in some crushed garlic, grated Parmesan and crunchy breadcrumbs.
- **Salads** Add small raw broccoli florets to salad; they contribute a lovely 'nubbly' texture.
- **Soup** Add cooked broccoli to soup at the last minute just to heat through.

B

- **Soy sauced** Reheat cooked broccoli in a little olive oil and stir in toasted almonds and a splash of soy sauce.
- **Stir-fries and vegetable dishes** Peel tender broccoli stems, slice and add to stir-fries, mixed vegetable dishes and soups.

Broth – see Stock

Brussels sprouts

Complementary flavours for Brussels sprouts include bacon, butter, chestnuts, dill, onions, thyme, juniper, nuts, nutmeg and caraway.

❄ Keep raw sprouts refrigerated for four or five days and cooked for a similar time. Blanched or cooked Brussels sprouts can be frozen.

- **Bacon and thyme** Fry sliced Brussels in bacon fat with crispy bacon pieces and a little thyme.
- **Brussels sprout slaw** Add chopped nuts, seeds, dried fruit, pomegranate seeds, sliced red onion and any other leftovers to shredded sprouts.
- **Bubble and squeak** Add cooked sprouts to bubble and squeak (p211).
- **Cheesy, creamy or crunchy** Reheat sliced Brussels sprouts in butter then add grated cheese or cream and plenty of freshly ground black pepper, or stir in a handful of toasted nuts or seeds.
- **Coleslaw** Shred raw Brussels sprouts and add to coleslaw (p287).
- **Stir-fry** Shredded raw Brussels sprouts are delicious stir-fried with bacon and garlic (p310).

Bulgur – aka bulgar, burghul and cracked wheat

- **Meatballs** Add to meatballs or meatloaf mixture as a tasty filler.
- **Soup** Add a handful to soup for the last few minutes to heat through.

- **Stir-fries** Use instead of rice in a stir-fry.

Almost Tabbouleh

A refreshing Middle Eastern Salad.

<u>SERVES 1</u>

30g leftover bulgur
1 small red onion, finely minced
1 garlic clove
2 handfuls of fresh parsley, finely chopped
½ handful of fresh mint
6 cherry tomatoes, coarsely chopped
½ cucumber, seeded and coarsely chopped
juice of 2 lemons
2 tbsp olive oil
salt and freshly ground black pepper

1. Mix everything together and chill for a while to let the flavours meld.

Burgers – see also Beef and Meat because this is what they are, or should be!

- **Pasta, soup or stir-fry** Coarsely chop cooked burgers and add to any of these dishes.
- **Reheat** Cooked burgers can be dry so whatever you do with them next must be fairly moist. To reheat a cooked burger either warm gently in an appropriate sauce, or wrap in fatty bacon and grill.

B

Butter

It's difficult to imagine having this as an actual leftover but if you do have a tad that needs using up, here are some ideas.

❄ Freeze it.

- **Flavoured butters** Add other leftovers, such as garlic or finely chopped herbs, to make a compound butter (p288).
- **Root veg** Mash into potatoes or other root veggies.
- **Sauces** Whisk into pan sauces or gravy at the last minute to make it rich and glossy.
- **Sticky toffee sauce** Melt with an equal quantity of dark brown sugar, a drop or two of vanilla extract and enough double cream to make an unctuous sauce. This keeps almost indefinitely in the fridge. Reheat gently and, if it splits and looks oily, add a little more cream which will bring it back together. Serve over ice cream, sticky toffee pudding, toss with popcorn or spread cold on toast!
- **Vegetables** Dress hot vegetables with a knob of butter.

> **HANDY HINT**
> Keep butter wrappers in the fridge to use when cooking onions my favourite way (p267).

Butter beans – see Beans and pulses

Buttermilk

The tangy flavour of buttermilk is good with berries and is refreshing to drink.

❄ Buttermilk keeps very well in the fridge and does freeze but is more suitable for cooking with than drinking once thawed.

- **Buttermilk dressing** Mix with mayonnaise (a little more mayo than buttermilk) and whatever seasoning you fancy.
- **Marinades** Buttermilk makes an excellent marinade for chicken; flavouring and tenderising it. Season buttermilk and pour over chicken. Marinate for at least an hour up to as long as a day and then cook as required.

- **Mashed potatoes** Replace the milk or cream in mashed potato with buttermilk (p304).
- **Pancakes and scones** Replace some or all of the milk in pancakes and scones/American biscuit recipes (pp282–86) with buttermilk for light and airy baking.

HANDY HINT

Add to soups as an alternative to cream but do so right at the end, buttermilk must not be boiled.

- **Smoothies** Use as some or all of the liquid in a smoothie (p308).

Butternut squash – see Squash

C

Cabbage

Cabbage goes well with apples, potato, onion, garlic, caraway, nutmeg, mustard, bacon, pork, beef and game. Additionally, red cabbage likes red wine, chestnuts and juniper.

To create delicious dishes from leftover cabbage it does behove one to cook it in a flavoursome way in the first place; plain boiled cabbage is uninspiring. This is easy; cook in a little salted water and butter until just tender and season deliciously.

❋ Raw cabbage keeps well in the fridge for a week and tightly formed cabbages (both white and red) keep for ages and ages. If for some reason you want to freeze cabbage, blanch it first. Cooked cabbage keeps in a covered container for up to four days and freezes well.

- **Bubble and squeak** Also, colcannon and rumbledethumps include cabbage (p211).
- **Coleslaw** See recipe on p287.
- **Mustardy** Reheat cooked cabbage in a little cream flavoured with a spoonful of wholegrain mustard.
- **Salads** Add finely chopped raw cabbage to salads.
- **Sesame cabbage** Shred cabbage and cook to crispy-tender in a little oil, drizzle with sesame oil and toss with a handful of toasted sesame seeds.
- **Soup** Add to soup for just the last few minutes of cooking time so as to keep its texture.
- **Stir-fries** Add shredded cabbage at the end of cooking (p310).

Haluski

This Eastern European dish uses an unfeasibly large amount of butter – I have seen recipes calling for as much as 225g per cabbage! I tend to use less or even a mix of butter and olive oil. Leftover ham or bacon is good in this, if you have some.

1 onion, thinly sliced
50g or more of butter or butter and olive oil mix
½ cabbage, shredded
200g egg noodles
salt and freshly ground black pepper
chopped cooked bacon or ham (optional)

1. Cook the onion in the butter until tender and starting to caramelise.
2. Add the cabbage, toss until all buttery and cook to *al dente*.
3. Meanwhile cook the noodles in plenty of boiling salted water until tender.
4. Drain the noodles and toss with the buttery cabbage, together with the ham and bacon, if using, taste and season.

Cake – see also Christmas cake

Most cakes go well with cream, ice cream, a cup of tea or coffee and a good book.

❄ Keep in an airtight container and, if it includes cream or fresh fruit, refrigerate it. Plain un-iced cakes freeze well.

● **Cake pops and truffles** There are many, many recipes and directions for these online. The basic idea is to mix crumbled cake with enough of something moist and delicious – such as frosting, butter, cream, syrup, and so on – to enable the crumbs to stick

COOK'S TREAT
Toast plain cake slices and serve buttered for breakfast or top with fruit and cream.

together. Roll into small balls for truffles or larger balls to
make cake pops, chill and then coat with something like cocoa,
cinnamon sugar or melted chocolate. Pop into pretty paper
cases or onto sticks and eat like lollipops.

- **Croûtons** Toss diced cake in melted butter, bake until crisp
and golden and serve with warm compôte or fruit salad.
- **Ice cream** Fold crumbled cake into soft ice cream.
- **Trifle** See p119 for more information.

Calamari – see Shellfish

Capers

Capers have an affinity with lamb, anchovies, garlic, olives, fish,
cauliflower, lemon and parsley.

- **Courgettes** Add a handful of chopped
capers and a squeeze of lemon when
sautéing courgettes.

HANDY HINT
Rinse capers before use
to rid them of excess
salt.

- **Deep-fried capers** Drain capers, dry
them and fry in a little oil until turning
brown and crispy. Drain on kitchen paper and serve as nibbles
or sprinkle on salads and fish dishes.
- **Fish sauce** After pan-frying fish, set it aside and add coarsely
chopped capers to the pan together with a little white wine and
lemon juice. Stir, scraping the pan to dissolve any fishy residue
and add a knob of butter to make a lovely sauce for the fish.
- **Tapenade** This olive paste recipe includes capers (p188).
- **Vinaigrette** Finely chop and add to vinaigrette. This is good
on roasted cauliflower.

Tartare Sauce and Remoulade

Mix together 4 tbsp mayonnaise, $\frac{1}{2}$ tbsp finely chopped capers,
$\frac{1}{2}$ tbsp finely chopped gherkins, juice of $\frac{1}{2}$ lemon and you have
Tartare Sauce. Add 1 tsp Dijon mustard and maybe an optional
$\frac{1}{2}$ tsp crushed anchovy *et voilà* – Remoulade!

Caraway seeds – see Seeds

Carrots

Carrot-enhancing ingredients include butter, honey, orange, apple, cabbage, onion, celery, potatoes, sugar, dill, chervil, ginger, parsley, anise, cumin, caraway and cloves.

❄ Keep raw, unpeeled carrots in a cool dark place for two to three weeks, and cooked in the fridge for three to four days. To freeze, carrots must first be blanched or cooked.

HANDY HINT
Cheer up a limp carrot by putting it in iced water for a while.

- **Carrot and parsnip purée** Lovely and sweet, this is an easy way to transform cooked leftovers into something different (p193).
- **Carrot cake** Don't forget this delicious cake. There are so many recipes to choose from it's best you choose one you like!
- **Coleslaw** Add grated raw carrot to coleslaw (p287).
- **Mashed potatoes** Mash hot, tenderly cooked carrots with hot cooked potatoes for beguiling golden mash.
- **Mirepoix** Includes finely diced carrot to flavour soups and stews (p63).
- **Roasted carrot soup** Toss chunks of carrot with a little olive oil, salt and pepper, then roast in a preheated oven at 200° C/gas 6 until tender. Add to the basic soup when the potatoes are almost cooked (p309).
- **Roasted** Roast carrot chunks with other root vegetables.
- **Salad** Coarsely grate a carrot and mix with a little finely grated root ginger and a squeeze of lemon juice. Very refreshing with spicy dishes.
- **Vegetable crisps** Peel a carrot and keep peeling until it is all ribbons. Toss with a little cornflour and deep-fry until crisp. Drain, season and use as a snack or garnish.

C

Cashew nuts – see Nuts

Cauliflower

Cauliflower goes well with Indian spices, cheeses, mustard seed, anchovy, cream, potatoes, garlic, lemon, olives, capers and nutmeg.

❄ Raw cauliflower keeps at least a week refrigerated but must be blanched before freezing. Cooked cauliflower will keep chilled for up to four days and can be frozen.

- **Cauliflower cheese** Cover cooked cauliflower in cheese sauce (p66) and sprinkle with grated cheese and fresh breadcrumbs. Bake in a preheated oven at 190°C/gas 5 for 10–15 minutes until hot, bubbling and crisp. Reheat leftovers and serve on toast!
- **Cauliflower salad** Cook florets until just tender, drain and immediately toss in vinaigrette. Chill until needed.
- **Crème du Barry** This is the name give to classic cream of cauliflower soup in France. For a simple version, use the Normal Soup recipe (p309) and add cauliflower stalks with the potatoes and florets a few minutes before the end of cooking. Season with freshly grated nutmeg, purée until smooth and finish with a spoonful of cream.
- **Crudités** Serve raw or barely cooked florets with other vegetables as part of a selection with a choice of dips.
- **Fritters** Flavour with cauliflower-friendly ingredients or add cheese to make cauliflower cheese fritters! See p285 for fritter mix recipe.
- **Mashed cauli** Mash very tender cooked cauliflower and heat with cream and freshly grated nutmeg as a side dish.
- **Salad** Cut into tiny florets and toss into salad.

Caviar

Caviar is good with Champagne, vodka, crème fraîche, toasted brioche and some say white chocolate.

- **Garnish** Sprinkle on fish dishes to impress people.

C

Celeriac – aka celery root

Celeriac is good with walnuts, ham, cheese, chicken, mustard, tarragon and sage.

❄ Keep raw celeriac in the fridge for up to two weeks, cooked for three or four days, or freeze.

- **Celeriac soup** Replace some or all of the potato in my normal soup with celeriac (p309).

HANDY HINT

Drop cut celeriac into acidulated water (p281) to stop it discolouring.

- **Celeriac remoulade** Coarsely grate celeriac straight into remoulade sauce (p60) and stir to coat thoroughly. Chill for an hour or so to allow the celeriac to soften a little. Add chopped fresh parsley, salt and pepper and maybe a spoonful of cream or crème fraîche.
- **Coleslaw** Shred raw celeriac and add to coleslaw (p287).
- **Potatoes** Mash cooked celeriac with potatoes, adding garlic or roasted garlic (p123).
- **Roast** Roast together with other root vegetables.

Celery

Celery is good with apple, walnuts, ham, cheese, onions and carrots.

❄ Lightly wrapped in clingfilm, celery keeps well in the fridge for up to two weeks but blanch or cook before freezing. Cooked celery will keep for up to five days in the fridge.

- **Celery soup** Cook thinly sliced celery with the onions at the start of the basic recipe (p309) and add coarsely chopped celery leaves just before serving.
- **Cocktail stirrer** A celery stalk makes a fine stirrer for a Bloody Mary or Bloody Caesar.
- **Coleslaw** See Basic Recipes (p287).
- **Mirepoix** Celery is a basic component of this classic French aromatics mix. Finely and uniformly dice together one part celery, one part carrot and two parts white onion. Use as a base for soups, stocks and stews or add to a pan when deglazing. Freeze leftover mirepoix in ice cube trays for later use.

C

- **Salads and garnish** Celery leaves make a pretty garnish and are good added to salads as indeed is celery itself.
- **Stir-fries** Add finely sliced celery at the end of cooking so that it retains its crunch.
- **Stock** Celery is good in most stocks.
- **Stuffing** Use celery in a stuffing mix; it's particularly good combined with lemon and parsley to make a stuffing to go with chicken. See Bread (p45).
- **Waldorf salad** Add to this classic apple and walnut salad (p12).

Chard – see Swiss chard

Cheese

'Cheese never sleeps.' Gastronomica in Pimlico
Cheese is a huge subject in its own right which I can only touch on here.

❊ Store strong-smelling cheeses separately from other foods and, similarly, keep strong smelling foods such as onions away from cheese so that everyone can keep their smells to themselves. Wrap cheese in greaseproof paper or parchment then, loosely, in clingfilm and finally I think it's a good idea to keep all your cheeses in a designated cheese box in the fridge. Freezing can change cheese's texture, making it crumbly. It is then best used for cooking where sometimes the crumbliness is a bonus.

Cheeseboard leftovers, miscellaneous scraps and general ideas

- **Alfredo sauce** This classic Parmesan sauce can include other cheeses. See basic recipe (p281).

  HANDY HINT
  Serve cheese at room temperature but don't keep it out too long or it will dry out.

- **Baked dish toppings** Mix grated cheese with breadcrumbs and sprinkle onto dishes to be baked – pastas, gratins, cauliflower cheese etc. – for a crisp crust.
- **Bread** Add cheese to bread dough: grated cheese will give an even flavour throughout and crumbles will give lovely cheesy

pockets. After the first rising, roll out the dough and scatter with the cheese plus any other additions such as nuts, fruit etc. Re-knead and continue as usual.

- **Burgers** Try topping your burgers with different cheeses; the processed stuff isn't compulsory.
- **Cheese croûton** Float a bit of cheese on toast on soup; if it's good enough for French onion, it's good enough for other soups.
- **Cheese fritters** Add about 75g cheese to the basic fritter recipe (p286).
- **Cheese straws** Cheat's Straws, made using cheddar pastry, make great nibbles to go with drinks (p69).
- **Dressings** Crumble cheese into vinaigrette or mayonnaise.
- **Egg dishes** Omelettes and many other egg dishes are enhanced by the addition of cheese.
- **Mashed potato** Add a handful of cheese to mashed potato for cheesy mash (p304).
- **Mozzarella in Carrozza** This style of fried sandwich works for many cheeses (p69).
- **Pizza** Scatter onto garlic bread and pizza.
- **Potted cheese** A kind of cheese pâté, mix 225g cheese scraps with 75g soft butter, or slightly less if there are soft cheeses in the scraps. Process or whisk to combine together with a modicum (about 1 tbsp) leftover alcohol: brandy, port, wine or even a good ale. Taste and season. Turn into a pretty pot or pots and chill but take it out of the fridge an hour or so before serving to soften a little.

  In France, where potted cheese is known as *fromage fort*, they spurn the butter, add garlic and their alcohol of choice is white wine. Both types of potted cheese are good spread on toast and flashed under the grill until bubbling and golden. Use your imagination and your leftovers wisely to make your own versions.
- **Risotto** Parmesan is the traditional cheesy addition to a risotto, but you can try other cheeses, too. Stir in for the last few minutes of cooking p307.
- **Salads** Add to salads, choosing other ingredients to suit.
- **Strata** See Bread (p50) for this savoury bread pudding.

Cheese Sauce

Normally I would use a mixture of Cheddar and Parmesan plus a little mustard, but any leftover cheese can be used to good effect together with seasonings to match.

MAKES 600ML

30g butter
30g plain flour
600ml milk
80g cheese, grated or crumbled
salt and freshly ground black pepper
pinch of mustard powder, cayenne or freshly grated nutmeg (optional)

1. Melt the butter in a medium-sized saucepan and stir in the flour to form a paste.
2. Cook gently for 1–2 minutes, then gradually whisk in the milk until completely combined.
3. Turn up the heat and whisk constantly as the mixture comes to a boil and thickens to a smooth sauce.
4. Turn the heat to low, simmer for 5 minutes, then stir in the cheese until melted.
5. Taste and season with salt, pepper and other flavourings if you like, but do not boil again as the cheese may become stringy.

Cheese on toast, toasted sarnies and grilled cheese sandwiches
These are all good ways to use up scraps of cheese. Cheese on toast is best, if you can be bothered, finished off in a preheated oven at 200°C/gas 6. This keeps the toast from drying out and burning round the edges and heats the dish through evenly.

Oddly enough, the classic American grilled cheese sandwich is fried! The original recipe calls for two slices of white bread filled with processed cheese. The sandwich is buttered on the outside and cooked in a hot pan until crisp and the inside is melting. Whilst not terribly pleasant, it is a good idea which lends itself to huge improvement.

For a 'grilled' cheese sandwich, use good bread, real cheese and whatever would go best with it. Butter the outside of the sarnie, lay it in a hot, dry frying pan, cover and cook the first side over a medium-low heat.

When crisp, turn the sandwich and cook the second side uncovered so that the first stays crisp.

Specific cheeses and cheese types
There are many different types of cheese and doubtless a directory somewhere of 'official' categories. I list them here, however, as seems natural to me, together with ideas peculiar to each cheese or type of cheese. Refer also to general ideas above.

FRESH CHEESE
These are soft, rindless, unripened cheeses such as cream cheese, cottage cheese, fromage frais, mascarpone, quark, ricotta and paneer. Generally speaking these go well with fruit, black pepper, spring onion and cucumber.

❄ Fresh cheese has a short shelf life; keep it chilled and eat within a few days. Throw all the cheese away if any mould appears on it. Full-fat fresh cheeses can be frozen but use within a couple of months or they will not be at their best.

- **Caramelised peaches** Fill peach halves with fresh cheese, sprinkle with brown sugar and pop under the grill until warm and caramelising.
- **Frostings** Sweeten and flavour with citrus zest, vanilla extract, jam, marmalade, liqueur etc., soften with a little cream if necessary and use as a topping, frosting or filling for cakes and desserts.
- **Pasta** Toss with hot pasta for a quick sauce, adding other ingredients according to your leftovers, or stir into a tomato-based pasta sauce to make it richer and creamier.
- **Scones** Split plain or cheese scones and fill with fresh cheese and tomatoes for a savoury cream tea or use sweetened fresh cheese and fruit for a more conventional one.
- **Smoked salmon** Top crostini with fresh cheese, smoked salmon, red onion rings and fresh dill.
- **Soup** Mix with a little cream and appropriate seasoning and add a spoonful to soup when serving.

C

BRIE, CAMEMBERT AND OTHER BLOOMY RIND CHEESES

These have a complex mushroomy taste which is enhanced by Champagne, bacon, apples and pears, sweet preserves, almonds, grapes, mushrooms and, of course, truffles.

✳ They are not fabulous keepers. Store, well wrapped, in the fridge and eat within a week or so of cutting. They do freeze.

- **Breadcrumbed and fried** Dice and coat with seasoned flour, dip in beaten egg and coat with breadcrumbs. Shallow-fry until crisp and golden and toss in a salad.

> **HANDY HINT**
> The rind is entirely edible but, should you wish to remove it, do so when the cheese is cold; it's much easier that way.

- **No-cook pasta sauce** Mix together some diced Brie or Camembert, half that quantity of coarsely chopped tomatoes, a little finely chopped red onion, a glug of olive oil, torn fresh basil, if possible, salt and pepper and set beside the stove to warm while you cook some pasta. When ready, drain the pasta, reserving a couple of spoonfuls of the cooking water, and toss together with the cheese mixture. Add the reserved water and toss again. Serve with freshly grated Parmesan.
- **Potato cakes** Put a nugget in the middle of potato cakes for a molten centre when cooked.
- **Warm salad dressing** Scoop the soft cheese from the rind and heat gently with about half as much crème fraîche, whisking until smooth and runny enough to drizzle. If necessary, thin the consistency with a little port, wine, brandy, water or stock. Toss a green salad with some crunchy croûtons, drizzle over the warm dressing and serve immediately.

SEMI-HARD CHEESES, SUCH AS EDAM, GOUDA, HALLOUMI, MOZZARELLA

I think of these as 'flexible cheeses', which is more polite than 'rubbery'! Edam and Gouda however do become firmer and more flavoursome as they age and then fit into the hard cheese category below.

✳ Store in a sealed container in the fridge.

- **Mozzarella in Carrozza** Make mozzarella sandwiches with white bread. Dip them in milk, then dredge with flour and finally dip in beaten egg. Shallow-fry in hot oil, turning so that each side is crisp, then drain briefly on kitchen paper. Serve hot, possibly with the anchovy sauce that you will find under Anchovies (p10).
- **Roasted tomatoes** Slice the cheese thinly, top with hot roasted tomatoes and serve with crusty bread and a glass of red wine.
- **Speidini** Toss cubed bread in flavoured oil, thread onto skewers alternating with cubes of semi-hard cheese and toast under a hot grill, turning now and then until the bread is crisp and golden and the cheese starting to melt.

WASHED RIND OR 'STINKY' CHEESES

These soft, pinky-orange, innocent-looking cheeses have been repeatedly washed in brine or alcohol during ageing, which produces the pretty colour and a distinctive 'smelly feet' aroma. Examples of washed rind cheese are Époisses, Pont l'Evêque, Limburger and, of course, our own dear Stinking Bishop. Good flavour pairings include smoked meats, potatoes, mushrooms, beef and, I read somewhere, kangaroo. The rind may or may not be worth eating; it varies from cheese to cheese and from diner to diner.

❄ Store in their own personal sealed container in the fridge so as not to contaminate other foods.

- **Potatoes** Fold nuggets of stinky cheese through creamy mash on the point of serving alongside a beef dish (p304).

CHEDDAR AND OTHER HARD OR CRUMBLY CHEESES

This category includes such cheeses as Leicester, Double Gloucester, Cheshire, Caerphilly, Lancashire and yes, even Wensleydale, Gromit. These are better for cooking when mature but younger cheeses will work too.

- **Cheat's Cheddar pastry** Sprinkle grated Cheddar onto a rolled out sheet of puff pastry, fold to enclose the cheese and re-roll, repeating several times, adding more cheese with each roll. You'll need about 100g cheese to 450g pastry. For yummy cheese straws, cut the pastry into strips, maybe give them a twist, and bake on a greased tray in a preheated oven at 190°C/gas 5. Or use the cheesy pastry to top an apple pie, as they do, reputedly, in Yorkshire.

- **Cheese scones** See p293 for basic recipe.
- **Welsh rarebit** See Beer (p38).

Glamorgan Sausages

These have a remarkably sausage-like texture.
It's fine to use a mixture of hard or crumbly cheeses if that
is what you have left over.

120g fresh breadcrumbs, plus extra for coating
100g Caerphilly, Cheddar or similar hard or crumbly cheese, grated
1 spring onion or equivalent amount of leek, finely chopped
1 egg yolk
a generous pinch of mustard powder
salt and freshly ground black pepper
1 whole egg, beaten

1. Mix together everything except the whole egg and extra breadcrumbs. Taste, season and form into 6 small sausages.
2. Dip in the beaten egg, coat in breadcrumbs and shallow-fry until crisp and golden.

REALLY HARD CHEESE

By this I mean Parmesan and similar cheeses, such as Pecorino. They go well with tomatoes, basil, olive oil, garlic, nuts, pears, beef, mushrooms, roasted squash, pasta dishes and red wine.

❋ Stored well-wrapped in the fridge, these will be good for at least a month and probably considerably longer.

- **Frico crisps** Scatter an even layer of grated Parmesan onto lightly oiled baking paper on a baking tray, sprinkle with black pepper or a pinch of cayenne. Cook in a preheated oven at 200°C/gas 6 for 5 minutes or so until melted but not browned. Leave for 5 minutes to firm up, remove from the baking tray to a rack and cool completely. Crumble into crisp pieces and sprinkle over savoury dishes.

- **Salad dressings** Add to Caesar dressing (p10).
- **Soups, risotto, pasta dishes and salads** Grate or shave over any of these dishes before serving.
- **Wine** Eat thin slivers with a glass of something red and I'm not talking tomato juice.

Don't throw away the rinds!

- **Marinate** In olive oil together with flavourings such as herbs, garlic, black peppercorns or chilli. Discard the rind and use the oil to drizzle or dip.
- **Parmesan broth** Simmer rinds in chicken or vegetable stock together with your choice of flavourings for an hour or more. Strain and use the broth in soup, sauces, and risottos.
- **Sauces and soups** Simmer in tomato sauces or soups, as is traditional when making Minestrone, or in any sauce or soup that you would grate Parmesan over.

BLUE CHEESE – AKA BLEU CHEESE IN AMERICA!
There are blue versions of most cheese types, Cambozola being a blue bloomy rind cheese, blue Wensleydale, and so on, so treat appropriately.

The salty, tangy taste of blue cheese is complemented by port, brandy, black pepper, garlic, roasted garlic, black garlic, caramelised onion, balsamic vinegar, bacon, beef, pears, figs, red grapes, walnuts, robust red or sweet dessert wine and honey.

- **Blue cheese and caramelised onion bread pudding** Omit the sugar from the bread pudding recipe (p49) and season to taste with salt and freshly ground black pepper. Add cooked onions (p303) and blue cheese.
- **Blue cheese butter** Mix with garlic, walnuts, black pepper or even dried pears See Compound Butters p288.
- **Blue cheese dip** Process blue cheese with an equal quantity of mayonnaise, flavour with roasted or

> **HANDY HINT**
> Keep a piece of hard blue cheese, such as Stilton or Gorgonzola, in the freezer where it will be handy to grate over dishes.

C

black garlic, caramelised onions or black pepper, and add
cream, if necessary, to thin the consistency.

- **Burgers** If you make your own burgers put a nugget of blue
cheese in the middle, making sure to enclose it completely.
- **Locket's savoury** See Watercress (p269).
- **Pears** Fill halved and cored ripe pears with crumbled blue
cheese and pop under a hot grill.
- **Polenta gratin with blue cheese and buttery leeks** (p303)
- **Salad** Crumble a hard blue cheese and toss in a salad,
especially one containing walnuts (see Pears p198, for a great
dressing for this kind of salad).
- **Steak** Scatter pieces of blue cheese over steak just before
serving or stir into the pan sauce; either way a drizzle of
balsamic vinegar is a good addition.

GOATS' CHEESE AND FETA

Goats' cheeses come in most of the above types: fresh, hard, crumbly, and
so on but I mention it separately because of its distinctive flavour, which
pairs very well with sweet flavours such as grapes and honey and with air-
dried ham and roasted vegetables.

- **Baked feta** Place a chunk of feta on a piece of lightly oiled foil.
Drizzle with good olive oil and season according to preference.
I usually add oregano and chilli flakes but roasted garlic is
good too. Loosely seal the parcel and bake in a preheated oven
at 200°C/gas 6 for 10– 15 minutes depending on the thickness
of the cheese. Serve with crusty bread and red wine.
- **Horiatiki** To make a Greek salad, toss lovely ripe tomatoes,
diced cucumber and chopped onion in a simple red wine
vinaigrette (made without mustard, see page 312) together
with fresh or dried oregano and salt and pepper. Serve topped
with black olives and feta.
- **Marinate in oil** Soak pieces of feta or goats' cheese in olive oil
flavoured with chilli, garlic, peppercorns, herbs and spices and
keep in the fridge for up to a month.
- **Stuffed figs** Fresh figs can be split open by cutting a cross
down from the tip into the flesh. Prise open the fruit and stuff
with goats' cheese, wrap in prosciutto, drizzle with balsamic
vinegar, then bake until warm and serve as a starter.

PROCESSED CHEESE

This is not so much a cheese as a 'cheese food' or 'cheese product', depending on how much of the real stuff it contains. It is made from a mixture of cheese or cheeses with at least some, if not all of the following – milk, whey, salt, emulsifiers, preservatives, colouring – and is heat-treated and emulsified. Some people claim that it is so bad it's good! I don't agree; it has little to recommend it other than it melts well and has a long shelf life.

- **Burgers** Melt on the top.
- **Fried sandwich** Make a 'grilled' 'cheese' sandwich (p66).

SWISS AND SWISS-STYLE CHEESES

These include 'eye' cheeses such as Emmental, Gruyère, Norwegian Jarlsberg and also Comté, Raclette, and similar sweet cows' milk cheeses with a mild, nutty taste and good melting qualities. Eat with cured meats, potatoes, grapes, apples, pears and white wine.

❄ These are not long keepers – say a month in the fridge.

- **Käseschnitte** This is a glorified cheese on toast or Swiss rarebit. Lay slices of toast in an ovenproof dish and sprinkle with white wine to moisten. Lay a slice of Swiss cheese on each piece of toast, then a slice of ham and another slice of cheese. Bake in a preheated oven at 200°C/gas 6 until the cheese is melted and lightly browned.
- **Raclette(ish)** Put a goodly lump of cheese in a dish under a hot grill or on the hearth in front of a roaring fire until it is pretty well melted and forming a skin. Serve traditionally scraped over new potatoes with gherkins and pearl onions or non-traditionally with crusty bread.
- **Stuffed chicken** Swiss cheese is used together with ham to stuff chicken breasts in the classic dish Chicken Cordon Bleu.

C

Cheesecake

- **Sundae** If, sadly, you are unable to eat all your cheesecake or want to share it amongst friends, remove the cheesy mixture from its base and layer up with fruit and cream or ice cream. Add some of the crumbled base to make a sundae-type thing.
- **Topping** Gently whisk some cream into the cheesecake filling to loosen its consistency and use to dollop onto desserts or sandwich biscuits together.

Cherries – see Fruit and also Berries for more ideas (even though they are not actually berries)

Eat with cream, cream cheese, goats' cheese, cinnamon, vanilla, almond, chocolate and brandy.

❄ Keep ripe cherries in a bag in the fridge and eat within a few days.

- **Breakfast** Add to breakfast cereal, yoghurt or fruit salad.
- **Cherry bounce** A delicious liqueur of cherries macerated in brandy – adapt the Rumtopf (p120).
- **Crumbles, clafoutis and pies** Make cherry crumble, clafoutis (p285) or cherry pie or add to apples or other fruit for a mixed fruit filling. See Crumble (p290).
- **Pancakes** Chop and add to pancakes (p283).

Dried cherries – see Dried fruit

Glacé and maraschino cherries

- **Cherry on the top** Use a shiny cherry to garnish drinks, sundaes and sticky buns.

> **HANDY HINT**
>
> Add to cakes, scones, breads, pancakes and so on, but rinse and dry well first or they might sink to the bottom.

C

Chestnuts

These are good with chocolate, honey, red wine, Madeira, caramelised onion, game, Brussels sprouts, sage and thyme.

- **Brussels and vegetables** Toss in butter together with cooked Brussels sprouts or other vegetables but Brussels are traditional.
- **Cabbage** Cook with red cabbage.
- **Casseroles** Include in rich winey braises.
- **Chestnut soup** Add cooked chestnuts in place of some or all the potatoes in Normal Soup (p309) and proceed as usual.
- **Stuffing** Chestnuts are a traditional ingredient in stuffing, particularly at Christmas. See recipe under Bread (p45).

Chicken

'The best way to execute French cooking is to get good and loaded and whack the hell out of a chicken. Bon appétit.' Julia Child

Chicken goes well with mushrooms, wine, cream, bacon, ham, leeks, garlic, lemon, chilli, curry spices, coconut and much more besides.

- **Coronation chicken** There are numerous variations of this classic dish but the basic idea is to flavour mayonnaise by stirring in some curry paste, mango chutney and fresh lime juice to taste. You can also make it lighter by adding Greek yoghurt. Fold in diced leftover chicken and garnish with fresh coriander. I think toasted almonds are traditional too.
- **Pasta** Toss chicken leftovers into sauced pasta dishes.
- **Patties** Make chicken cakes or patties using the fishcake recipes under Fish on p115.
- **Soups, salads, sandwiches and pizza** All benefit from some diced chicken thrown in.
- **Stir-fries** (p310).

Chicken fat – aka shmaltz

This really isn't very good for you but adds great flavour and is essential in traditional Jewish cooking.

❄ Strain warm fat into a clean glass jar and store in the fridge where it will keep for months, or freeze it.

- **Roast potatoes** Toss baby new potatoes in schmaltz together with some crunchy sea salt and roast; these are especially good with ... chicken.
- **Soup** Sweat diced onion and other vegetables in schmaltz as a base when making soup.

Gribenes

Gribenes are chicken skin and onions cooked together in schmaltz until crisp.

chicken fat and skin, cut into about 1cm pieces
sea salt and freshly ground black pepper
1 onion, thinly sliced or diced

1. Put the fat and skin into a heavy-based pan over a low heat and sprinkle with salt and pepper.
2. Cook, uncovered, until the fat starts to melt, then turn up the heat a little.
3. When the skin just starts to brown, stir in the onions and cook until everything is golden and crunchy.
4. Cool a little, then strain over a bowl.
5. Use the gribenes to sprinkle onto dishes or nibble on.
6. The resulting fat is, of course, schmaltz and can be used as above.

Chicken carcass

Once you've used the meat, fat and skin from your chicken, you can still get more flavour and goodness from it by using the carcass to make stock.

> **HANDY HINT**
>
> Chicken skin makes a tasty garnish; just season, cook in medium oven until crispy and use immediately.

- **Light stock** Put a roast chicken carcass with any meat still on the bones in a little cold water, just 1– 2 cups, in a heavy-based pan. Bring to the boil, cover and simmer for about 15 minutes. Remove the carcass and set aside just until cool enough to handle; whilst warm, it is possible to remove a surprising amount of meat from the bones. The stock will not be strongly flavoured but is still better than water in soups and stews. Use the meat scraps in a soup, with cooked pasta or in a sandwich.

- **Rich stock** For a stock that takes a bit more time but has a richer flavour, put the stripped carcass plus the giblets if you have them (minus the liver, see below) into a medium-sized pot. Add a quartered onion, chunks of carrot, maybe a celery stick and a handful of black peppercorns. Cover with cold water, bring to the boil, turn down the heat, cover and simmer for at least a couple of hours. Strain, cool and chill.

Chicken and other poultry livers

The rich, luxurious flavour of chicken livers is complemented by sweet tastes, such as caramelised onion, pears, cranberry sauce, and so on, as well as brandy, black pepper, bacon, wine – including medium and sweet white wines – port and sweet sherry.

❊ If you buy fresh chickens with giblets, freeze the livers until you have collected enough to make something worthwhile.

- **Bayou dirty rice** A traditional Cajun dish of rice cooked with giblets and pork, here's an easy leftovers-friendly version. Cook a chopped onion, a chopped celery stick and a crushed garlic clove in a little oil or bacon fat until soft. Add one part long grain rice and two parts chicken stock and simmer, covered, until the stock is absorbed and the rice is tender. Meanwhile, sauté coarsely chopped chicken livers and fold into the cooked rice together with seasonings which should properly include a bit of heat such as cayenne or Tabasco. Leftover bacon is good in this.

> **COOK'S TREAT**
>
> If you have 1–2 livers just removed from a fresh chicken, season and sauté in butter until brown on the outside, but still pink in the middle. Flame carefully with a touch of brandy and add enough cream to make a sauce. Mash all together and serve on toast.

- **Chicken liver vinaigrette** Gently poach 1– 2 chicken livers, crush with a fork and mix with vinaigrette.

C

- **Chopped liver** I was going to suggest chopped liver but it uses far too many livers to qualify as a recipe for leftovers!
- **Pâté** Purée warm, just-cooked chicken livers with soft butter, brandy and black pepper for a simple pâté.
- **Rumaki** I have read that this dish comes from Polynesia, Hawaii, Japan or was invented by a guy called Vic. I have seen recipes using salmon, water chestnuts and chicken livers. Here is a chicken liver version. Wrap bite-sized pieces of liver in bacon, roll in brown sugar and grill. Serve on cocktail sticks.

Chickpeas – aka garbanzos and ceci; see also Beans and pulses

These, to my mind the loveliest of pulses, have strong affinities with Middle Eastern flavours such as cumin, tahini, yoghurt and mint and with chorizo, spinach, garlic and olive oil. All the following ideas and recipes are for canned or home-cooked chickpeas. If you have leftover dried chickpeas, cook them and then do one of the following.

- **Hummus bi Tahini** This nutty dip is one of the best known uses for chickpeas. See recipe on p301.
- **Pasta e ceci** To make this soup, cook a finely chopped onion, 2 chopped celery sticks and a garlic clove together in a little olive oil to soften. For an authentic flavour, add a few finely chopped fresh rosemary leaves. Add about 200g leftover chickpeas, cover with stock and cook for about 20 minutes until the chickpeas are very tender. Remove half of the peas and purée the rest of the soup. Dilute with more stock if necessary, return the whole chickpeas, add a sprinkling of tiny pasta shapes and cook until tender. Taste and season. Leftover prosciutto is great in this, as is grated Parmesan.
- **Roasted chickpeas** Rinse the chickpeas, drain and pat dry. Toss with a little olive oil, spread on a baking sheet and roast in a preheated oven at 190°C/gas 5 for 30–40 minutes until shrivelled (in a good way), crisp and golden. Season with crunchy sea salt and spices to taste. Maybe stir in a few nuts or seeds for the last few minutes of cooking time.
- **Salads, soups, stews and curries** Try adding some chickpeas to any of these dishes. They will bulk out a meal and add their nutty flavour and texture.

Chicory – aka Endive and Witloof

I mean here the heads of compact white leaves with pale green or occasionally purple tips, which are not to be confused with the curly lettuce called frisée or escarole which is also known as both chicory and endive. I hope I've cleared that up for you!

Chicory tends to have a bitter taste and the more it is exposed to the light, the more bitter it becomes, so keep it in the dark. It is complemented by orange, ham and cheese.

❄ Store in the fridge for a few days. Do not freeze.

- **Crudités and edible 'spoons'** Individual leaves make great scoops for dips and salads.
- **Grilled chicory** Halve, drizzle the cut side with a little oil and grill – cut side to the heat – until just starting to char. Serve immediately with a fruity dressing; the pear vinaigrette under Pears would be good, especially with a little blue cheese too.
- **Salads and stir-fries** Add chicory leaves, sliced or whole, to salads and stir-fries.

Chilli peppers

The fruity heat of chillies enhances so many other foods that I personally would try them with almost anything! Chilli is gorgeous with chocolate, tropical fruits, all meats, tomatoes, garlic, many cheeses, seafood, beans, coconut, citrus, butternut squash, nuts and lots besides.

> **HANDY HINT**
> When working with chillies, don't put your fingers near your eyes or any other part of your or anyone else's body that you particularly value. Wash hands and utensils thoroughly.

❄ Store fresh chillies in the fridge for a week or so. They freeze successfully but lose their crispness. Either chop then freeze or freeze whole and slice off pieces as needed.

- **Chilli butter** Blend chopped chillies into butter. Other good additions are cumin, fresh coriander, lime or orange zest. See page 288 for how to make compound butters.

C

- **Fruit salad** A hint of chilli is great, at least to my mind, in tropical fruit salads.

Simultaneous Crystallised Chilli and Syrup

Use this in baked goods, add to chocolate desserts, such as chocolate ice cream and sprinkle a little over tropical fruit salads.

75g white sugar
150ml water
75g fresh hot chillies, deseeded and cut crosswise into thin strips

1. Bring the sugar and the water to a boil, stirring to dissolve the sugar.
2. Add the chillies and cook on a low heat, topping up with a little water as necessary, for 30 minutes.
3. Meanwhile preheat the oven to 180°C/gas 4 and line a baking tray with greaseproof paper.
4. Strain the chillies into a bowl, keeping both the chillies and the syrup; for me this makes about 150ml of syrup but it depends on how assiduously you top up the water.
5. Spread the chillies on the prepared baking tray.
6. Bake for 20–25 minutes, stirring and separating as they dry and crisp, remembering that they will crisp further as they cool.
7. When cold, break up any clumps and store in an airtight container.
8. Label both chillies and syrup clearly, use sparingly and maybe, like all good things, keep them out of the reach of children.

Chips – aka fries or French fries

There really isn't a lot that can be done with leftover chips but I'll give it a go.

- **Chip butty** Of course! This is useful if you don't have enough chips to go round.
- **Poutine** A popular French-Canadian dish of chips sprinkled with curd cheese and gravy poured over it! I'm not seriously suggesting it as a way to use up leftover chips; I just wanted to mention it.
- **Reheat** In a preheated oven at 200°C/gas 6 (*not* the microwave which will only make them soggier).

Chocolate

Dark chocolate enhances beef and game dishes and chilli con carne. Dark and milk chocolate go with coffee, chilli, vanilla, ginger, cinnamon, caramel, bananas, nuts, peanut butter, cherries, brandy, rum and several liqueurs. White chocolate additionally goes frightfully well with berries.

'Leftover chocolate' is, of course, an oxymoron but if you need to get the most out of a fragment of the wonderful stuff here are some ideas.

- **Cakes and biscuits** Add chopped chocolate to any chocolate friendly cake or biscuit recipe.
- **Chocolate bread pudding** Follow the bread pudding recipe (p50) but add 1 tbsp cool, very strong coffee to the custard mix, toss coarsely chopped chocolate together with the bread and sprinkle the top with light brown sugar before baking.
- **Chocolate meringues** Fold coarsely chopped chocolate into meringue before baking.
- **Chocolate sandwiches** Especially good if made with brioche and served warm.
- **Dessert toppings** Grate chocolate over ice cream, cappuccino, trifle, cake, mousse and Affogato (see Ice cream p150).

> **COOK'S TREAT**
>
> Take a square of chocolate and manoeuvre it into the roof of your mouth. Now drink a delicious coffee without disturbing the chocolate; this makes the coffee taste wonderful and the chocolate last longer than usual. Once adept at this, try adding a sip of brandy.

C

- **Ganache** Coarsely chop some chocolate. Bring an equal quantity of double cream *almost* to the boil, then pour it over the chocolate and stir until smooth. Serve warm as a sauce or dip, chilled as a rich mousse, chilled and whipped as a frosting, or chilled very thoroughly, rolled into balls, coated in cocoa *et voilà* – truffles!
- **Pancakes** Sprinkle coarsely chopped chocolate onto pancakes when cooking the first side (p283).
- **Stews** A square or two of dark, dark chocolate enhances rich game and beef stews and also chilli con carne.

Hot Chocolate Caramel Sauce

120g caster sugar
180ml double cream
90g dark chocolate
pinch of salt
½ tsp vanilla extract

1. Gently melt the sugar in a heavy-based pan and cook over a medium heat, swirling the pan from time to time, until caramelised – a rich reddish brown.
2. Immediately and carefully (this will splutter a lot) add the cream and stir over a low heat until the caramel, which will have hardened, has melted again.
3. Stir in the chocolate, salt and vanilla and whisk until smooth.

Chocolate spread

- **Bread and butter pudding** Add some chocolate spread with some sliced bananas, hazelnuts and chunks of chocolate. See recipe on p50.
- **Chocolate banana ice cream** Fold 25g chocolate spread into the Famous One Ingredient Ice Cream on p28.
- **Smoothies and milkshakes** Both can often benefit from a spoonful of chocolate spread (p308).

> **COOK'S TREAT**
> Here's an enjoyable way of rinsing out a jar of chocolate spread – although it's so good don't restrict yourself to just those occasions. Ideally use 2 tbsp chocolate spread per person, dissolve it in a cup of warm water or milk and bring gently almost to the boil.

Chorizo

This difficult-to-pronounce sausage comes in many different styles but here I am talking about dry chorizo, whether it be spicy, garlicky or whatever, which are complemented by potatoes, tomatoes, beans, fish, chicken, garlic, spinach and chickpeas.

❈ Please go by the use-by date, which can vary from a week to several months. It freezes okay but declines in quality after a couple of months.

- **Chorizo butter** Make a butter with finely chopped chorizo plus about an equal quantity of soft butter and perhaps smoked paprika and finely chopped red onion (p288). This is good melted over fish.
- **Chorizo in red wine** Cook finely diced red onion and a little garlic in a drizzle of olive oil until tender. Add thickly sliced chorizo and cook until the fat is running, then add a generous glug of red wine. Bring to the boil, turn down the heat and simmer until the wine has almost evaporated. Serve with good bread, salty cheese and red wine or as part of a selection of tapas.
- **Eggs and other things** Add to hash, risotto, frittata, omelettes, scrambled eggs, soups, pastas and pizza (see the Basic Recipes section).
- **Paella** I'm not going to give a recipe for Paella here but if you have one about the place, add some chorizo.

C

- **Potatoes roasted with chorizo** Toss new potatoes with sliced chorizo, a little sea salt and enough oil to coat lightly. Roast in a preheated oven at 200°C/gas 6 for 30–40 minutes until the potatoes are tender, crusty and golden, and the chorizo is crisp.
- **Salads and garnish** Fry thin slices in a little oil until crisp before adding to salads, using as a garnish or just eating.

Christmas cake – see also Cake

❄ Christmas cake, if prepared and stored correctly (well wrapped and kept somewhere cool), will keep a long while, but if you have only crumbs left or not enough cake to go round here are a few ideas.

- **Boxing Day pancakes** Crumble onto pancakes when cooking the first side and serve with a dollop of brandy butter melting over them (p283).
- **Christmas cake pudding** Use cake instead of bread in bread pudding (p49).
- **Christmas trifle** Soak the cake in a little brandy or other suitable liqueur and use seasonal ingredients such as orange and cranberry. See Trifle (p119).
- **Christmassy recycled biscuit cake** Add chunks of cake plus leftover Christmas nuts, dried fruits and chocolate Santas off the tree. See Recycled Biscuit Cake (p42).
- **Ice cream** Crumble the cake, then fold into soft vanilla ice cream together with a tot of brandy.

Christmas leftovers – see also Cranberry, Mincemeat, Turkey, Various and Vegetables

- **Christmas pie** Turkey, gravy, stuffing balls and any other leftovers such as sausage meat, chestnuts, and so on, make a delicious pie topped with pastry or mash.
- **Christmas pizza** Spread the base with leftover gravy and top with shredded turkey and crumbled stuffing. Drizzle with

cranberry sauce a minute or two before taking out the oven. If you feel cheese is necessary, then I suggest something mild and creamy, such as Brie.

- **Hash** Make turkey bubble and squeak including all the leftover veggies from the Big Meal plus turkey and stuffing (p211).
- **Turkey sandwiches** Obviously, with added stuffing, cranberry sauce and perhaps a pot of dipping gravy.

Christmas pudding

- **Christmas pudding sauce** Melt a knob of butter and a spoonful of brown sugar. Stir in crumbled Christmas pudding plus brandy or rum to taste and serve with ice cream.
- **Christmas pudding truffles** Similar to cake pops (p59) but use brandy butter as the binder.
- **Reheat luxuriously!** Fry thick slices of leftover Christmas pudding in butter and serve with custard, cream or ice cream or, if it is still the season of goodwill, all three.

Christmas stuffing

- **Boxing Day fritters** Form leftover stuffing into balls, flatten and put a spoonful of cranberry sauce in the middle, then reform the ball, enclosing the cranberry sauce completely. Dip in flour, egg and breadcrumbs and deep-fry until hot, crisp and golden. Eat carefully as the cranberry will be very hot. You could also form the stuffing into cakes, shallow-fry in a pan until crisp and serve with cranberry sauce.
- **Seasonal croûtons** Dice cold stuffing and shallow-fry until crisp. Serve with turkey soup or salad.
- **Toad in the hole** Make stuffing balls or sausage shapes and use instead of real sausages (p285).

C

Cider and perry

For people in the US, see Apple juice for 'non-alcoholic cider'.

The apple taste of cider is good with fish, cheese, bacon, pork and, of course, apples. Perry is better with pears and blue cheese.

- **Apple or pear cream sauce** Deglaze a pork or chicken pan with dry cider or perry, reduce a little and finish with cream. It's even better if you cook a few apple or pear slices alongside the meat.
- **Apple sauce** Add a splash to apple sauce (p15).
- **Chicken or pork** Use as part of the liquid when braising chicken or pork.
- **Flat cider** or **perry** is fine to cook with.
- **Wassail** This is a mulled apple juice. Use cider instead of apple juice in the recipe and add a tot of Calvados or brandy when serving.
- **Welsh rarebit** Replace ale with cider (p38), or make a blue cheese version with perry.
- **Wine** Replace white wine in recipes with dry cider.

Clams – see Shellfish

Clementines – see Oranges

Clotted cream

Clotted cream complements fruits, cake, chocolate, scones (of course) and mushrooms.

- ❄ Keep chilled and go by the best-before date. Clotted cream does freeze but will be separated and lumpy when thawed. Whisk gently to bring it back together, although it will still not be quite as creamy and might be best used for cooking.

- **Anchovies** Strange but true – clotted cream is pleasant with anchovy or anchovy paste (Gentleman's Relish) on toast.
- **Dark chocolate truffles** Gently melt some chocolate, then

stir in an equal quantity of clotted cream. Chill to firm. Roll into balls and coat in cocoa, grated chocolate, finely chopped nuts or something similar.

- **Frosting** Mix with an equal quantity of sifted icing sugar to fill and frost a cake.
- **Mushrooms** A spoonful or so adds a rich flourish to garlicky sautéed mushrooms.
- **Potatoes** Add to mashed potatoes – very luxurious – or use to fill baked potatoes.
- **Soup** Stir a dollop into soup.
- **Thunder and lightning** This is, for some reason, the name given in Cornwall, UK, to the combination of golden syrup and clotted cream; try it on toast.
- **Toast** In the absence of scones, jam and clotted cream is excellent on toast.

Cockles – see Shellfish

Coconut

Coconut goes well with citrus or tropical fruits, seafood, chicken, rice, vanilla, chocolate, ginger, chilli and spicy foods in general.

Fresh coconut

❄ Keep whole fresh coconut in the fridge. Cut coconut can be refrigerated for four days or so. Shred or chop the flesh and wrap well to freeze.

Canned coconut milk

❄ Once opened, keep in a non-reactive container in the fridge for up to five days.

- **Coconut and toasted spice marinade** For chicken and fish, dry-fry a spoonful of curry powder or paste

> **HANDY HINT**
> Once coconut milk has been sitting for a day or so, the thick coconut cream rises to the top and can be carefully spooned off to enrich soups and sauces.

until smelling fragrant, stir in about 300ml coconut milk and cool before using.

- **Rice** Use the coconut water left over after spooning off the cream (above), to replace some or all of the water when cooking rice.
- **Smoothies** Use coconut milk instead of some or all of the milk.

Creamed coconut block

✽ This keeps very well in a cool pantry or the fridge.

- **Fish** I always cut off the layer of coconut oil at the top of the block and save it to fry fish.
- **Spicy dishes** Coarsely chop and stir into curries or spicy sauces.
- **Tomato and coconut dip** Gently melt together some creamed coconut with about twice its volume of tinned chopped tomatoes until merged. Add salt, pepper, lime juice and some chilli heat to taste.

Desiccated and shredded coconut

✽ Dried coconut keeps very well, tightly wrapped, in a cool, dry cupboard or the fridge.

To toast coconut, spread on a baking tray and pop in a preheated oven at 180°C/gas 4 until golden. Check it frequently and stir around so that it browns fairly evenly. Take it out when it looks good, cool completely and store in an airtight container.

- **Breakfast** Mix into granola or muesli.
- **Cake** Add to recycled biscuit cake (p42).
- **Coconut crust** Dip shrimp, fish or chicken in seasoned flour, beaten egg and then dried coconut or a mixture of coconut and breadcrumbs. Shallow-fry until golden and serve with a spicy dip.
- **Ice cream** Stir toasted coconut into ice cream.
- **Meringues** Fold coconut into meringues before baking (p107).

Coffee

Coffee is delicious with chocolate, cream, spirits and liqueurs, vanilla, cinnamon, cardamom, nuts especially walnuts, bacon, beef and a pinch of salt.

Made coffee

❄ It's only worth saving really good strong delicious coffee leftovers; store in the fridge or freeze until needed. These ideas are for black coffee, no sugar! Freeze coffee in ice cubes as an interesting way to cool appropriate drinks – vodka springs to mind.

- **Affogato** See Cook's treat (p150).
- **Bread** Add a little to French toast (p51) or bread pudding (p49).
- **Casseroles** Add to beef braises and pot roasts for rich, dark gravy.
- **Coffee Martini** Shake together good strong cold coffee or espresso with half as much vodka, a quarter as much Kahlua and ice. Strain into martini glasses. Add cream if you wish.
- **Hair colour** Brunettes can enhance their hair colour with a coffee rinse. Pour strong black coffee over your hair, work in and leave for 10–15 minutes before rinsing out.
- **Hot chocolate** Use instead of water when making hot chocolate.
- **Iced coffee** Pour cold coffee over ice, sweeten with sugar or syrup and add milk or cream or rum or something to taste. (See also *Ca phe sua da* under Condensed milk.)

Ham and Red Eye Gravy

This is traditionally served in America's Deep South with hot biscuits or grits for breakfast.

SERVES 1

1 thick slice of ham
1 tsp bacon fat
pinch of sugar
30ml strong coffee

1. Fry the ham in the bacon fat until brown and hot.
2. Set aside and keep warm.
3. Add the sugar and coffee to the pan and cook, stirring and scraping up any ham juices.
4. Taste, season, maybe dilute with a little water and pour over ham.

Coffee Caramel Syrup

240ml good strong coffee
225g sugar
120ml water

1. Set the coffee beside the stove.
2. Stir together the sugar and the water over a low heat until the sugar is dissolved.
3. Boil to a deep reddish brown, watching closely and swirling occasionally. As soon as it reaches the right colour, all at once yet carefully (it will boil rapidly) add the coffee and stir over a medium heat until the caramel melts back into the coffee.
4. Simmer for a few minutes until reduced and thickened slightly.
5. Cool.

HANDY HINT

Clean the pan by making a cup of coffee in it!

C

Coffee beans

- **Coffee brittle** Replace nuts with crushed coffee beans (p179).
- **Coffee sugar** Crack beans and add to a container of sugar to infuse with flavour, in a similar way to making vanilla sugar.

Ground coffee

※ Keep dry, dark, airtight and cool.

- **Meringues** Add a spoonful to the meringues recipe on p107.

Condensed milk

※ Decant condensed milk into an airtight container and it will be good in the fridge for 1–2 weeks, officially, but considerably longer in reality. Don't say I said so. Neat condensed milk does not freeze successfully.

- **Easy chocolate fudge or fudge sauce** Gently melt together equal quantities of condensed milk and dark chocolate, stir in a few drops of vanilla

> **COOK'S TREAT**
> Spoon out of the tin and eat it!

extract and enough warm water to form a sauce OR leave out the water and add chopped nuts, spread onto a board, cool, then cut into pieces.
- **Moose milk** For this delicious warming drink, stir together equal quantities of sweetened condensed milk and dark rum, then top up with hot water. This tastes as if it could be good for a cold.
- **Smoothies** Replace some of the milk in a smoothie (p308) with condensed milk.
- **Sorbet** Freeze Vietnamese iced coffee, below, as lollies or cubes. Crush the frozen cubes in a food processor to make coffee sorbet.
- **Vietnamese iced coffee** If you like sweet coffee, use condensed milk instead of regular which leads me to … *Ca phe sua da*, Vietnamese iced coffee. For a simple version, stir

C

together one part condensed milk and three parts hot coffee. Pour over the back of a teaspoon into a tall glass containing ice cubes. This is surprisingly delicious.

Cookies – see Biscuits

Corn – see Sweetcorn

Cornmeal

HANDY HINT
Sprinkle onto a baking tray for pizza or bread to give a tasty non-stick surface.

- **Crisp coating** Use instead of or as well as breadcrumbs for a crispy crust on fried foods.

Courgettes – aka zucchini plus other summer squash such as pattypans, crookneck or marrow

Courgettes taste good with tomatoes, onions, aubergine, garlic, lemon, basil, oregano, mint, dill and chives and almost all cheeses.

❄ Raw courgettes will keep well in the fridge for four or five days. Blanch to freeze. Cooked will keep up to four days in the fridge and freeze well.

- **Baking** Try replacing carrot in carrot cake recipes with courgette or there are many recipes for chocolate courgette brownies and the like.
- **Courgette flowers** Their blossoms are edible – dip in Tempura batter (p285) and deep-fry or stuff first and then deep-fry. You can even eat them raw.
- **Courgette fritters** Grate courgette and mix with crushed garlic, mint and feta into the fritter recipe on p286.
- **Fried and marinated** Grilled, roasted or pan-fried courgettes are quite absorbent so as soon as they are cooked, toss in a light vinaigrette and some fresh herbs, if you have them. Season and allow to marinate a few hours.

- **Frittata** Add raw or cooked to frittata (p296).
- **Pizza** Top a pizza with thin slices of courgette, brush with oil and season before baking.
- **Raw** Courgettes can be eaten raw; slice and add to salads or serve alongside other crudités with a dip.
- **Roasted vegetables** Roast with other vegetables such as onion, aubergine and pepper.
- **Smashed courgette dip** Slice and cook very gently, covered, in a little olive oil together with some chopped garlic and dried chilli, stirring occasionally. When very tender, smash up a bit and season to taste with not only salt and pepper but also fresh mint and lemon juice.

Couscous

- **Breakfast** Heat plain leftover couscous gently with honey or maple syrup, dried fruit and nuts and a spot of cream for breakfast.
- **Stuffing and meatloaf** Use to add texture, flavour and bulk to meatloaf, meatballs, stuffing and so on.
- **Tart base** Mix about 150g leftover couscous with about 15g melted butter and press into a pie dish. Fill with whatever you fancy or have left over and bake in a preheated oven at 180°C/gas 4 until the filling is hot and cooked and the crust golden.

Crabs – see Shellfish

Crackers

- **Break into soup** In America, soup is often served with crackers, particularly a variety called saltines. As people often break crackers directly into the soup this would seem ideal for leftover broken crackers.
- **Coating for fried foods** Crush savoury crackers and use as part or all of the coating.

C

- **Seed sprinkles** If seeded crackers have shed their seeds in the packet sprinkle them on salads (see also Seeds).

Cranberries and cranberry sauce – see also Berries

The sharp-sweet flavour of cranberries is good with orange, port, soft and cream cheeses, chicken, turkey, duck, goose, cured meats and pâtés, pumpkin, squash and apples.

- **Apples** Mix with apples in a pie or crumble.
- **Baking** Add whole cranberries to baked goods or swirl sauce through them before cooking.
- **Breakfast** Stir into yoghurt or porridge.
- **Cabbage** Add some cranberries or cranberry sauce when cooking red cabbage.
- **Goats' cheese and cranberry tartlets** Roll out puff pastry and cut into squares or rounds. Score a border round each one and spread the inner sections with cranberry sauce. Top with a slice or dollop of goats' cheese and bake in a preheated oven at 200°C/gas 6 for 10–15 minutes until the edges are puffed up and golden. Serve warm.
- **Sandwiches** Cranberry sauce is excellent in bacon and brie sandwiches, turkey sandwiches or peanut butter sandwiches.
- **Soup** Warm cranberry sauce and drizzle onto pumpkin soup.
- **Syrup** Warm leftover cranberry sauce with a little orange juice and use as a syrup for pancakes or ice cream or to glaze ham.
- **Turkey meatballs** Put a teaspoonful of cranberry sauce in the middle of turkey meatballs.
- **Vinaigrette** Add 1–2 spoonfuls to vinaigrette for a Christmassy tasting salad.

Crawfish – see Shellfish

Crayfish – see Shellfish

Cream – see also Clotted cream and Crème fraîche

❄ Keep in the fridge. The higher the fat content the more likely cream is to freeze successfully, but it may still be grainy when thawed. This can be avoided by whisking double cream until thick and freezing in small portions for ease of use.

● **Custard based dishes** Add to dishes such as French toast and bread pudding (see Bread pp49, 51).

● **Potatoes** Add a spoonful of cream when mashing potatoes.

● **Scones** Use instead of milk to make scones, which will then be called shortcakes (p292)!

● **Soups and sauces** Use to enrich all sorts of dishes.

Crème fraîche

The tangy flavour of crème fraîche, which is something between yoghurt and soured cream, goes well with berries, smoked fish, salmon and caviar.

❄ Keep chilled. If frozen, it will separate but may still be usable in soups and sauces.

● **Cream or cheese substitute** Use in place of cream, soured cream or cream cheese in sweet and savoury recipes.

● **Desserts** Dollop on top of desserts as you might use thick double cream.

● **Mashed potatoes** Add to potatoes to make a creamy mash.

● **Mushroom sauce** Stir into sautéed mushrooms to make a quick sauce.

● **Sauces** Mix with black pepper, lemon zest and horseradish to go with smoked fish, or add Dijon mustard to serve with roast beef.

● **Soup** Enrich soups with crème fraîche, added at the end of the cooking time. Don't allow them to boil or they will separate.

C

Crêpes – see p283 for the basic recipe

- **Filled pancakes** Wrap round a savoury filling, lay them in a greased baking dish, pour over a creamy or cheese sauce and bake in a preheated oven at 200°C/gas 6 for 15 minutes.
- **Sweet options** Do a similar thing with a sweet filling, topped with cream and sugar.

Crevettes – see Shellfish

Crisps – aka chips in American-speaking nations

❄ Pointless, I know, but crisps freeze well and can be eaten from frozen!

- **Breadcrumb coating** Add crushed crisps to breadcrumbs when coating for fried foods.
- **Crunchy sprinkles** Crush and sprinkle over dishes that are crying out for a bit of crunch such as creamy dishes.
- **Spanish omelettes** I read of and so tried a Spanish-ish omelette using crisps instead of fresh potato. Soak crisps in beaten egg for a few minutes and then make an omelette as usual. I can't say I recommend it.

Croissants

See Bread for all the details of the following suggestions and
substitute croissants for the bread.

- **Bread pudding** Cut lengthways and lay in the dish so that
  when baked the cut edges at the top of the pudding go
  delicately crisp.
- **Croissant French toast** Cut the croissants in half lengthways
  and serve cut-side up so that the crisp layers trap all the gooey
  syrup and butter.
- **Croûtons** Croissants make lovely crunchy ones.

Crumpets and pikelets

Now these are tricky! Other than a base for various sweet or savoury
toppings they don't really inspire me at all so I would suggest freezing
leftovers until one of us thinks of something!

Cucumber

Good with fish, soured cream, yoghurt, cream cheese, mayonnaise,
vinegar, tomatoes, onion, chilli, mint, dill, chives, parsley and Pimm's.

- ❄ Uncut cucumber will keep for up to a week in the fridge, a cut
  one just two or three days. It doesn't freeze with any success.

- **Eye soother** Put a cool slice of cucumber on each eye and
  relax in a prone position to soothe and refresh eyes and to
  reduce dark circles and puffiness.
- **Pimm's** Use thin slices of cucumber for garnish. Try
  cucumber in a gin and tonic instead of a slice of lemon or lime.
- **Raita or tzatziki** Make these delicious dips (p279).

C

Sweet Cucumber Pickle

Sweet, crunchy and excellent with spicy dishes, seafood and salads.

1 cucumber
salt
3 tsp light brown sugar
150ml white vinegar
pinch of chilli flakes (optional)

HANDY HINT

The easy way to deseed a cucumber is to score a line with a sharp knife either side of the seeds and use a sharp edged teaspoon to scrape them out.

1. Top and tail the cucumber and halve lengthways. Remove the seeds (see the Handy hint).
2. Slice as thinly as possible and put into a nylon sieve suspended over a bowl.
3. Salt generously, tossing to coat, then leave for an hour or more.
4. Empty the juices from the bowl, fill it with cold water and wash the cucumber. Drain well.
5. Stir the sugar into the vinegar until dissolved and add the chilli, if using.
6. Stir in the cucumbers, put in an airtight jar or container, cover and chill until needed.

Custard sauce

❄ Press clingfilm onto the surface of custard, right out to the edges, to prevent a skin forming (unless you like custard skin, some people do). Keep chilled for a day or two.

- **Bananas and custard** Fill a pretty glass or two with sliced bananas (possibly macerated in rum and brown sugar), custard and cream.
- **Cream filling** Fold cold custard into whipped cream to fill cakes or éclairs.
- **Fool** Substitute custard for some of the cream when making a fruit fool (p300).
- **Trifle** Layer with cake, fruit and cream to make trifle (p119).

D

Daikon – see Radish

Damsons – see Plums

Dates, dried – see also Dried fruit and Fruit

Cinnamon, blue cheese, bacon, bananas, walnuts and honey all go well with dates.

❄ Dried dates keep well for up to a year in a cool, dark place and can be frozen.

- **Baking** Coarsely chop and add to all sorts of baked goods.
- **Biscuits** Include chopped dates in recycled biscuit cake (p42).
- **Blue cheese** Serve with blue cheese dishes and salads.
- **Breakfast** Sprinkle chopped dates onto breakfast cereals and porridge.
- **Sandwiches** Add to banana sandwiches.
- **Stuff them** Remove the stones and insert a delicious filling, such as bananas and peanut butter, bacon and goats' cheese, blue cheese and honey, or marzipan.
- **Stuffing** Add to stuffing, particularly for lamb (p45).

> **COOK'S TREAT**
> Snack on them!

Dhal – aka dal or dahl, this concerns the cooked dish; for uncooked dhal see Beans and pulses

Leftovers of this lovely Indian dish lend themselves to some other excellent dishes.

- **Dhal roti** Mix enough flour into the cold dhal to make a soft dough. Roll into balls and then flatten into thick rounds and cook on a lightly greased tava or frying pan until the first side is brown. Turn, fry the other side and serve with curries, salads or even more dhal.

- **Dhal soup** Dilute leftover dhal with stock or water to a soupy consistency. Taste and season and, if possible, serve topped with a dollop of thick plain yoghurt and some crisply fried shreds of poppadom.
- **Lentil fritters** Dhal thickens up considerably when cold, so form into patties, coat in seasoned flour and fry to crisp.

Doughnuts

I honestly can't think of a lot to do with leftover doughnuts but a friend of mine did once make an excellent doughnut bread pudding (p49).

Dressing – see Vinaigrette or Stuffing depending on your point of view

Dried fruit

❆ Keep dried fruits cool and dry in a sealed container for up to a year.

- **Baking** Stir into fruit-friendly baking recipes.
- **Breakfast** Add to muesli, granola or trail mix (p302).
- **Macerate** Put dried fruit in a clean jar and add enough brandy or rum to cover by a depth of 1cm. Wait at least 24 hours before using the macerated fruit with ice cream, in bread pudding, scones, pancakes, in fact anywhere you would use un-macerated fruit. As you get more leftover fruit, add it to the jar, topping up with spirit as necessary to keep it submerged. You can carry on like this forever. If you run out of fruit the liquor will be delicious for drinking purposes.
- **Salads and rice** Toss into salads and rice dishes.

Dripping – see Gravy

Dublin Bay Prawns – see Shellfish

Duck

Duck is good with honey, ginger, squash, sweet potatoes, hoisin, garlic and not just oranges but plums, cherries, pomegranate, blackcurrants and cranberries.

❄ Store raw duck, wrapped in the fridge for no longer than the best-before date and if it doesn't have one, then just for a couple of days. Raw duck freezes successfully. Cooked duck keeps in the fridge for up to four days and freezes well.

● **Crispy garnish** Shred, crisply fry and garnish appropriate dishes with it.
● **Noodles** Add duck to stir-fries and noodle dishes.

Easy Rillettes

1. Cook leftover duck meat in a heavy-based pan very gently in about an equal quantity of duck fat for an hour or so until meltingly tender.
2. Cool a little, then shred the warm meat with two forks, and not any other way, and mix together with the fat.
3. Season to taste with garlic, salt, pepper and a little Cognac.
4. Press into ramekins, ensuring every scrap of meat is under the duck fat.
5. Chill for at least a day to meld flavours but serve at room temperature with good bread and red wine.

● **Leftover Rillettes** Stir a spoonful or two into risotto.

D

Duck fat

❄ Don't ever, ever throw duck fat away; strain, cool and keep covered in the fridge for up to six months.

- **Grattons** These are crispy pieces of duck skin fried in their own fat. These can arise naturally as a result of rendering duck fat or, if not, dice the skin and fry until crisp. Drain on kitchen paper, season and eat as soon as cool enough, or use to garnish soups, salads, pâtés and general duck dishes (see also Gribenes under Chicken).
- **Hash** Cook potato hash (p211) in duck fat and add any meat scraps.
- **Roast chicken** Rub duck fat onto chicken before roasting to give a really crisp skin.
- **Roast potatoes** Fry or roast seriously tasty potatoes in duck fat – a little garlic wouldn't go amiss here too.
- **Roast squash** Roast squash or pumpkin in duck fat together with red onion or shallots.

Dumplings – see the recipe under Dough for how to make these (p292–94).

- **Fried** Fry in butter until hot and crisp and serve instead of fried potatoes.
- **Soups and stews** Reheat gently in soup or stew.

Duxelles – for how to make Duxelles see Mushrooms

- **Egg dishes** Add to all sorts of egg dishes (p294–98).
- **Pasta sauce** Stir through pasta in creamy sauce.
- **Pizza** Spread on a pizza base instead of the more traditional tomato sauce.
- **Risotto** Stir through risotto (p306).
- **Steak sauce** Add to a steak pan when deglazing with wine.
- **Toast** Spread on toast and top with cheese or crispy bacon and a poached egg.

E

Easter eggs – see Chocolate unless they are of the boiled egg persuasion, in which case see Eggs

Edamame – aka soya beans
Use leftover edamame (nice word!) anywhere you might use leftover peas or broad beans.

Eggs

❄ Store eggs in the fridge but bring to room temperature before cooking. Freeze individual eggs, lightly beaten, in ice cube trays. Allow to thaw naturally.

Eggnog

If you've two good eggs you don't know what to do with, here is your answer but if you are worried about raw eggs, then I'm afraid this isn't for you.

2 lovely fresh eggs
90g caster sugar
1 tsp vanilla extract
225ml double cream
300ml cold milk
brandy, rum or bourbon
freshly grated nutmeg

1. Whisk together the eggs and sugar until starting to thicken.
2. Whisk in the vanilla and the double cream until well combined.
3. Lastly whisk in the milk.
4. Chill until needed.

E

5. Serve with a tot of brandy, rum or
    bourbon and sprinkle with nutmeg.

HANDY HINT

If possible decant into
an empty brandy bottle
so that its aroma can
infuse the nog; I even
hate to waste smells!

● **Bread pudding** Use nog instead of
  some of the egg mixture to make a
  boozy bread pudding (p50).
● **French toast** Use leftover nog –
  preferably made with brandy to be properly French – instead
  of the egg mixture (p51).
● **Pancakes** Replace some of the egg with nog (p283).

Boiled eggs

If you have eggs to spare, hard boil them to stop them spoiling then use
them in a variety of tasty ways.

❄ Keep in the fridge for up to a week and, if peeled, make sure
   they are under water. Change the water daily.

● **Curried eggs** Heat gently in a curry sauce and serve with rice.
● **Devilled eggs** Peel hard-boiled eggs, cut in half lengthways,
  scoop out the yolk and mash to a paste with mayonnaise and
  Dijon mustard plus seasonings of your choice. Spoon or pipe
  the mixture back into whites and sprinkle with paprika to
  serve. This lends itself to all sorts of variations; cheese and
  chilli, bacon, black pepper, anchovies, garlic, capers and so on.
● **Egg mayonnaise** Coarsely chop or mash boiled eggs and stir
  into mayonnaise to use in sandwiches, salads or as a filling for
  a baked potato.
● **Eggs mornay** Pour cheese sauce (p66) over boiled eggs,
  sprinkle with more cheese and fresh breadcrumbs and bake in
  a preheated oven at 180°C/gas 4 until hot and crisply golden.
  Leftover spinach would be a traditional addition and sippets
  (triangles of crustless bread fried in butter until crisp) a
  traditional accompaniment.
● **Kedgeree** Add quartered hard-boiled eggs to this traditional
  rice dish (p116).
● **Mimosa** To make this old-fashioned garnish, separate whites
  and yolks, chop the whites and press the yolks through a sieve.

Mix together with chopped parsley and crunchy sea salt. Sprinkle on fish dishes, asparagus, chopped liver, to name a few uses.

- **Salads** Add to potato salad, as is traditional in America or to the French Salade Niçoise (p118).
- **Scotch eggs** Wrap cold hard-boiled eggs (peeled, of course!) in 70–80g seasoned sausage meat per egg, making sure there are no gaps. Roll in beaten egg and then fresh breadcrumbs. Deep-fry until crisp and golden.

Sauce Gribiche

A cross between egg mayonnaise and tartare sauce traditionally served on tête de veau and possibly even better with fish or asparagus.

1 hard-boiled egg, separated into yolk and white
2 tsp Dijon mustard
2 tsp red wine vinegar
120ml vegetable oil
1 finely chopped shallot
1 tbsp capers, chopped
2 gherkins, chopped
1 tsp chopped parsley
1 tsp chopped tarragon
salt and freshly ground black pepper

1. Mash the egg yolk with the mustard and vinegar.
2. Gradually whisk in the oil, then stir in the chopped egg white and the other ingredients.
3. Season to taste.

E

Egg whites

Many recipes call for an extra egg yolk, leaving you with white to spare.

❄ Store covered in the fridge for a few days or they freeze well as ice cubes. Thaw naturally.

- **Baking glaze** Whisk lightly with a pinch of salt and brush onto baked goods before cooking for a shiny glaze.

<table>
<tr><td>

HANDY HINT

30ml egg white is the equivalent of the white of one large egg.

</td></tr>
</table>

- **Egg white omelette** Like a normal omelette really but just using egg whites – very slimming and disappointing!
- **Fritters** Fold a stiffly beaten egg white into fritter batter for extra lightness (p285–86).
- **Meringues** See My Failsafe Meringue Recipe opposite.
- **Pastry cases** To seal a pre-baked pastry case so that it doesn't get a soggy bottom when filled, brush with lightly beaten egg white and return to the oven for an extra couple of minutes.
- **Sorbet** Lightly whisk an egg white or two until foamy, then fold into sorbet just before freezing for a smooth, creamy texture (p299).

HANDY HINTS

Older egg whites whisk more successfully than newer ones and room temperature whites work better than cold, so get them out of the fridge an hour before using.

It is absolutely imperative when whisking egg whites that nothing greasy comes anywhere near them. Make sure that your bowl, whisk, hands etc. are completely grease-free. Furthermore, when separating the whites from the yolks, ensure that no yolk at all is left in the whites – yolks are greasy. The easiest way to lift a spot of yolk out of egg white is to use a piece of egg shell.

My Failsafe (honestly) Meringue Recipe

2 egg whites
375g caster sugar
½ tsp pure vanilla extract
3 tbsp boiling water

1. Preheat the oven to 110°C/gas ½.
2. Have ready a large baking tray lined with baking parchment or greaseproof paper.
3. Put the egg whites, sugar and vanilla into a large, dry, grease-free bowl.
4. Start whisking, add the boiling water and continue whisking until the mixture is very thick and stands in stiff peaks.
5. Pipe or spoon the meringue into your required shapes onto the trays and bake for a couple of hours until crisp and dry. When they are a pale biscuit colour and sound crisp when tapped on the bottom, they are ready.

Egg yolks

❄ Store raw yolks in the fridge but just for a couple of days, covered with a spoonful of cold water to stop them drying out; carefully pour it off before using. They freeze well but should be stabilised first; stir either a pinch of salt or a pinch of sugar into each yolk, depending on what you intend to use them for. Ice cube trays are a good idea for freezing them. Allow to thaw naturally.

● **Golden glaze** Beat an egg yolk with a pinch of salt and brush onto pastry before baking for a golden glaze.
● **Lemon Curd** See Lemons p160.
● **Mayonnaise** Whisk two room-temperature egg yolks with ½ tsp of salt, 1 tsp Dijon or English mustard and a grinding of black pepper. Gradually, literally a drop at a time, start whisking in 300ml vegetable oil. If you add the oil too fast the mayonnaise will curdle. After a while you will have a very thick emulsion, at which stage whisk in 1 tsp white wine vinegar or

lemon juice and then the rest of the oil, speeding up slightly. Taste and adjust the seasoning, adding more lemon juice or maybe a little garlic, if you wish. Try replacing some of the oil with extra virgin olive or a nut oil.

Easy Hollandaise Sauce

225g butter
3 egg yolks
2–3 tbsp lemon juice
salt and freshly ground black pepper

1. Melt the butter gently over a low heat until it starts to foam, then set aside for a few minutes for the solids to sink to the bottom of the pan.
2. Blend together the rest of the ingredients in a liquidiser, processor or bowl with a whisk.
3. Whilst liquidising, processing or whisking, pour the butter into the eggs in a slow stream, being careful to leave back all the solids.
4. Taste and season.

> **HANDY HINT**
> The best way to keep hollandaise warm is in a vacuum flask.

Endive – see both Chicory and Lettuce

Evaporated milk

- **Coffee** Use in your coffee instead of normal milk.
- **Potatoes** Many people swear by evaporated milk in mashed potatoes for extra creaminess.
- **Soup** Stir a little into soup.

Everything – see Various

F

Fennel

The aniseed taste of fennel is good with apple, orange, lemon, seafood, pork, bacon, garlic, Parmesan, black pepper, olive oil and peppery salad leaves.

❄ Raw fennel keeps in the fridge for a week although it does gradually lose flavour over time. It must be blanched before freezing and tastes milder after blanching or cooking.

- **Chowder** Cook a little fennel in with the base vegetables when making seafood chowder (p114).
- **Fennel soup** Add thinly sliced fennel to the onions at the start of cooking the basic soup (p309) and purée some of the fronds in at the end for a pretty speckled effect. Finish with cream and season to taste. This is good served chilled and called fennel vichyssoise.
- **Fish** Bake fish on a bed of fennel stalks to infuse with flavour and look impressive.
- **Garnish** The fronds make a pretty garnish.
- **Hash** Add to potato hash either with bacon or with fish.
- **Hollandaise** Add chopped fronds to hollandaise sauce just before pouring over fish (p108).
- **Potatoes** Thinly slice some fennel, cook in butter until tender and layer up in scalloped potatoes (p305).
- **Salads and coleslaw** Add shredded fennel to salads and coleslaw (p287).
- **Shrimp or scallops** Chop finely and sauté in olive oil with scallops or shrimp. Finish with a squeeze of lemon and some pretty fronds.
- **Vinaigrette** Shave wafer thin fennel slices and dress with a lemon vinaigrette.

F

Warm Fennel Vinaigrette

½ bulb fennel, finely chopped
2 tbsp olive oil
1 tbsp cider vinegar
1 tbsp lemon juice
salt and freshly ground black pepper
fennel fronds, finely chopped

1. Cook the fennel gently in the oil until tender and golden.
2. Cool in the oil for 15 minutes, then stir in the vinegar and lemon juice.
3. Taste, season and stir in the fronds.
4. Re-warm if necessary and serve with fish.

Figs

Figs marry well with honey, balsamic vinegar, cinnamon, soft cheese, blue cheese, almonds, hazelnuts, walnuts, calves' liver, chicken livers, foie gras and air-dried ham.

❋ Keep at room temperature until ripe after which they deteriorate quickly so eat as soon as possible. If necessary lay them lovingly in the fridge for just a couple of days.

- **Butter-fried figs** Sauté slices of fresh fig in butter with a little brown sugar and serve with calves' liver, soft cheese or ice cream.
- **Fig vinaigrette** Scrape the flesh from one ripe fig into 100ml of balsamic vinaigrette and drizzle over blue cheese or ham.
- **Posh toast** Serve fresh figs on crostini, bruschetta or other toasted snacks, together with blue cheese and a drizzle of honey.
- **Pizza** Figs together with blue or goats' cheese make a great pizza topping especially with black pepper and a little brown sugar.
- **Salads** Add a few wedges to salad; they're particularly good with Parma ham and goats' cheese.

Dried figs – see also Dried fruit

- **Baking** Add to sweet baked goods, season with black pepper if you think it will be appropriate.
- **Breakfast** Stir into breakfast cereals, porridge or yoghurt.
- **Tapenade** Try adding some figs to the olive recipe on p188.

Filo pastry – aka phyllo

❄ Filo dries out very easily so keep wrapped at all times. Store in the fridge or freeze it.

- **Filo parcels** Bake little parcels filled with other leftovers – the size and shape will depend on the leftovers but cigars, triangles and purses spring to mind.
- **Garnish** A quick, easy and delicious sweet garnish: loosely crumple leftover filo pastry, bake until crisp, then dust with icing sugar.
- **Mini tart cases** Layer buttered scraps in muffin cups and bake in a preheated oven at 180°C/gas 4 until crisp and golden – about 12–15 minutes. Cool and fill with something delectable.

F

Fish – see also Shellfish

'The piece of cod that passeth all understanding.' Edwin Lutyens

Whilst different fish have different affinities, generally speaking, oily fish are good with astringent flavours such as gooseberry and rhubarb and also beetroot, horseradish and capers, white fish are enhanced by cream, butter, leeks, fennel, ham, bacon and white wine; and pink fish additionally pairs with red wine. They all go well with citrus, dill and parsley.

Raw fish scraps and trimmings

❉ If your fish have not been previously frozen, collect scraps in the freezer until there are enough to work with.

● **Deep-fried fish skeletons!** This is rather odd; I have read about it frequently but have to admit I've never tried it. Deep-fry fresh fish bones, preferably with a little flesh clinging to them, and serve hot and crisp sprinkled with sea salt. I wish I was still cheffing – this sounds like a fabulous garnish!

● **Fish pie** Put fish bits and pieces into an ovenproof dish and pour over milk to cover. Add peppercorns, lemon zest and parsley stalks, if possible. Cover with foil and cook in a preheated oven at 180°C/gas 4 until tender. Strain off the hot milk and use it to make a sauce (if you can't think how, see the cheese sauce recipe on p66 and leave out the cheese!). Pour over the fish, top with mashed potato and bake until brown.

● **Seafood mixed grill** Marinate a collection of seafood trimmings in olive oil with lemon and black pepper, grill and serve displayed fabulously with halves of grilled lemon, sprigs of parsley and herb mayonnaise.

Fish Stock

Use only really fresh bones, trimmings and fish heads, if you don't have enough, some fishmongers will give these away if you ask nicely. Some won't, of course.

1kg fish heads and bones
1 sliced onion
1 tbsp vegetable oil
180ml dry white wine
any other flavourings (see Handy hint below)

1. Discard the eyes and gills and wash the trimmings well to remove any blood.
2. Gently cook the onions plus any other raw vegetables in the oil in a large pot, stirring frequently, until they start to soften but not to brown.
3. Add the rest of the ingredients and enough water to just cover.
4. Slowly bring to a simmer, skimming off any scum that rises to the top.
5. Maintain at a gentle simmer for 20 minutes; unlike with meat stock, long cooking is not a good idea.
6. Strain and discard the solids.

HANDY HINT

'Any other flavourings': these are usually celery, carrot and leeks. Parsley stalks are good or fresh herbs, or try a combination of fennel, lemon and pepper or perhaps fresh ginger and lime zest for an Asian twist.

F

Seafood Chowder

Make the basic soup recipe on page 309, but in addition to the basic
ingredients, add the following, using whatever fish you might have
left over, whether fresh or frozen.

1 carrot, thinly sliced
2 celery sticks, thinly sliced
½ fennel bulb, thinly sliced
leftover raw fish, cut into small pieces
leftover raw shellfish, cut into pieces
cooked fish and shellfish, cut into pieces
150ml cream

1. Add the carrot, celery and fennel to the onions in the basic
    recipe at the start of cooking.
2. After mashing or puréeing the potatoes, use a good slug of
    cream when diluting to taste.
3. Bring the soup just to boiling point and add the raw fish.
4. Bring back to just boiling and add the raw shellfish.
5. Bring back to just boiling, add the cooked fish and shellfish,
    then return to a very gentle boil and turn off the heat
    immediately.
6. Taste and season again if necessary.

Cooked fish

- **Fish pâté** Try the recipe under Smoked fish (p117).
- **Fishcakes** There are several ways to make fishcakes from
  cooked fish – involving such things as wet bread or a thick
  sauce – but the following two are the easiest and most
  accessible. If you have any leftover fishcakes you can mash
  them on toast!
- **Fishcakes by the breadcrumb method** Mix leftover cooked
  fish with 1 tbsp mayonnaise per 100g. Add chosen flavourings
  and seasonings and gently work in fresh breadcrumbs by hand
  until the mixture is capable of holding together. Coat in
  seasoned flour and shallow-fry until hot, crisp and golden.

- **Fishcakes by the mashed potato method** Gently mix together equal-ish amounts of flaked cooked fish and mashed potato. Season to taste. Form into cakes and chill for 30 minutes or more to prevent them falling apart whilst cooking. Coat and cook as above.
- **Hash** Add cooked and flaked fish to hash (p211).
- **Lemon vinaigrette** Turn pieces of cooked fish in a light lemony vinaigrette and chill until needed. Serve as part of a salad.

Smoked fish

There are several methods of smoking fish, which give different results in texture aswell as taste.

COLD-SMOKED FISH – including lox and gravlax

Whilst this is cold-smoked, it is dry brined first, normally served raw and is so special it deserves a sub-heading all its own. Different treatments are used to produce lox and gravlax, sometimes called gravadlax, but the end products are similar.

Smoked salmon is lovely with lemon, black pepper, dill, soured cream or crème fraîche, rye bread, eggs and Champagne – possibly all at the same time!

- **Bruschetta** Top bruschetta with soured cream and leftover caviar.
- **Eggs Norwegian** Replace the bacon in eggs Benedict with smoked salmon.
- **Fish pâté** Chop finely and fold into fish pâté for a pretty and tasty effect.
- **Luxury scrambled egg** Stir chopped smoked salmon into, or sprinkle over, scrambled eggs.

F

COLD-SMOKED FISH – usually haddock, cod and other white fish, and kippers

These smoked fish go remarkably well with leeks and also with bacon and ham, cream, butter, crème fraîche, black pepper and egg. As they are cold smoked (or in the worst case scenario just flavoured artificially and dyed yellow), they need to be cooked.

- **Cullen skink** A creamy smoked haddock and potato soup from the Scottish town of Cullen. For my version, which is surprisingly similar to the original (see p309), use butter to cook the onions and milk as the liquid. Add uncooked smoked haddock for the final 5 minutes of simmering, remove when cooked, mash the potatoes and then flake the fish back into the soup. Alternatively, stir in cooked smoked haddock when the soup is finished. A delicious non-traditional variation would be to replace the onions with leeks.
- **Gratin** Mix cooked smoked fish into leftover mashed potato together with a little cream, sprinkle with breadcrumbs and grated cheese and bake until hot, crispy and golden. Lovely lunch!
- **Ham and haddie** A Scottish dish, lightly brown a thick slice of smoked ham or bacon in butter, turn and top with a piece of smoked haddock. Lower the heat, cover the pan and cook for a few minutes until the fish flakes easily. Serve for breakfast possibly with a poached egg on top and a little hollandaise (p108).
- **Kedgeree** Smoked haddock is the usual fish of choice in kedgeree but I see no reason why other smoked fish would be less good. Cook a little onion in a lot of butter until tender. Stir in ½ tsp curry paste or powder per person and, after a minute, add cooked rice and cooked smoked fish. Toss all together until hot and serve garnished with hard-boiled eggs and lemon wedges for breakfast.
- **Omelette Arnold Bennett** Created by the chef at the Savoy Hotel in London to feed their long-term guest Mr Arnold Bennett (coincidence?). A quicker, lighter, easier and frankly fake Omelette Arnold Bennett (the original recipe includes thick béchamel sauce and hollandaise!) using leftovers is made by folding cooked smoked haddock into crème fraîche

together with lemon zest, black pepper and chopped parsley and using this to top a barely cooked omelette. Sprinkle with Parmesan and pop under a hot grill to finish.

> **COOK'S TREAT**
>
> Warm pieces of leftover kipper in butter with black pepper and a little whisky and eat on toast.

- **Risotto** Poach the fish in water and use the resulting broth to make risotto (p306). Buttery leeks are great stirred into this with the fish and a spoonful of cream.

HOT-SMOKED FISH – such as trout, salmon, mackerel and buckling
Hot-smoking fish also cooks it. Complementary flavours include lemon, black pepper, cream cheese, horseradish and beetroot.

- **Fish pâté and dip** Whilst most cooked fish leftovers can be made into pâté, smoked fish is particularly good, or a mixture of smoked and unsmoked. Purée, process or mash together boneless, skinless fish with about an equal quantity of cream cheese plus the usual suspects: lemon, parsley, black pepper and salt to taste. If the pâté is too thick, soften with cream, soured cream, yoghurt or crème fraîche. Horseradish is a good addition, as is beetroot for a lovely pink pâté.
- **Pasta** Toss flaked smoked fish with pasta in a creamy sauce with lemon, parsley, black pepper and maybe a tad of vodka.
- **Potato salad** Fold flakes of hot-smoked fish into potato salad – a little horseradish wouldn't go amiss here.
- **Potatoes** Add to creamy scalloped potatoes (p305).
- **Smoked fish butter** Use about half as much fish as butter and add flavouring such as lemon, pepper, parsley or other herbs (see Compound butters on p288). Serve a slice or two on non-smoked fish or stir into cream sauces as appropriate.
- **Smoky fishcakes** (see Fishcakes on p114).

Tinned/canned fish

ANCHOVIES – have a separate entry due to their sheer usefulness

F

SALMON AND TUNA

- **Beans** Try dressing white beans with peppery lemon vinaigrette then stirring in some canned tuna or salmon. Serve with crusty garlic bread.
- **Dips and pâté** Make pâté, dips and spreads by blending them with cream, cream cheese or mayonnaise.
- **Fishcakes** See Fishcakes (p114– 15).
- **Salade Niçoise** Simply put, this is oil-packed tuna and/or anchovies plus tomatoes, cucumber, onion, green beans, potatoes, boiled eggs, black olives and lettuce tossed in a classic vinaigrette.
- **Tonnato** A mayonnaise sauce traditionally served with cold veal but equally good with grilled fish. To cheat, process together 100g oil-packed tuna, 1 tbsp capers, 2 anchovies, 1 tbsp lemon juice, 60ml of olive oil and fold into 225g mayonnaise.

SARDINES AND PILCHARDS

- **Bagels** Top toasted bagels with cream cheese, red onion and a sardine.
- **Toast** These fish are good mushed up on toast and drizzled with vinegar – try balsamic.

Flatbreads – see Bread and also Tortillas and Wraps

Flax seeds – see Seeds

Frankfurters – see Sausages

Fruit – see also Berries and Dried Fruit

Most fruits are suitable for using in a variety of ways.

- **Coulis and fools** (p300).
- **Crumbles, pies and turnovers** See basic crumble and pastry recipes (p290).
- **Fruit brûlée** Fold leftover fruit into sweetened whipped cream, sprinkle with sugar and caramelise under a hot grill or with a blow torch.
- **Fruit salad** Toss berries and attractively cut fruits with caster sugar and set aside for an hour, by which time a natural syrup will have formed. Stir in additional ingredients such as a squeeze of citrus, fresh chopped mint leaves or rum. Cook leftover fruit salad to make compôte! Leftover compôte can be stirred into porridge, yoghurt or rice pudding.
- **Juice** Top up excess juice after cooking fruit with sparkling water for a refreshing drink, or freeze in cubes and use to cool and flavour future drinks.
- **Smoothies** (p308).
- **Sorbet and granita** (p299).
- **Trifle** Moisten leftover cake with sweet sherry, as is traditional, or fruit juice or another alcoholic beverage that suits the fruits you have available. Layer up the cake with fresh fruit plus custard, jelly and whipped cream.

F

Rumtopf – aka rumpot

Patient German people invented this as a way of storing summer fruits for Christmas. The rumtopf must be started at least two months before you want to drink it, but the good news is you can do something else whilst you wait. Choose a glass or ceramic jar with a really good seal and make sure it is scrupulously clean and dry. Add leftover fruit as and when you have any, as long as it is in perfect condition. Rumtopf is a gorgeous sipping liquor. The fruit is dark, mushy and powerfully flavoured but a little with ice cream is good.

Berries are ideal for rumtopf; other good additions are sliced stone fruit and cherries

1. Always use perfect fruit – no bruises, no over-ripe or under-ripe fruit, just perfect. De-stem, remove stones and make sure the fruit is completely dry.
2. Weigh the fruits and put into the jar together with half their weight in sugar.
3. Cover with enough dark rum (or brandy for a brandytopf, I presume) to a depth of 1cm. It is imperative that all the fruit is submerged, so put a small saucer directly on top to stop random berries floating to the surface.
4. Cover tightly and store in a cool dark place until you have more fruit to add, at which time just repeat the above steps. Don't stir when adding additional fruits, just layer up.

Tinned/canned fruit

❄ Chill leftovers in an airtight container, submerged in their juice or syrup, for a few days, or freeze.

● **Fresh fruit substitute** You can use tinned or canned fruit to replace fresh fruit in recipes, but bear in mind it is already cooked, so adjust any cooking time accordingly.
● **Juice** Top up the syrup or juice from canned fruit with sparkling water for a refreshing drink or freeze the juice in ice cubes for later.
● **Sorbet** Strain the fruit, coarsely chop and partially freeze. Run through the food processor with syrup from the can or a simple or flavoured syrup, such as ginger with pears. Freeze.

Fudge

COOK'S TREAT

Chop or crumble, then sprinkle over or stir into ice cream.

- **Baking** Stir chunks of fudge into suitable baked goods.
- **Crumbles** Mix chopped fudge into sweet crumble topping but keep back a spoonful or two of un-fudged crumble mix to sprinkle protectively on top (p290).
- **Fudge sauce** Gently melt chopped fudge in an approximately equal amount of double cream. Once cold, this can also be whisked as a frosting.
- **Fudge on toast** Whilst playing with fudge for this very book, I had an inspiration – fudge on toast! Just grate over hot toast and pop back under the grill to melt. Lovely breakfast.

G

Game

Game is divided into two classifications: furred, which includes rabbit and hare, venison and wild boar (for which also see Meat); and feathered, which covers duck, pigeon, pheasant, partridge, grouse, quail, woodcock and snipe (so also look at Duck, Goose, Chicken and Turkey).

Generally speaking game is good with red and sweet fortified wines, sweet preserves such as redcurrant or cranberry, spices such as cinnamon, cloves and ginger, dark chocolate, cabbage, mushrooms, garlic, rosemary, thyme and bacon.

❄ Collect scraps together in the freezer until there are enough to make a game pie or ragu. Or make a hunter's pie – the game version of cottage pie (p36).

> **HANDY HINT**
> 'Many game meats are low in fat so cook slowly in liquid.

Game Ragu

A rich sauce traditionally served with wide pasta such as pappardelle. This recipe can make use of scraps of leftover game you have grouped together in the freezer.

SERVES 4

1 tbsp oil
1 onion, coarsely chopped
500g mixed game, coarsely chopped
1 garlic clove, minced
½ tbsp tomato paste
¼ tsp ground cinnamon
¼ tsp freshly grated nutmeg
1 square dark chocolate
200ml red wine
120ml rich beef stock
salt and freshly ground black pepper

1. Heat the oil and fry the onion until browned, then add the meat and brown that too.
2. Stir in the garlic, tomato paste and spices and cook together for a minute or so.
3. Stir in the rest of the ingredients.
4. Bring to the boil, turn down the heat, cover the pan with a thick piece of foil and then the lid.
5. Cook very gently for an hour or more until rich and tender.

Gammon – see Ham and Bacon

Garlic

I thought it might be easiest to list the things garlic doesn't go well with but it even appears occasionally in dishes with chocolate, coffee or fruit. As a store cupboard staple it's always possible to use up 'leftovers' but here are a few notes.

❊ Fresh garlic bulbs will keep well without refrigeration for three months or more, and don't really like cold and damp so only chill if absolutely necessary. Opened garlic bulbs should be kept for no more than ten days. Chopped garlic keeps a day or two in the fridge, well wrapped to stop its aroma interfering with other foods. Freeze separated into cloves or, even better, purée peeled garlic with twice its volume of oil and then freeze. The wonder of this is that once frozen it is still soft enough to scrape off a little when needed.

● **Garlic vodka** Put a few peeled garlic cloves in a bottle of vodka (you will probably have to drink a little vodka first to make room) and keep in the freezer. Use the resulting garlic vodka in sauces, bloody Marys or peculiar Martinis.

Roasted garlic

Roasted garlic and/or its oil can be used to enhance so many dishes. Mix into mashed potato, stir into vinaigrette, blend into hummus, brush onto pizza bases, serve with blue cheese, whip into soft goats' cheese or make roasted garlic butter and roasted garlic bread, to name but a few.

G

❄ Roasted garlic keeps well in the fridge for 4 or 5 days or can be frozen, in which state it will still be soft enough to break off pieces as needed.

1. Cut heads of garlic in half through their equators and stand cut-sides up in a shallow ovenproof dish.
2. Drizzle quite generously with olive oil, being sure to anoint the cut surfaces well, and season with salt and pepper.
3. Cover tightly with foil and cook in a preheated oven at 180°C/gas 4 until utterly tender, which takes about an hour.
4. Cool until you are able to handle it, then squeeze the soft garlic into a clean airtight container, adding any oil remaining in the dish.
5. Pour in extra olive oil to cover completely, put on the lid and store in the fridge until needed or freeze in a freezer bag.

Giblets – see Offal and Chicken Livers

Ginger

Chocolate, chilli, lemon, orange, garlic, lime, mango, melon, tomato, vanilla, pork, fish, honey, whisky, soy, pears, plums, rhubarb, apricot and coriander all go well with ginger.

Fresh ginger – aka Green Ginger or Ginger Root

❄ Store wrapped in kitchen paper in a plastic bag in the salad crisper part of the fridge for up to a month. Ginger freezes well; cut into thin slices or grate and freeze in small portions. However it is possible to grate ginger from frozen.

- **Carrot soup** Add a little grated ginger when making carrot soup.
- **Ginger sherry** Store peeled ginger in a bottle of dry sherry, as a bonus the flavoured sherry is excellent used in stir-fries.
- **Ginger tea for one** Not only delicious and warming but also soothing for an

> **HANDY HINT**
>
> The easiest way to peel ginger that I have found is to scrape it with the edge of a sharp teaspoon.

iffy tum! Simmer 6–7 thin slices of green ginger in 200ml of water for 15 minutes. Adjust the taste with honey or sugar, lemon or lime, rum or not and drink hot.

COOK'S TREAT

When testing this tea, I had some ginger-infused water left over so used it to make hot chocolate.

- **Lime and ginger syrup** Stir together 150g sugar and 125ml water over a medium heat until the sugar has dissolved. Thinly slice about 2cm ginger root, add to the syrup and simmer, stirring occasionally, for 15 minutes. Add the juice of a lime and cook for a further few minutes until syrupy. Strain into clean jars, cool and keep in the fridge for up to a month. Serve over ice cream or dilute with fizzy water and call it sherbet.
- **Marinade for tuna** Mix together 1 tbsp grated ginger, 2 tsp sugar, and 1 tbsp each soy sauce and sesame oil. Marinade tuna steaks in this for several hours. Dry steaks before grilling or pan searing.
- **Rum and ginger butter sauce** Pan-fry fish or chicken, set it aside and keep warm. Cook a teaspoon or so of grated ginger for a minute or so, flame with a little rum and then swirl in a knob of butter. Season and serve with your lump of protein.
- **Vinaigrette** Add grated ginger to vinaigrette, especially with rice vinegar.

Sushi ginger – aka pickled ginger or gari

- **Asian style** Finely shred and toss into Asian-style salads with seafood or chicken.
- **Martini** Garnish a martini with a pretty pink slice.
- **Stir-fries** Shred finely and add to stir-fries.

Crystallised ginger – see Dried fruit

Stem ginger in syrup

- **Fruit** Add to fruit salads and pear dishes.
- **Glaze** Use the ginger syrup to glaze cakes or drizzle onto pancakes, French toast, porridge or ice cream.

G

- **Mince pies** Stir a little finely chopped stem ginger into mincemeat for rather special mince pies.
- **Recycled biscuit cake** Add chopped stem ginger to recycled biscuit cake (p42).
- **Rum spritzer** Add a tot of rum to the syrup and top up with soda water.

Gnocchi

- **Fried** Fry in a little butter or olive oil until hot and crisp and serve as a side dish or part of a fry up.
- **Gnocchi gratin** Stir leftover gnocchi into pasta sauce, top with cheese and breadcrumbs and bake in a preheated oven at 190° C/gas 5 for 10 minutes until hot, crisp and golden.

Goat meat – see both Lamb and Meat

Goats' milk – see Milk

Golden syrup

- **Breakfast** Drizzle onto porridge, pancakes, ice cream and French toast.
- **Golden syrup sauce** Melt together equal quantities of butter, light brown sugar and golden syrup and boil for a few minutes until it starts to caramelise. Carefully stir in enough cream to make a sauce to your liking, then stir over a low heat until everything has melted again.
- **Recycled biscuit cake** (p42).
- **Thunder and lightning** (see Clotted cream, p87).

'ti Punch

This delicious little (petit ...'ti) punch from the French West Indies is made with cane syrup or golden syrup as we know it in the UK!

One of sour Two of sweet Three of strong Four of weak

1. Mix together the sour (which is lime juice), the sweet (golden syrup) and the strong (which is, of course, rum).
2. Stir in the weak (water) if you want to! Try substituting ice for water for a cold, strong drink or top up with sparkling water for a long refreshing quaff.

Goose – see Duck, Game and Meat

Gooseberries – see also Berries and Fruit
Gooseberries are humdingers with elderflower and good with mackerel, pork and aniseed.

- **Gooseberry fool** Add a touch of elderflower cordial, if possible (p300).
- **Gooseberry sauce** Cook with sugar to taste and a little water until they collapse, which won't take long. Strain and use as a sauce for pork, in which case add a little sage, or mackerel which would be good with fennel seed.

Granadilla – see Passionfruit

Granola

- **Mix it** Add to other cereals.
- **Topping** Sprinkle over ice cream or yoghurt – depending on your preferences.

G

Grapefruit

Good with mint, orange, honey, brown sugar, rum, shellfish, smoked chicken, watercress and avocado.

❄ Keep for a week or so at room temperature or up to three weeks in the fridge.

● **Grapefruit salsa** Mix coarsely chopped grapefruit flesh with similarly chopped avocado, a little fresh chilli, lime juice and maybe a touch of light brown sugar. Serve with grilled fish or chicken.

> **HANDY HINT**
>
> Warning: it is said in the Caribbean that grapefruit 'cuts your nature' – meaning it reduces your sex drive.

Grapes

Eat grapes with blue cheese, in particular, and cheese generally, other fruits, chicken, pork and white fish. Check for and remove damaged grapes as soon as you get them home to stop any rot spreading.

❄ Keep in a perforated plastic bag (they may well have been sold in one) and store in the fridge for up to a week. Pick grapes from the bunch, wash and dry, spread on a baking tray and freeze solid. These are good for nibbling and make good 'ice cubes'.

● **Bread** Add to bread dough for a cheese-friendly loaf.
● **Crunchy caramel grapes** Carefully dip little clusters of grapes in hot caramel (a little coarse black pepper is a nice twist) and cool on a greased tray until hard.
● **Grape salsa** Coarsely chop or slice grapes and toss with finely chopped red onion, a little olive oil, slightly more red wine vinegar and salt and pepper to taste. Parsley is a pretty addition, balsamic or sherry vinegar a pleasant variation.
● **Grilled sandwich or pizza** Add halved red grapes to a grilled blue cheese sandwich or pizza.
● **Kebabs** Thread large grapes onto skewers alternating with cubes of chicken or pork. Rub with a little oil, season and grill.
● **Roasted grapes** Toss loose grapes or little clusters with a little

oil, sugar and salt. Roast in a preheated oven at 200°C/gas 6 until they start to blister and serve warm with cheese or ice cream.

- **Sautéed grapes** Sauté and serve with cheese.
- **Squash** Add a handful of grapes to butternut squash when roasting.

Grape and Balsamic Sauce for Chicken or Pork

Use this sauce to deglaze a pan in which you have sautéed chicken or pork.

Serves 3–4
1 tbsp olive oil
½ a small onion, finely chopped
handful of seedless red or black grapes
1 tbsp sugar
60ml balsamic vinegar
120ml chicken stock
salt and coarsely ground black pepper

1. Heat the oil and fry the onion and grapes until the onion starts to brown and the grapes lose some colour (which surprises me!).
2. Stir in the sugar and cook for 30 seconds.
3. Add the balsamic vinegar and boil to reduce a little.
4. Add the chicken stock, bring to the boil and simmer for 10 minutes.

Spiced Grapes

Serve with cheese.

1 small bunch of grapes
225g sugar
240ml water
12 black peppercorns, lightly crushed
1 cinnamon stick
1 star anise

1. Pierce the grapes a few times with a sterilised darning needle, if such things still exist.
2. Bring all the other ingredients to the boil, then simmer for 2–3 minutes to form a syrup.
3. Add the grapes, cover, cool and store in the fridge until needed.

Gravy

I refer to the juices from roasted meats or a little bit of leftover stew with or without the lumps.

- **Eggs** Drizzle gravy over *oeufs en cocotte* or add a spoonful or two to scrambled eggs.
- **Gravy** Add to more gravy!
- **Mushrooms** Stir a few spoonfuls of rich meaty gravy into sautéed mushrooms.
- **Pasta sauces** Use to sauce pasta, adding meat, mushrooms and so on.
- **Sandwiches** Serve a little dish of hot 'dipping gravy' with good bread or a meat sandwich.
- **Soups and sauces** Use to enrich soups and sauces.

Green beans – see Peas and Green beans

Green onions – see Spring onions

Greengages – see Plums

Greens – see Cabbage

Guava – see also Fruit

Guavas taste good with lime juice, other tropical fruits, cream, ice cream and in fruit punch.

❋ Once ripe, put in the fridge and eat as soon as possible, as they are not good keepers.

- **Eat it all** The whole fruit is edible including skin and seeds.
- **Fruit salads** Add to tropical fruit salads.

H

Haggis

Traditionally haggis is paired with whisky, neeps (turnips) and tatties, and is also good with strong ale, black pepper, rowanberry or similar sweet sauce and with Cheddar and Cheddar-like cheeses.

- **Alfredo sauce** Toss chopped haggis with pasta in a peppery Alfredo sauce (p281).
- **Eggs** Haggis is good in omelettes and scrambled eggs.
- **Haggis hurling** Try to beat the World Record for Haggis Hurling, which for many years stood at 180ft 10in and was held by one Alan Pettigrew since 1984. However, this record was broken by Lorne Coltart who lobbed a haggis a magnificent 214ft 9in in June 2011.
- **I dare you!** The most surprising haggis recipe I have seen so far is Haggis, Okra and Coconut Tart with Pineapple Salsa but as I haven't tried it 'yet', I cannot comment.
- **Kedgeree** Crumble into this breakfast rice dish (p116).
- **Mushrooms** Moisten with a little cream and whisky and use to stuff mushrooms. Sprinkle with breadcrumbs and bake in a preheated oven at 190°C/gas 5 until the mushrooms are cooked through and the filling is hot and crusty.
- **Pizza or toast** Scatter crumbled haggis over pizza or cheese on toast.
- **Potatoes** Fry into clapshot or rumbledethumps (p211).
- **Scotch eggs** Add to the sausage meat coating (p105).

Ham

Ham is particularly pleasant with maple syrup, brown sugar, honey, cloves, pineapple, mustard, eggs and cheese.

- ❄ Cooked ham will keep for five or six days in the fridge and freezes well for up to three months.

- **Breakfast** Fry thick slices of ham instead of bacon for breakfast – see Coffee (p90) for how to make accompanying red eye gravy.

- **Croque monsieur** A traditional French sandwich made by spreading two slices of white bread with Dijon mustard, laying a slice or slices of Gruyère on each piece of bread, sandwiching the two together with ham in the middle and then … what? I have seen recipes for this 'classic' baked, fried, toasted, brushed with butter and toasted, brushed with butter, dipped in Parmesan and toasted etc. The important thing, I think, is the ham, Gruyère and Dijon – the rest is up to you. Or add ham to less confusing cheese sandwiches.
- **Eggs** Ham and eggs are a great combination. See Basic Recipes for ideas.
- **Gratin** Finely chop and mix with breadcrumbs and grated cheese to sprinkle on top of baked dishes.
- **Haluski** Ham is a good addition to this cabbage and noodle dish (p59).
- **Ham croquettes or fritters** Same thing, different shape! Mix coarsely chopped ham (air-dried is tastiest and if you heat it in a little olive oil with a bit of garlic it is tastier still) into mashed potato together with chopped parsley. Form into cakes or croquettes, dip in beaten egg and coat with crumbs, panko or otherwise. Shallow or deep-fry until hot, crisp and golden.
- **Hash or strata** Add to hash (p211) or to strata (p50).
- **Pasta** Toss with pasta in a suitable sauce.
- **Potted ham** Make the basic recipe your own (p170).
- **Stock** A ham bone makes fine stock. Put it in a large saucepan together with chopped onion, carrot and celery. Add a few black peppercorns, cover with cold water, bring to the boil, turn down the heat, cover and simmer for a couple of hours, topping up with boiling water if necessary. Use in soup, sauces, bean dishes and pease pudding.
- **Stuffing** Ham is an excellent addition to stuffing for pork, chicken or turkey (p45).

Marino Branch
Brainse Marino
Tel: 8336297

Pease Pudding

A cheap, easy, delicious and flexible dish which absolutely relies on good ham stock for its wonderfulness. Traditionally served with boiled ham or in ham sandwiches, leftovers can be used to make all sorts of other delicious meals – see p199.

see p199

SERVES 4–6

300g dried split peas
1 litre ham stock

1. Cover the split peas with cold water and soak overnight.
2. Drain, put the peas in a large saucepan and just cover with ham stock.
3. Bring to the boil, skim off any scum, turn down the heat, cover and simmer, stirring occasionally, until the peas have broken down to form a purée. You can help with a bit of mashing. It may be necessary to add stock or water or if, on the other hand it's too runny stir over a medium heat to evaporate excess liquid, bearing in mind it will thicken further as it cools.

Dry cured ham – such as Prosciutto (aka Parma ham) and Serrano
These lovely, dry, salty hams are excellent with sweet fruits such as fig, melon, mango and peach and with goats' cheese, asparagus, eggs, fish and chicken.

❈ Tightly wrapped, dry cured ham keeps very well for a month or two in the fridge. It also freezes well but just for a couple of months before starting to deteriorate.

● **Asparagus** Wrap around asparagus spears and roast or grill. Dip in a runny egg if you have one.
● **Egg dishes** Mix with chopped parsley, spring onions and grated Parmesan and add to omelettes, scrambled eggs, etc.
● **Frazzle it** Fry shreds of this ham in a little oil until crisp to sprinkle on soups and salads.

- **Pizza** Top pizza with pieces of dry cured ham and be adventurous – try adding blue cheese and figs or maybe sliced peaches and goats' cheese.
- **Seafood** Wrap prosciutto round prawns or scallops, secure with a pre-soaked cocktail stick (so it won't catch fire) and grill
- **Wrap** Wrap around fillets of fish or chicken before baking or grilling.

Hamburger – see Burgers or Beef

Hazelnuts – see Nuts

Herbs

Fresh ones!

❄ Wrap fresh herbs loosely in kitchen paper and place in an open plastic bag in the fridge. Lightly sprinkle the kitchen paper with water occasionally and they will stay fresh for a few days, however ... a better way to keep herbs fresh is to arrange them like a bunch of flowers in a jar of water, either at room temperature or in the fridge with a loose plastic bag over them to stop them drying out. They should be okay for a week or so if you remember to refresh the water from time to time.

❄ Pack ice cube trays with chopped fresh herbs and top up with water or stock to cover, freeze to add to soups, sauces and gravies. Alternatively, purée fresh herbs with a little vegetable oil and freeze in cubes.

- **Herb butter** You can make a compound butter using all kinds of herbs (p288).
- **Herb tempura** Dip leaves, sprigs or even small bunches of herbs into a light tempura batter and deep-fry for just a minute or so in hot oil. Drain on kitchen paper, sprinkle with sea salt

and use immediately as a splendid garnish. See p285 for tempura batter recipe.

- **Pastry** A pretty way to use herb leaves is to lay them on half a sheet of thinly rolled out pastry, fold the other half on top and roll until the leaves show through. Bake as intended.
- **Pesto** The classic recipe (p137) is, of course, made of basil but the idea can be varied for different herbs.
- **Salads** Toss in some complementary herbs.

Mixed herbs

- **Bouquet garni** Tie bay, thyme and parsley together and used to flavour soups and stews. Discard the herbs before serving.
- **Fines herbes** This classic mixture of parsley, chives, thyme, tarragon, chervil and occasionally mint can be added to dishes at the end of cooking.
- **Herbes de Provence** Oregano, thyme, rosemary, marjoram, maybe fennel and sometimes lavender, all of which, by rights, should be from Provence.

Basil

Basil goes famously well with tomatoes but is also good with garlic, onions, chilli, lemon, olive oil, most cheeses, chicken, seafood and Mediterranean vegetables that are really fruit such as aubergines, peppers and courgettes.

- **Alfredo sauce** Add to Alfredo sauce (p281) and toss with freshly cooked pasta. Roasted tomatoes would be a boon here.
- **Dip** Puréed with mayonnaise with nothing else added, fresh basil makes a surprisingly delicious dip.
- **Green beans** Stir into just cooked green beans with a drizzle of good flavoured olive oil.
- **Pistou** A variation on pesto (see recipe below) with the pine nuts replaced by a diced tomato. In France,

HANDY HINT

Basil should be added to hot dishes in the last minutes of cooking or it will lose much of its flavour. Scatter over just out the oven pizza or add to tomato soups, sauces, risottos and pastas dishes for just the last couple of minutes of cooking time.

this is stirred into beany vegetable soup called ... soupe au pistou, *quelle surprise*!

- **Salad dressing** Make pesto salad dressing by adding a little extra oil and a splash of vinegar to the Pesto recipe below.
- **Salads** Toss torn leaves into salads – especially those containing tomatoes and especially, especially those containing tomatoes and mozzarella.
- **Sandwiches** Mix into cream cheese to spread in a tomato sandwich.
- **Sauce for pan-fried chicken** Set the cooked chicken aside and keep warm. Sauté a little finely chopped onion or shallot in the residual fat in the pan, deglaze with a splash of balsamic vinegar and a splash of chicken stock and reduce to syrupy. Stir in shredded basil and a knob of butter, taste, season and serve with the chicken.
- **Vinaigrettes and marinades** These both take well to a little added basil oil.

Pesto Genovese

There are numerous versions of this traditional herb sauce from Genoa but they all contain varying quantities of pine nuts, Parmesan cheese, garlic, olive oil and fresh basil. Here is a rough guideline – if you have less basil make less pesto! I think it is best made with a pestle and mortar for a rustic effect but if you are in a hurry a food processor works fine.

❋ This keeps well in the fridge for a week or more, so long as the pesto has an unbroken layer of oil on top.

1 garlic clove, chopped
good pinch of coarse sea salt
1 small handful of pine nuts, lightly toasted
about 250g fresh basil leaves
50g Parmesan cheese, freshly grated
100ml or more olive oil
salt and freshly ground black pepper
squeeze of lemon juice (optional)

H

1. In a mortar, crush together the garlic and salt to a coarse paste.
2. Add and crush in the pine nuts.
3. Work in the basil leaves a few at a time.
4. Add the grated cheese and then stir in enough olive oil to make a thick, unctuous sauce.
5. Taste, season and add more oil until it is to your liking. Some people add a squeeze of lemon.
6. Pour into a clean jar and top off with a little extra oil to seal it from the air.

Bay

Bay's flavour is good in milky puddings and sauces and with beef, game, shellfish, mushrooms and beans. Bay prefers long, slow cooking; add to soups, stews and braises at the start of the dish, remembering to remove before serving.

❇ Unlike most herbs, bay leaves need no tender loving care, just leave them about the place; they will dry out and taste slightly stronger but will be just as useful.

- **Custard** Infuse in warm milk when making custards.
- **Insect repellent** Sprinkle broken bay leaves around as an insect repellent.
- **Pears** Add a bay leaf when poaching pears in red wine.
- **Seafood** Add to the water when boiling shellfish.
- **Weevils** Bay leaves used to be added to dry goods to ward off weevils and, having met a few weevils in my time, I think this is a good idea.

> **HANDY HINT**
> Tear or break the leaves before using to release more flavour.

Chervil

The sweet, aniseed taste of this pretty herb goes well with carrots – which are from the same family – and with butter, white fish, lemon and eggs. It is best used cold or at the point of serving as heat destroys its flavour.

- **Carrots** Toss a little chervil with buttery glazed carrots.
- **Sauces** Add to butter sauces such as hollandaise (p96).

- **Soups, salads and eggs** Chervil is great with all of these.

Chives
The mild onion taste of chives enhances goats' cheese, cheddar, cream cheese, sour and fresh cream, butter, eggs, asparagus, leeks and seafood. Cook as little as possible or add chives at the end of cooking.

- **Fish** Add finely chopped chives to fish pâtés (see Fish).
- **Flowers** Lovely purple chive flowers are edible, tasty and make a stunning garnish.
- **Potatoes** Mix chives into soured cream or cream cheese to fill baked potatoes. Stir into potato salad, potato soup, mashed potato – get the picture?

Coriander – aka cilantro and sometimes Chinese parsley
Some people say that coriander tastes of soap, some that it tastes of bed bugs (what strange lives they must lead!) and some that it tastes of citrus and ginger. Whatever the case, it goes well with avocado, chicken, rice, beans, coconut, lime, ginger, chillies and curry spices, and is popular in Latin America, India and south-east Asia.

❄ Coriander favours the jam jar in the fridge with a bag on its head method of storage – see above.

- **Coriander and mint chutney** Process together 100g each of fresh coriander and fresh mint plus 1 tbsp fresh ginger, 1– 2 fresh chillies, 2 garlic cloves, 1 tsp sugar, the juice of a lime and salt to taste. Chill and serve with lamb and grilled meats, or stir into yoghurt and serve with curries.
- **Coriander pesto** (see Basil above). This works with pine nuts but is also very good using pumpkin seeds or cashews instead. Add a little chilli heat and a squeeze of lime juice but don't bother with the cheese unless you really want to.
- **Salsa** Coriander is commonly used in South American salsas.

H

Dill or dill weed

Pretty fronds of dill are very good with seafood and with chicken, cabbage, potatoes, carrots, cucumber, cream and butter.

- **Carrots** Add some chopped dill when you toss cooked carrots in melted butter.
- **Garnish** Use fronds of dill as a pretty feathery garnish for seafood dishes.
- **Pickles** Add to pickled cucumbers (p98).
- **Sauces** Add to cream sauces or hollandaise (p108) to serve with fish or chicken.
- **Vinaigrette** Stir into mustardy vinaigrette to serve with smoked salmon.

Fennel – see Fennel the vegetable because I'd only say the same things again here!

Marjoram – aka sweet marjoram and sometimes oregano
Marjoram and oregano are closely related but marjoram is milder tasting. Use this herb with eggs, fish, chicken, lamb, pork, carrots, potatoes and in Italian dishes.

- **Beans** Mix marjoram into white bean dishes, add garlic, lemon and black pepper.
- **Bouquet garni** Marjoram is a good addition to this classic herb mix (p136).

Mint

Mint is good with lamb, peas, new potatoes, cucumbers, blackcurrants, lemon and yoghurt.

- **Crystallised mint** Brush pretty mint leaves with egg white and sprinkle with caster sugar. Bake in a preheated oven at 150°C/gas 2 for 5–6 minutes until crisp and crunchy. Use as a garnish.
- **Lemonade** Add a sprig or two to a long glass of lemonade.
- **Mint and coriander chutney** See coriander and mint chutney (p139).
- **Mint julep** See Bourbon (p243).

- **Mint pesto** Substitute mint for the basil in the basic recipe (see Basil). Or add some cooked peas and make pea and mint pesto.
- **Mint syrup** Put equal volumes of coarsely chopped mint leaves, sugar and water into a small pan, bring to the boil, stirring to dissolve the sugar, turn off the heat, cover and leave to steep for 20 minutes. Strain into a clean jar, store in the fridge for up to two weeks and use for a quick mint julep (see Bourbon, p243) or add to sorbets, drizzle over ice cream, sweeten tea or glaze fresh out the oven cakes.
- **Mint tea** Add fresh mint leaves to just boiled water and steep for a few minutes until it tastes good. Sweeten with honey or sugar and serve immediately or chill and serve over ice.
- **Mint vinaigrette** This makes a delicious dressing for warm new potatoes or green beans and peas or cucumber salad (see p312).
- **Minted honey** Stir together warm honey, finely grated lemon zest and chopped fresh mint. Pour back into the honey jar, cool and cover. Serve with roast lamb, stir a little through freshly cooked vegetables or add to vinaigrette.
- **Potatoes and peas** A sprig of mint added to the water when cooking new potatoes or peas is beneficial.
- **Summery minted pea soup** Simmer fresh or frozen peas in flavoursome chicken or vegetable stock together with a handful of fresh mint until tender. Purée with cream, taste and season.
- **Yoghurt** Add to lassi or raita (see Yoghurt).

Oregano – aka Wild Marjoram
More assertive than its cousin marjoram, oregano is good with anchovies, capers, aubergine, olives, beans, eggs, cheese, especially feta, chicken, lamb, fish, lemon, tomatoes and is popular in Greek, Italian and Mexican cooking.

- **Cheese** Add to marinating goats' cheese or feta (see Cheese).
- **Chicken and potatoes roasted with oregano and lemon**
  Put chicken quarters into an ovenproof dish together with diced potatoes. Sprinkle with fresh oregano and finely chopped garlic, squeeze over a lemon and add a drizzle of olive oil. Add lemon slices if you have some. Season and turn everything about with your hands to coat. Roast in a preheated

oven at 190°C/gas 5 for about an hour until tender and some parts are crisp.

- **Lamb** Mix with garlic and olive oil to rub onto lamb before roasting.
- **Pizza** Sprinkle with oregano as you take it from the oven.
- **Tomato dishes** Replace basil with oregano in fresh tomato dishes for an entirely different but delicious effect.

Parsley

There is more to parsley than sprinkling. It has a flavour that complements potatoes, mushrooms, bacon, fish, lemon, garlic and other herbs.

In the following five parsley mixtures, proportions and even ingredients are a matter of personal preference – be guided by what you have and what it tastes like! In all cases, the flavour of parsley should be prominent.

Parsley mixtures

1. **Persillade** A simple French garnish of finely chopped parsley and garlic which is used for sprinkling or added for the final few minutes of cooking, particularly with lamb. Sometimes it is briefly sautéed to intensify the flavour before adding to a dish.
2. **Gremolata** This is an Italian version of persillade – chopped parsley and garlic – with finely grated lemon zest added. Traditionally sprinkled on the veal dish osso bucco, it is a great addition to other roast meats, seafood, roast or new potatoes and soups.
3. **Italian salsa verde** The essential components of this sauce are parsley, garlic, anchovy, capers and olive oil. Basil and/or mint are sometimes added. Crush everything but the oil with a pestle and mortar or finely chop if you have good knife skills or process in the food processor. Each method produces a different texture but they are all good. Stir in a little lemon juice or red wine vinegar to taste, then enough olive oil to make a sauce. This is traditionally served with boiled meats but is also good with fish.
4. **Chimichurri** An Argentinean parsley sauce served with lots of things but especially steak. It is similar to salsa verde but made with parsley, garlic, a little fresh oregano, wine vinegar, salt, pepper and chilli flakes or cayenne.

5. **Charmoula** Also known as chermoula, or even just chrmla, this is a sauce or marinade of North African origin. In addition to parsley, this one contains an equal-ish quantity of fresh coriander, garlic, lemon juice, paprika, cumin, salt, pepper and olive oil. This is a traditional marinade for fish.

- **Breath freshener** Chew a sprig of parsley to freshen the breath.
- **Deep-fried parsley garnish** Deep-fry clean and completely dry parsley sprigs, drain on kitchen paper and serve promptly as a delicately pretty and crispy garnish.
- **Garnish** Sprinkle on things to make them pretty!

> **HANDY HINT**
>
> To make a good job of chopping, swirl the parsley in a bowl of water, lift out into a strainer (so as to leave the dirt in the water), wring out in a clean dry cloth and chop.

Rosemary

This strongly flavoured aromatic herb is good with lamb and other fatty meats such as pork and duck, with garlic, onions, chestnuts and red wine.

- **Casseroles** For a mild flavour, add a whole sprig of rosemary towards the end of cooking a casserole or soup and remove before serving.
- **Grilling** Use strong rosemary stalks to skewer meats for grilling or use a sprig of rosemary as a brush to anoint meat with oil for grilling or roasting.
- **Meat** Spike meats, especially lamb, with rosemary leaves before roasting.
- **Potatoes** Add finely chopped rosemary leaves to roasting potatoes.
- **Punches and salads** Sprinkle pretty rosemary flowers over salads or add to summery wine cups and punches.

Sage

A little of this strongly flavoured herb goes a long way; use with pork, veal, chicken, turkey, sausages, liver, kidneys, squash and many cheeses.

- **Apple sauce** Add chopped sage to apple sauce for serving with pork (p15).

H

- **Deep-fried** Sage leaves are robust enough to stand deep-frying without a batter coating. Drain on kitchen paper and sprinkle with crunchy sea salt.
- **Scones** Add finely chopped fresh sage to cheese scones (p293).
- **Squash** Sprinkle over roasted squash, or squash soup.
- **Stuffing** Sage and onion is a classic flavour for stuffing to go with pork or chicken (p45).

Sorrel

The lemony flavour of sorrel goes well with butter, cream, soured cream, cream cheese, seafood, lamb, leeks, potato, lettuce, spring onions and chives.

❊ Store in the fridge for no more than three days and don't freeze unless cooked. It's a good idea to blanch sorrel to allay the sharp taste and to stop it curdling cream sauces; larger leaves should definitely be cooked once you have removed the stems.

- **Egg dishes** Add to omelettes, scrambled eggs and so on (p297).
- **Fish** Mix into buttery or creamy sauces to accompany fish, particularly salmon and trout.
- **Potatoes** Add to potato salad.
- **Salads** Add tender young leaves to lettuce and a sweet rather than astringent dressing.
- **Soups** Purée in some sorrel, especially those of the leek persuasion.

Tarragon

This distinctive aniseed-scented herb is excellent with chicken and with veal, white fish, salmon, scallops, tender salad leaves, mushrooms and shallots.

- **Dressings** Add to vinaigrette (p312) or mayonnaise to serve with chicken or salmon salads.
- **Sauces** Stir into creamy sauces or hollandaise (p108).
- **Stuffings** Tarragon in stuffing is particularly good for chicken (p45).

Thyme
Good with parsley, garlic, potatoes, carrots, tomatoes, beans, goats' cheese, cheddar, Brie, nuts, squash, mushrooms, and chicken.

- **Bouquet garni** Thyme is essential in this herb collection (p136).
- **Garnish** Sprinkle thyme flowers on salads or other dishes requiring a pretty garnish.
- **Stuffings** Add to stuffing together with lemon zest and black pepper for roast chicken (p45).

Hokey pokey – see Honeycomb

Hollandaise sauce
This buttery sauce, which is essential to Eggs Benedict, also goes very well with fish and with fresh green vegetables such as asparagus. See Eggs for an easy recipe for hollandaise (p108).

- **Reheating** Hollandaise is notoriously difficult to reheat once cold but if you have leftovers, press clingfilm onto the surface and chill. To reconstitute, try this. Melt the leftover sauce very gently. Whisk together an egg yolk and 1 tbsp water over a medium heat until the yolk starts to stiffen at which stage gradually beat the melted and, to be frank horribly split, sauce into the mixture.
- **Sauce mousseline** Fold whipped cream into hollandaise *et voilà* sauce mousseline!

Honey
Honey is particularly delicious with walnuts, almonds, lemon, yoghurt, cheeses especially those that are blue and soft, mustard and whisky.

❋ Kept dry and covered, honey keeps indefinitely if not longer; it may

HANDY HINT
If honey crystallises, as it tends to in cooler temperatures, just stand the jar in a pan of warm water stirring occasionally until it clears again.

darken or even become cloudy over a long time but is still perfectly edible.

- **Carrots** Stir a little into freshly cooked carrots together with a knob of butter and shake to glaze.
- **Drinks** Use every bit of honey in the jar – fill with hot water, add lemon juice to taste and enjoy a pleasant drink.
- **Facemask** Warm the skin first with a hot cloth, smooth on a little honey and leave for 15–20 minutes. Wash off with warm water and then splash the face with cold water to close the pores.
- **Fruit salads** Sweeten a fruit salad with a little honey.
- **Glaze** Gently brush warm honey over freshly baked cakes and puddings to glaze.
- **Honey butter** Blend together twice as much butter as honey. Additions could be lemon zest, poppy seeds or whole grain mustard. See compound butters p288.
- **Honey syrup** Useful for drizzling on ice cream, pancakes, yoghurt etc. for glazing cakes fresh out of the oven, adding to fruit salads etc. and essential for the Bee's Knees (see below). Stir together equal quantities of honey and warm water until the honey has dissolved and bring to a simmer. Cool and keep in the fridge.
- **Honey vinaigrette** Make vinaigrette by shaking the ingredients in an almost-empty honey jar. See basic vinaigrette recipe on p312.
- **Honeyed blue cheese on toast** This is sublime. The sweet caramelised honey is a perfect foil for the sharp, salty taste of blue cheese. Crumble, slice or spread the cheese onto hot toast and drizzle each slice with 1–2 tsp runny honey. Grill until the cheese has melted and the honey is starting to caramelise.
- **Ice cream** Drizzle runny honey over ice cream; vanilla ice cream with honey and salted peanuts, for instance, is an absolute treat!
- **Pancakes** Stir together honey and a knob of butter until melted and hot and serve with pancakes.
- **Porridge** A spoonful drizzled over or stirred into porridge adds a delicious flavour.
- **Roasted vegetables** Drizzle over roasting vegetables (not potatoes) to boost both flavour and caramelisation.

- **Sandwiches and salads** Honey plus a little wholegrain mustard stirred into mayonnaise makes a great dressing or spread for ham sandwiches.
- **Soothe a throat** Honey syrup may help calm sore throats and tickly coughs.
- **Sorbet or granita** Freeze honey syrup (opposite), mashing the mixture from time to time during freezing, to make honey sorbet or granita, depending on your dedication. See recipes on p299.
- **Sweetener** Use as a casual sweetener. By which I mean don't replace sugar with honey willy nilly in baking or other precise recipes – they are of different consistency and sweetness – but do use to sweeten drinks and more relaxed recipes, tasting as you go.
- **The Bee's Knees** This cocktail is said to have originated during the prohibition era in America; honey was believed to mask the smell of liquor. Shake four parts of gin and one part each lemon juice and honey syrup with ice. Strain into a chilled glass and garnish with a twist of lemon. You can, of course, vary proportions to taste.
- **Yoghurt** Drizzle over Greek yoghurt and top with nuts.

Honeycomb – aka Cinder Toffee, Sponge Toffee and Hokey Pokey

If you have an actual honeycomb apparently it is both edible and pleasant mashed up on toast or served with cheese. Honeycomb tastes good with honey, chocolate, cream and ice cream.

✳ Keep it dry!

- **Creamy desserts** Add to mousses, fools, trifles or any other gooey desserts.
- **Honeycomb butter** Crush into butter (p288) with a spoonful of honey too and melt over pancakes.
- **Ice cream** Crumble over or stir into ice cream.

H

Horseradish – for Japanese horseradish see Wasabi

The pungent flavour of horseradish is good with beef, venison, oily and/or smoked fish, potatoes, apples, beetroot and cream.

❋ Fresh horseradish keeps well in the fridge, loosely wrapped, for a few weeks but doesn't freeze well.

HANDY HINT

Take care when preparing horseradish as it can really make your eyes sting. Only prepare as much horseradish as you need; it loses strength once peeled. It also loses flavour when cooked so always use raw.

- **Bloody Mary** Vary this classic cocktail with a tad of horseradish.
- **Dumplings** Add a little to dumplings for a beef stew.
- **Fish sauce** Mix horseradish sauce with an equal quantity of soured cream to go with smoked and oily fish.
- **Pâté** Flavour smoked fish pâté (p117).
- **Potatoes** Add horseradish or horseradish sauce to mashed potato to accompany beef and fish or to top cottage pie.
- **Sauces** Add to cream sauces for steak and fish.
- **Vinaigrette** Stir a pinch into vinaigrette. See basic vinaigrette recipe on p312.

Hot cross buns – see Bread and act accordingly with the following provisos

- **French toast** Follow the basic recipe but make sure you keep the cross upwards!
- **Hot cross bun pudding** Follow the basic recipe for bread pudding; this also looks attractive if the top of the dish is a layer of crusts with their cross upwards!
- **Make croûtons (see p45)** Toss the torn hot cross buns with melted butter. Serve with warm fruit compôte.

Hot dogs – see Sausages

Hummus – sometimes spelt houmous
For a recipe for this delicious chickpea dip, see page 301. It keeps well, but if you have some that needs using up, try these ideas.

- **Coleslaw** Stir through coleslaw (p287) for an unusual dressing.
- **Potatoes** Mash into a baked potato or mix leftover hummus with an approximately equal quantity of leftover mashed potato, form into little cakes and fry.
- **Sandwiches** Spread in sandwiches and wraps instead of butter or mayonnaise then fill with ham, cheese or a sandwich filling of your choice.
- **Vinaigrette** Stir a spoonful of leftover hummus into vinaigrette. See basic vinaigrette recipe on p312.

I

Ice cream

Ice cream's affinities depend on its flavour but it often goes well with hot fruit pies, soft summer fruits, sweet syrups and sauces.

❋ Obviously ice cream should be kept frozen, ideally between –20°C and –25°C. If ice cream thaws it should be thrown away, do not refreeze for two reasons: firstly the texture will not be as good and, more importantly, harmful bacteria may have developed.

> **HANDY HINT**
> Press clingfilm onto ice cream's surface to stop ice crystals forming.

- **Biscuits** Sandwich suitable biscuits together with ice cream.
- **Ice cream soda or float** Known as a spider in the Antipodes! Put a scoop of ice cream together with chosen flavourings – such as chocolate sauce or maple syrup – into a tall glass. Some people add a little milk. Top up with a carbonated drink (cola, ginger beer, lemonade, etc.) and the ice cream will fizz, bubble and froth in a most spectacular fashion. Top with whipped cream, a cherry or what have you.
- **Milkshake** Can't do without it (p308)!
- **Truffles** Working quickly so that the ice cream doesn't melt, roll leftover ice cream into balls and coat with cocoa, cinnamon sugar, crushed biscuits, etc. Return to the freezer until ready to serve with after-dinner coffee. This combination may make your teeth hurt but is worth it.

> **COOK'S TREAT**
> Affogato is a simple treat. Pour a shot of espresso over a modicum of ice cream. Maybe add a little brandy and sprinkle with crumbled Amaretti, other leftover biscuits or grated chocolate.

Icing

- **Cake pops** Mix leftover buttercream icing with crumbled cake to make truffles or cake pops (p59).

J

Jalapeños – see Chillies

Jam

'The rule is, jam tomorrow and jam yesterday – but never jam today.'
Lewis Carroll

If you did have jam yesterday and fancy finishing off the leftovers
tomorrow, here are some ideas. It goes superbly with toast, scones, butter,
cream and sponge cakes.

- **Asian-style dipping sauce** Some jams – such as plum,
  apricot or grape – are suitable for this. Gently melt the jam
  with 1–2 tbsp soy sauce plus finely chopped spring onions,
  fresh chilli and a squeeze of lime juice, tasting as you go. If no
  fresh chilli is available, use a drop or two of Tabasco or other
  hot sauce.
- **Butter** Make a compound butter with just jam and butter,
  although you could add a pinch of cinnamon or chilli or salt or
  whatever takes your fancy (p288). Spread on toast or melt over
  pancakes.
- **Doughnuts** Inject some jam into a doughnut using an icing
  syringe or similar (p294).
- **Glaze** Gently warm jam till it is runny enough to brush onto
  bread, fruit tarts, etc. to glaze them.
- **Meat sauces** Add a spoonful of an appropriately flavoured jam
  (such as cherry with duck, or redcurrant with lamb) to pan
  juices after cooking meat to form a rich, sweet and fruity
  sauce.
- **PB & J** Peanut butter and jelly (which is what we call jam!) is a
  popular sandwich in America. A standard PB & J comprises
  buttered white bread, peanut butter and strawberry jam. Use
  good-quality bread or brioche, sprinkle a little crunchy sea salt
  over the peanut butter and lightly toast just to warm and melt
  the fillings together and you can lift this snack to another level.

J

- **Porridge and pudding** Add a dollop of jam instead of honey or sugar to sweeten porridge, rice pudding and other similar dishes.
- **Sweet sauce** Warm jam until it is runny and use it to sauce ice creams and desserts. How about a white chocolate sandwich cooked as French toast (p51) and sauced with warm raspberry jam for breakfast?
- **Tarts and turnovers** Use up some pastry scraps to make little jam turnovers or jam tarts.

Jelly – aka jello – for the American meaning of 'jelly' see Jam above

- **Trifle and sundaes** Chop or dice leftover jelly and add as a layer in trifle or sundaes such as knickerbocker glory.
- **Whipped jelly** Whisk leftover jelly until fluffy, which increases its volume and makes it look like something different!

Jerusalem artichoke – aka sunchoke because they are related to sunflowers.
The flavour of Jerusalem artichokes is enhanced by garlic, parsley and some of the stronger herbs such as sage or rosemary, apples and pears.

✳ These root vegetables should be stored in the same way as potatoes – cool, dark and dry – and should then be good for a week to ten days. Cooked, they can be kept in a sealed container in the fridge for four or five days. They don't freeze well in either state.

> **HANDY HINTS**
> Drop artichokes into acidulated water as you prepare them or they will discolour (p281).
>
> You might find it easier to peel Jerusalem artichokes once cooked as they are knobbly.

- **Potatoes** Pretty well anything you can do with a potato you can do with a Jerusalem artichoke.

Juice – see Fruit

Juniper berries

Famous for flavouring gin, these berries go well with duck, game, hearty meat dishes and cabbage. Get more flavour out of the berries by crushing lightly before use and soaking in a little warm wine or stock or other liquid you will be cooking them with.

- **Butter** Make juniper butter with crushed berries, garlic, black pepper, salt and parsley (p288).
- **Gin** Make your gin taste even worse – or better, if you like this spirit more than I do – by adding juniper berries to the bottle!
- **Marinades** Add a berry or two to marinades for game and meat.

Jus – see Gravy

K

Kale

Kale has a strong flavour and, unless very young and tender, is not good eaten raw. Cook it, without the stalks, as you would spinach. It tastes well with nutmeg, mustard and garlic.

❄ Keep in the fridge and eat sooner rather than later, as the older it gets the more bitter it becomes. Blanch for a couple of minutes to freeze.

● **Soups** Add shredded kale to Minestrone-type soups for the last few minutes of cooking.

Kidneys – see Offal

Kiwi fruit – aka Chinese gooseberry, although unrelated to gooseberries

Kiwi fruit goes excellently with lime, with other citrus and tropical fruits and with ginger, coconut and sesame.

❄ Keep at room temperature until ripe, then in the fridge for a maximum of a week. They don't freeze well unless in a sugar syrup.

● **Breakfast** Add to breakfast cereals and yoghurt.
● **Fruit salad** Kiwi is a very pretty addition to a fruit salad. Cut slices across the fruit so that you can see the burst of black seeds inside.

> **HANDY HINT**
> Don't use raw kiwi in jellies as an enzyme contained in the fruit stops them setting. It also curdles milk.

● **Meat tenderiser** Kiwis contain an enzyme that can be used to tenderise meat – either rub cut fruit onto meat or add a chopped or puréed kiwi to marinades.
● **Salsa** Dice or chop and mix with your choice of cucumber,

melon, fresh coriander, lime juice, chilli and so on to serve with seafood or chicken.
- **Smoothies** Blend into smoothies – you could strain out the seeds but I think they look good. See recipe on p308.
- **Sugar syrup** Toss sliced kiwi with a little caster sugar and fresh lime juice and leave a while to form a syrup. This is delicious atop Pavlova with strawberries and blueberries for added visual appeal.

Kohlrabi – see Turnip for more ideas as they can be treated similarly

This cabbage-turnip cross with hints of radish flavour goes well with Dijon mustard, garlic, parsley, potatoes, butter, cream and roasted meats. The leaves are edible and can be treated like spinach.

❄ Store kohlrabi, wrapped, in the fridge for three or four days but don't freeze unless cooked.

- **Coleslaw** Tender young kohlrabi can be eaten raw. Shred it into 'kohlslaw' (p287) or other salads.

Kumquat – see also Oranges

Like oranges kumquats go with duck, ginger, cranberries and cinnamon. The skin of kumquats is often eaten along with the rest of the fruit because in addition to being difficult to peel, the flesh can be sharp and the sweetness of the skin provides a pleasant contrast.

❄ Store for up to two weeks in the fridge but don't freeze unless cooked.

- **Cranberry sauce** Add a few sliced kumquats when making cranberry sauce or stir already cooked into ready made.
- **Fruit salads** Add slices of sweet, ripe kumquat to fruit salads.
- **Marmalade** If you really have a plethora of kumquats they make good marmalade.

L

Lamb – see also Meat

Lamb goes brilliantly with mint, rosemary, garlic and redcurrant jelly and with onions, leeks, potatoes, aubergine, apricots and warm spices such as cinnamon, cumin and turmeric.

- **Shepherd's pie** Mince or dice leftover meat and make a pie, adapting the cottage pie (p36).
- **Stovies** See p170 for this traditional leftover meat dish.

Langoustines – see Shellfish

Lard

- **Pastry** When making pastry, replace up to half the butter with lard for a traditionally light and tasty result.
- **Potatoes** Lard is really good for roasting potatoes.

Leeks

Leeks are delicious with chicken, fish in general and salmon in particular, potatoes, cheese, cream and butter. The nicest way I know of cooking leeks is the same way I like to cook onions (p303).

HANDY HINT

Leeks tend to trap soil between their leaves and the best way I have found to make sure they are clean is as follows: Remove the root end and outer leaf, cut the leek in half lengthways and slice. Fill a deep bowl with cold water, add the sliced leeks and swirl to separate and wash. Leave to sit until the water is still, the leeks floating and the soil has fallen to the bottom of the bowl. Using your hands or a skimmer, gently scoop the leeks from the surface of the water into another bowl, strainer or saucepan.

❄ Store raw leeks in the fridge for a week or so, cooked for four or five days. They must be blanched or cooked before freezing.

- **Cheese and leek scones** Mix cooled buttery leeks into your dough mix when making cheese scones (p293).
- **Frazzled leeks garnish** Cut a leek into long thin strips, rub a little cornflour through them (this makes them crunchy) and deep-fry for a few minutes until they are golden. Lift out of the oil with a skimmer and drain on kitchen paper.
- **Leek and potato soup** Use leeks instead of onions in the normal soup recipe on p309 and finish with cream. Serve cold and call it vichyssoise! Garnish with frazzled leeks.
- **Leek strata** See p50 and use buttery cooked leeks and a complementary cheese such as goats' cheese or Caerphilly.
- **Peas** Cook finely shredded leeks with peas or stir cooked leeks through cooked peas just to heat through.
- **Potatoes** Mash buttery cooked leeks into potatoes.
- **Replace onions** Use leeks instead of onions in any recipes to give a milder flavour.
- **Sauce** Mix cooked leeks into Alfredo sauce to serve with chicken, fish or pasta (p281).

Lemongrass – aka citronella and serai or sereh

The citrus taste of lemongrass is a great foil for coconut and good with shellfish, fresh coriander, chilli and lime.

❄ Well wrapped lemongrass will be fine in the fridge for a couple of weeks.

- **Custard** Infuse milk with lemongrass before making custards – it won't curdle the milk as lemon would.
- **Fish** Lay fish on pounded lemongrass stalks to steam or insert the stalks in the cavity of fish before grilling, baking or frying but remove before serving or warn your guests.

> **HANDY HINT**
>
> Only the pale inner core of the bulb end of lemongrass is edible but the leaves and stalk are great for adding flavour to dishes as long as you remember to remove them from the dish before serving. Maybe bash the stalks before using so that they give up more flavour.

L

- **Stock** Add to the pot when making chicken or fish stock.

Lemons – see other citrus fruits and Zest for further ideas

Lemons go well with fish, chicken, fresh green herbs, olive oil, garlic, blueberries, raspberries, honey, and gin and tonic.

❄ Store at room temperature, displayed in a pretty bowl, for a week or two (or three). They do well in the fridge for somewhat longer; up to six weeks if you keep them in a plastic bag so they don't dry out. After cutting, keep in the fridge and use as soon as possible. Freeze leftover lemon juice in ice cube trays and thaw out as needed.

- **Acidulated water** This lemony water prevents fruit and vegetables discolouring during preparation or cooking (p281).
- **Buttermilk substitute** Add 1 tbsp lemon juice to 225ml milk and leave five minutes as a useful buttermilk substitute.
- **Caramelise lemon slices** Pan-fry in a little olive oil until they start to go gold round the edges. Use as a delicious and impressive hot garnish for fish.
- **Chicken and fish** Place paper-thin slices of lemon under sympathetically flavoured chicken or fish dishes when serving.
- **Grill lemon halves** Place cut-side down alongside fish in a pan to brown for 1–2 minutes. Serve the lemon with the fish so that diners can squeeze the warm juice over the fish.
- **Highlights** Run lemon juice through your hair and go out in the sun – highlights! Remember to wash it out when you come back in.

HANDY HINTS

Get more juice from citrus fruit by firmly rolling on a hard surface or by warming slightly in the microwave for just a few seconds, or both, before cutting.

To use the zest as well as the juice, remove the zest first as it's so much easier that way. And whilst on the subject, only use the bright-coloured outer skin not the white pith beneath, as this is bitter.

- **Lemon butter** Use lemon zest, sea salt, black pepper and parsley (p288).
- **Lemon drizzle** What makes lemon drizzle cake so lush and moist is the warm lemon syrup poured over the cake as soon as it comes out the oven. A similar treatment can be given to any freshly baked lemon-friendly cake. Make the syrup by stirring together 60g caster sugar and the juice of a lemon, making sure that not all the sugar dissolves so as to give a crunchy topping. Depending on the size of cake it may be necessary to double up on syrup quantities.
- **Marinade** Make a peppery lemon marinade (see p312) for chicken or fish.
- **Soured cream** For a soured cream substitute, gradually whisk 1 tbsp lemon juice into 250ml double cream, tasting as you go and stopping when you think you have added not quite enough. Allow to sit for 15 minutes, during which time the cream should thicken. Taste again and add a little more juice if you really, really think it necessary.
- **Squeeze some juice** Sprinkle lemon juice on top of salads, vegetables and seafood as a bright and healthy dressing, in fact a last minute squeeze of lemon, or lime, brightens many dishes.
- **Tea** Add a slice of lemon to tea instead of milk.
- **Vinaigrette** Replace vinegar with lemon juice in the basic vinaigrette recipe (p312).
- **Water** Add pieces of leftover lemon to a bottle of water in the fridge – it's more interesting than drinking plain water.

Lemon Curd

If life hands you lemons, make lemon curd.

MAKES ABOUT 150G

3 large eggs
finely grated zest and freshly squeezed juice 2–3 lemons, about 80ml juice
150g sugar
60g butter, at room temperature, cut into small pieces

1. Put a nylon strainer over a bowl beside the stove.
2. Break the eggs into a heatproof mixing bowl and whisk in the lemon juice and sugar.
3. Stand the bowl in boiling water in a small pan.
4. Simmer over a medium heat, stirring absolutely constantly until the mixture starts to thicken. This will take a while, maybe 10 minutes or so. If you have such a thing as a sugar thermometer you are aiming for 71°C.
5. Immediately pour through the strainer.
6. Whisk in the butter pieces and the lemon zest.
7. Cool, press a piece of clingfilm on the surface and chill until needed.

Squeezed out fruit

- **Air freshener** Put a cut or squeezed lemon in the fridge to freshen the air.
- **Bleach** If you have discoloured elbows (no need to explain) rest them in a couple of squeezed lemon skins for a while to bleach the skin and then wash off.
- **Chicken** Put empty lemon halves in the cavity of a chicken before roasting.
- **Clean chopping boards** Scrub your chopping boards from time to time with a used lemon. This is even more efficient if you sprinkle salt on the lemon first to make it abrasive. Let the fruit sit directly on any stains for a while to bleach them out.
- **Fruit shells** Freeze hollowed-out citrus fruit shells filled with a matching or complementary sorbet.

- **Hand freshener** Rub your hands with lemon shells to remove nasty or over-powering smells such as fish or onion.

Lemon curd

- **Cheesecake** Lemon curd is delicious folded into thick yoghurt or whipped cream or cream cheese for instant cheesecake.
- **Ice cream** Add a layer or dollop to suitably flavoured ice creams or sundaes.
- **Lemon curd mess** Fold into whipped cream with chunks of meringue for a tangy twist on Eton mess.
- **Meringues** Sandwich meringues with lemon curd and cream.
- **Topping or filling** Spread on toast or use to fill scones or cakes.
- **Trifle** Make a lemon trifle (p119).

Lentils – see Beans and pulses and also Dhal

Lettuce

There are lots of different lettuces with textures from soft and floppy to crisp and refreshing and with flavours ranging from bitter to sweetish. They are, however, unanimously enhanced by citrus, mayonnaise, cream, bacon, fish, herbs, salad vegetables, onions, peas and leftovers.

❄ Stored in a loose plastic bag in the fridge, soft leaf lettuce will keep for three or four days, crisper lettuces such as romaine, cos and iceberg up to a week. Don't even think about freezing lettuce.

HANDY HINT
To revive limp leaves, put in a bowl of icy cold water for 10 minutes, drain and spin or lightly press dry. They will crispen remarkably.

- **Edible cups** Curly lettuce leaves make pretty and edible cups for serving salads and dips in.
- **Peas** Add a handful of shredded lettuce leaves to peas with a generous knob of butter and maybe finely chopped spring onion or mint. Add a little water and cook until the peas are tender – this is a bit French.

L

- **Sandwiches** Add to sandwiches or make an actual lettuce sarnie on good bread with mayonnaise and a sprinkling of crunchy sea salt.
- **Smoothies** I have heard of people adding lettuce to smoothies but I think you'd have to be pretty desperate! See recipe on p308.

Specific lettuces

- **Cos, romaine and little gem** Particularly good with Caesar dressing (p10).
- **Escarole and frisée** Escarole and its frillier, more bitter cousin frisée (aka curly endive) are the lettuces of choice (unless you have some leftover dandelion leaves) when making a traditional salade Lyonnaise. Toss the lettuce with lardons and classic vinaigrette (p312) and top with a poached egg. Serve with croutôns.
- **Iceberg** Frankly, this has little in the way of flavour but is refreshingly crunchy, so use to give body to floppy salads or as a bed for soft things such as prawn cocktail.
- **Iceberg slaw** Make a similar dish to coleslaw (p287). It might be a good idea to lighten the mayonnaise with yoghurt but is certainly not essential.
- **Iceberg wedge** A traditional salad in America is a wedge of iceberg lettuce, in the piece, drizzled generously with blue cheese dressing and sprinkled with crunchy bacon bits.
- **Little gem** Good cooked in butter and ideal for adding to peas (see above).
- **Round, Boston and Bibb** Soft-leaf lettuces are also good cooked with peas (see above).

Limes – see also Lemons and Zest

The flavour of lime is good with seafood, chilli, ginger, rum, coconut, other tropical fruits, avocado and fresh coriander.

❄ Store as for lemons.

- **Butter** Make lime butter for fish; good additions would be fresh coriander and chilli. See recipe for compound butters on p288.

- **Fruit salsa** A squeeze of lime brightens tropical salsas.
- **Just like a lemon** Use a lime pretty well anywhere you would use a lemon.
- **Marinades** Lime juice is often used in marinades (see Yoghurt).
- **Mayonnaise** Mix into mayonnaise with a dash of hot sauce.
- **Tropical fruit salad** Toss tropical fruits in lime juice with a sprinkling of caster sugar and leave for half an hour or so for a syrup to form.

> **HANDY HINT**
>
> Speaking of the tropics, workmen in the West Indies would often wash cement off their legs with freshly picked limes.

Liver – see Offal

Lobster – see Shellfish

Loganberries – see Berries and also Fruit

Lychee – see Fruit

M

Macadamia nuts – see Nuts

Mandarins – see Oranges

Mangetout – see Peas and Green Beans

Mango – see also Fruit

Mangoes are good with vanilla, ginger, avocado, orange, lime, coconut, chilli, fresh coriander, mint, curry spices, seafood, chicken, smoked chicken, ham, duck and rum.

❄ Keep under-ripe mangoes at room temperature for four or five days until ripe and then in the fridge for up to a week; cut mango will be okay for three to four days. To freeze a mango peel it, slice and spread without touching on a baking tray. Once frozen, decant into a freezer bag.

- **Breakfast** Add ripe mango to cereals or stir into yoghurt.
- **Cakes and biscuits** Add diced or chopped mango to baking recipes; it may be necessary to add a little more flour to take up the juices.
- **Carrot Soup** This tastes good with a little mango puréed into it.

> **COOK'S TREAT**
> Slice mango onto fresh toast, sprinkle with light brown sugar and grill until hot and bubbling.

- **Coleslaw** Add some shredded mango but make sure it is under-ripe (p287).
- **Curries** Fresh mango is excellent in chicken or seafood curry.
- **Mango chow** See Pineapple chow on p203.
- **Mango fool** Maybe add a drizzle of chilli syrup to your mango fool (p300) or a spoonful of rum.
- **Mango mess** See p172 for a recipe for Eton Mess and try it

with mango instead of strawberries.

- **Mango salsa** Dice mango and mix with similarly chopped red or spring onion and your choice of avocado, tomato, fresh coriander or mint, cucumber and fresh chilli or ginger. Toss with freshly squeezed lime juice and season to taste.
- **Mango sorbet or granita** See basic recipes on p299.
- **Salads** Chicken or seafood salads benefit from some fresh mango, which is also a great addition to a fruit salad.

Maple syrup

I am talking real maple syrup here, although fake could probably be used too. This beautiful flavour goes brilliantly with bacon and also with walnuts and pecans, pumpkin and squash, ice cream, pancakes, French toast, cake – ooh it's yum.

❄ To keep it fresh, refrigerate after opening or keep indefinitely in the freezer where real maple syrup will usefully remain semi liquid.

- **Bacon** Brush bacon rashers with maple syrup and grill or pop in the oven (about 190°C/gas 5) until crisp.
- **Cake glaze** Brush warm maple syrup onto warm fresh out of the oven cakes and bakes for a delicious finish.
- **Canadian cream tea!** Serve with scones and clotted cream or on toast – it sure beats jam!
- **Drinks** Add to smoothies and milkshakes or stir into a glass of cold milk.
- **Drizzle** Maple syrup is made for drizzling over ice cream, yoghurt, breakfast cereal, porridge etc.
- **Maple butter** Use 1 tbsp maple syrup to 60g butter (see recipe for compound butter on p288). Coarsely chopped walnuts or pecans or crisply cooked and dried bacon would all make great additions.
- **Maple leaf cocktail** Shake one part maple syrup, one part lemon juice and three parts Bourbon with ice. Strain into a chilled glass.
- **Maple pecan pie** It always surprises me that pecan pie doesn't 'officially' contain maple syrup. Try replacing some of

M

the syrup in a standard recipe, whether it be golden or corn, with maple syrup.

- **Popcorn** Toss freshly popped corn with maple syrup and perhaps a touch of butter or crunchy bacon bits.
- **Roasted vegetables** Toss a little maple syrup with roast parsnip, squash, pumpkin or sweet potatoes for the last few minutes of cooking.
- **Sweet potatoes** Add just a little maple syrup to mashed sweet potatoes, especially when serving with ham or bacon.

Marshmallows

- **Hot chocolate** I have never understood why people put marshmallows on top of hot chocolate but if you fancy it, go for it.
- **Ice Cream** Coarsely chop and add to ice cream sundaes or stir into chocolate ice cream together with some nuts.

> **HANDY HINT**
> Stuff a mini marshmallow into the point of an ice cream cone to stop it dripping.

Marmalade – see also Jam

- **Cake glaze** Brush warm marmalade onto suitable cakes, bread pudding etc. as soon as they are out of the oven.
- **Cheesecake** Warm marmalade slightly and spread on top of cheesecake, then chill before serving.
- **Duck** Stir a little into the pan juices after cooking duck for a cheat's version of 'duck à l'orange' as we say in England for some reason!
- **French toast and bread pudding** Add a few spoonfuls of marmalade to the recipes (p49– 51).
- **Manly bread pudding** A spoonful of marmalade is excellent in this recipe (p49).

> **HANDY HINT**
> Add a marshmallow or two to a bag of brown sugar to keep it soft. The beauty of this is you can still eat the marshmallow later.

Marrow – see Courgettes

Marzipan

Because this is made of almonds, marzipan tastes good with cherries and stone fruit generally and also pears, chocolate and fruit cake.

❄ Kept cool and dry marzipan should be fine for six months or so. Once opened, it will tend to dry out, so wrap exposed and cut edges well.

- **Baked goods** Add coarsely chopped marzipan to cake, muffin, biscuit and pancake recipes.
- **Balls!** Roll into little balls and then roll these in cocoa and sugar or melted chocolate.
- **Crumble** Add crumbs of marzipan to the crumble recipe (p290). It is especially good for a cherry crumble.
- **Crunchy garnish** Bake pieces of marzipan for a few minutes in a preheated oven at 200°C/gas 6 until crisp, then crumble over creamy cakes and desserts.
- **Dates** Stuff them with marzipan scraps.
- **Frangipane** Sprinkle a layer of chopped marzipan over a pastry base then top with fruit, peaches or cherries for instance, and bake for a delicious frangipane tart thingy.

Chewy Marzipan Cookies

1 egg white
40–50g icing sugar, sifted, plus extra for dusting
pinch of salt
250g marzipan, finely chopped or grated

1. Preheat the oven to 160°C/gas 3. Line baking trays with greaseproof or baking parchment and grease lightly.
2. Whisk the egg whites until quite frothy but not stiff. Slowly whisk in the sugar, salt and marzipan, then speed up and whisk to a soft, sticky dough which is as smooth as possible. You may need to add more sugar or, if too firm, perhaps a splash of rum or something; the texture of bought marzipans seems to vary quite a lot.
3. Scoop into small balls, roll in icing sugar to coat and place well spaced on the baking trays as they will spread during cooking.
4. Bake for 20–25 minutes until golden round the edge and cracking on the top.

Mayonnaise

This mainly applies to bought mayonnaise. You can use fresh mayonnaise in the same ways but do so sooner rather than later.

- **Baked fish crust** Brush mayonnaise over salmon or white fish fillets and sprinkle with crumbs for baking.
- **Creamy vinaigrette** Mix with vinaigrette for a new and different dressing. To make it even easier, make the vinaigrette in the empty mayo jar to use up every scrap. See recipe for vinaigrette on p312.
- **Fish cakes** (p114).
- **Mashed potatoes** Add a dollop of mayonnaise instead of milk or cream.
- **Sandwich spread** Substitute for butter in suitable sandwiches.

Meat – see also individual meats

Raw meat

❄ Collect raw trimmings and scraps in the freezer until there are enough to make stock (p34).

- **Burgers** Finely chop or mince raw meat, usually beef, and form into burgers (or meatballs). People often ask me what binder I use in my burgers but I don't; I just season the meat and then press it to shape – it always works for me.
- **Gravy** Don't throw away bones and trimmings; add them to the pan when roasting a joint for extra-good gravy.
- **Stir-fries** Add leftover meat or nice scraps to stir-fries. See recipe for stir-fry on p310.

Roast meats

- **Cottage pie** This is a classic leftover dish (p36), which you can make by mincing or finely chopping meat left from a roast.
- **Reheating cold roast meat** For a rerun of the original roast dinner, about 20 minutes before serving, bring your (hopefully leftover) gravy to a boil, turn off the heat and add the sliced meat. Put the lid on and set aside until ready to serve, by which time it should be hot and juicy and still tender.
- **Rissoles** For 250g minced roast meat, add 50g fresh breadcrumbs, a finely chopped onion and season to taste. Mix in a lightly beaten egg and maybe more breadcrumbs to enable the mixture to be formed into cakes. Coat in seasoned flour and shallow-fry.
- **Sandwiches** If you have leftover gravy, spread a little into the sarnies made with leftover roast meat or serve hot alongside for dipping purposes.
- **Stir-fry** Add cooked meat to stir-fries at the last minute, just to heat through. See recipe for stir-fry on p310.

M

Potted Meat

1. Shred leftover roast meat and weigh it.
2. Gently melt half as much leftover fat or butter, then allow to cool slightly, during which time any solids will sink to the bottom.
3. Mix the meat with any seasonings that are appropriate: herbs, spices and salt to taste.
4. Stir in about 75 per cent of the fat (leave back the solids) and press the resulting mixture into ramekins, levelling the surface.
5. Pour over the rest of the fat, discarding the solids. Chill.

• **Leftover potted meat** Stir potted meat through hot pasta with perhaps some cream or sauce.

Stovies

These are most commonly made with leftover roast lamb or beef but I see no reason why pork or chicken or even sausages wouldn't work too.

1 tbsp meat dripping, lard or oil
1 onion, thinly sliced
120g or so roast meat, diced
3–4 potatoes, sliced
300ml appropriate stock, hot
salt and freshly ground black pepper

1. Preheat the oven to 190°C/gas 5.
2. Melt the fat in a flameproof casserole, then add the onion and cook gently for about 5 minutes until tender.
3. Stir in the meat and season with salt and pepper.
4. Layer the sliced potato over the meat and onions.
5. Pour over the stock, cover and bake for about 40 minutes until the liquid is absorbed and the potatoes are tender and starting to brown round the edges. To facilitate this, take the lid off for the last few minutes of cooking.

Stewed meat – see also Gravy

- **Risotto** Stir through for the last few minutes of cooking (p306).
- **Sauce** Leftover stew can be a great sauce for pasta and for suitable meats, such as winey beef stew over steak.
- **Soup** Enrich a sympathetically flavoured soup with a spoonful or two of stew.

Melon – see Watermelon if such is your fruit

Sweet melon tastes good with lime, ginger, black pepper, mint, basil, grapes, cucumber, smoked and air-dried ham, salty cheeses and shellfish.

❄ Store ripe melon in the fridge for up to a week. If cut, press clingfilm onto the surfaces, not only for its own good but because it is prone to permeating other foods with its scent. It will keep chilled for three or four days but if frozen will be mushy when thawed.

- **Fruit salads** Any melon, or even a medley of melons, makes a good addition to a fruit salad (p119).
- **Ham** Melon is famously good served with air-dried ham such as Prosciutto. Maybe add goats' cheese or feta and a black pepper sprinkle.
- **Melon salsa** Dice melon and toss together with complementary ingredients such as cucumber, mint, red or spring onion, avocado, lime juice, and so on. Try a mix of different coloured melons if you have a range of leftovers.
- **Raita** Add to or even replace the cucumber in the basic recipe on p279 with melon.

M

Meringues

- **Coating** Use finely crushed meringues to coat truffles or the sides of frosted cakes.
- **Make a mess!** The classic Eton mess is simply crushed meringues and strawberries folded into whipped cream but it works for most fruits.
- **Sprinkle** Crushed or broken meringues are great sprinkled over ice cream, creamy desserts, Affogato (p150) and suchlike.

Milk

❄ Keep milk in the cooler body of the fridge rather than the door. If kept constantly cold, it may well keep for up to a week after its sell-by date. If frozen, it will expand so pour a little out of the bottle first.

- **Milkshakes or smoothies** Milk is, of course, essential in milkshakes and is good in smoothies too.
- **Potatoes** Add to mashed or scalloped potatoes (p305).
- **Rice pudding** Milk is essential for rice pudding, and it can even be made using leftover rice (p223)!
- **Soak strongly flavoured ingredients** Remove some of the salt from anchovies and capers or the 'wee' flavour from kidneys by soaking in milk to mellow them.

Mincemeat – as in the sweet
Christmas preserve

> **HANDY HINT**
>
> Mincemeat is easier to work with if loosened with a little spirit of some sort – rum or brandy or whisky for instance. Just saying.

❄ This will in all probability keep until next Christmas but here are some ideas.

- **Cake filling** Fold into whipped cream and use to fill cakes, éclairs or scones.
- **Christmas crumble** Mix mincemeat with apples under a crumble topping. See recipe for crumble topping on p290.

- **Christmas sorbet** Purée leftover mincemeat and add, in this case, just half as much simple syrup plus a little brandy or rum, but just a little and freeze (p299).
- **Ice cream** Swirl leftover mincemeat through softened ice cream.
- **Mincemeat palmiers** (p195).

Muesli

- **Make granola** (p302).

Mushrooms

The umami-ness of mushrooms is good with chicken, bacon, garlic, onion and shallots, cream, wine, sherry and brandy, eggs and cheese, especially Brie.

❄ Keep raw mushrooms in a paper bag in the fridge for up to a week. Do not store in anything airtight. They can be sliced and frozen. Cooked, they will be good covered in the fridge for a few days and also freeze well.

- **Mushroom fritters** Sautéed mushrooms work best in these (p285–86).
- **Mushroom soup** Purée garlicky sautéed mushrooms with the basic soup on p309 together with cream, cream cheese or clotted cream.
- **Salads** Thinly sliced raw mushrooms are good in salads.
- **Stir-fry** Add in accordance with the general instructions (p310).
- **Toasted cheese sandwich** Add raw or cooked mushrooms. They are especially good in Brie or Camembert sarnies.

M

Duxelles

This mushroom almost-paste can be made with just stalks, if necessary. It is traditional in Beef Wellington but can be used to add flavour to scrambled eggs, mashed potatoes, cream sauces, pasta dishes, gravy, under the skin of chicken before roasting, as a layer under cheese on toast and so on.

15g butter or 1 tbsp oil
250g mushrooms, finely chopped
1 shallot or small onion, finely chopped
A little finely chopped tarragon and/or parsley
1 tbsp wine, vermouth, sherry, brandy or even port (all optional)
Salt and freshly ground black pepper

1. Heat the butter or oil and add all the other ingredients except the optional alcohol.
2. Cook gently over a low heat until all the liquid given off by the mushrooms has disappeared.
3. Add the booze, if using, and continue to cook until that too has gone.
4. Season to taste with salt and pepper.

❄ This freezes well, preferably in small quantities.

Dried mushrooms

- **Mushroom butter** Reconstitute dried mushrooms in warm water or wine for about 20 minutes. Squeeze dry, then sauté in a little butter, oil or bacon fat. Season with salt and pepper and cook until all the moisture has gone. Cool, chop and mix into soft butter with chopped garlic and parsley if you wish (see compound butters p288).
- **Mushroom powder** Pop them in a spice or coffee grinder and grind to a powder to season steaks, eggs, and other mushroom friendly dishes.

Mushy peas – aka sloppy pease – a delicacy from northern England

- **Ham sandwiches** Mushy peas are a good addition to ham, bacon and other sarnies.
- **Mushy pea cakes** If thick enough to solidify when cold, form into cakes, coat in seasoned flour and fry until hot and crisp.
- **Pea and ham soup** Purée leftover mushy peas into the normal soup recipe (p309) and stir in a little shredded ham too, if you have some.

Mussels – see Shellfish

N

Nectarines – see Peaches

Noodles – see also Pasta

❄ Store leftover cooked noodles tossed with just enough oil to coat, so that they neither dry out nor stick together.

- **Garnish** Deep-fried noodles make a crunchy garnish for soups and salads.
- **Noodle cakes** Heat a little oil in a non-stick pan and coil in cooked noodles to form a cake. Flatten against the pan and cook until golden on the bottom, turn carefully and cook the other side.
- **Soup** Noodles are a good addition to spicy broth-type soups.
- **Stir-fry** Replace the rice with noodles in a stir-fry. See tips for stir-frying on p310.

Nutella – see Chocolate spread

Nuts

❄ Store in an airtight container in the fridge for up to six months or twice as long in the freezer. Nuts tend to take up other flavours so make sure they are tightly enclosed. Don't store in metal containers as this can spoil them.

Toasted or Roasted Nuts

These have intense flavour and crunch. Use toasted nuts in the same way you would use un-toasted nuts!

1. Preheat the oven to 180°C/gas 4 or heat a large, dry-frying pan.
2. Add some salt, pepper and spices to the nuts at the start of toasting.
3. Either shake and stir the nuts in a dry pan over a medium heat until crunchy, fragrant and golden or spread on an ungreased baking tray and pop in the oven for a few minutes, shaking or stirring occasionally, until the same result is achieved.
4. The roasting time varies so keep an eye on them; they need to be a shade or so darker and fragrant; too dark and they'll be bitter. Don't add oil, they have enough of their own.
5. Add fresh herbs, if using, at the end.
6. The nuts become crisper as they cool. Don't chop until cold or they may become oily.

- **Baking** Add chopped nuts to cakes and other baked goods – toasted nuts are less likely to sink to the bottom.
- **Breakfast** Add a handful of leftover nuts to store-bought or homemade granola and muesli.
- **Cheesecake** Add some chopped nuts to your biscuit base (p42).
- **Crumble** Chopped nuts are a great addition to a crumble topping (p290).
- **Gratins** Coarsely chop and sprinkle onto bakes and gratins, such as cauliflower cheese.
- **Honey nut butter** Add coarsely chopped nuts and a drizzle of honey to softened butter (p288).
- **Nutty vinaigrette** When making vinaigrette in the food processor, pulverise a handful of toasted nuts and a little garlic before adding the vinegar (sherry or balsamic would be best) and then the oil. Taste, season and thin with a little warm water if necessary. This doesn't keep for more than a day or two in the fridge but that should be long enough! Bring to room temperature before using. See vinaigrette recipe on p312.
- **Pancakes** See page 283 and add chopped nuts to the pancake after pouring the batter into the pan.
- **Pesto** Pine nuts are the classic but other nuts work very well too (p137).

> **HANDY HINT**
> Toast only what you need as any advantages gained in crispness and fragrance will diminish with time.

N

- **Popcorn** Toss in some nuts with whatever other flavourings or seasonings you are using.
- **Praline butter** See below for the praline recipe and see compound butters (p288) for the method.
- **Recycled biscuit cake** Add a nutty touch to this sweet treat (p42).
- **Salads and stir-fries** Both will benefit from a handful of nuts to add flavour and a different texture.
- **Stuffing** Mix in nuts, toasted or otherwise, when making a stuffing (p45).
- **Toppings** Ice cream and sundaes, porridge, cereals and bread pudding all benefit from a sprinkling of nuts.

Sugared Nuts

I often do this with walnuts and a little black pepper to go in blue cheese salad.

100g sugar
50ml water
pinch of salt
125g nuts

1. Preheat the oven to 180°C/gas 4 and set a lightly greased baking tray beside the stove.
2. Heat together the sugar and water over a low heat, stirring until the sugar has dissolved.
3. Turn up the heat and boil to a light syrup – this only takes a few minutes. A little of the syrup dabbed on a plate should form a thread when you lift the spoon.
4. Stir in the salt and nuts.
5. Spread onto the baking tray and bake in the oven for 10 minutes until crisp, keeping an eye and a nose out in case they start to overcook.
6. Cool, breaking up any clumps, and use whole or chopped in or on ice cream, in salads or just in your mouth.

Easy Nut Brittle and Simple Praline

Any nuts can be used to make brittle; a mixture is good and salted nuts are excellent. Just two ingredients are needed: equal quantities of coarsely chopped nuts and caster sugar.

1. Put a lightly greased baking tray on a heatproof pad or surface beside the stove.
2. In a heavy pan, gently melt the sugar over a low heat and when it is a greyish liquid, turn up the heat and cook to a rich caramel colour. Carefully swirl the pan to even the cooking.
3. Stir in the nuts and immediately and very carefully tip the whole lot onto the greased baking tray.
4. Leave to cool then break into pieces to make brittle, or process to a powder for praline.

Almonds
Almonds pair well with cherries, peaches, apricots, chilli, honey, yoghurt, chocolate and squash.

- **Fish topping** Mix finely chopped almonds with breadcrumbs and herbs, spices, grated lemon zest or Parmesan cheese, moisten with olive oil and press gently onto lightly buttered fish. Bake in a preheated oven at 200°C/gas 6 until crisp and tender.
- **Greek yoghurt** This is excellent with almonds and honey for breakfast.

GROUND ALMONDS

- **Coating** Mix with breadcrumbs as a coating for fried foods.
- **Crumble** Replace up to 30 per cent of the flour with ground almonds (p290).

Brazil nuts
Brazils are good with bananas and dates.

❄ Look after them as they are even more prone to going rancid than other nuts.

N

- **Dates** Brazil nuts are perfectly shaped to stuff into dates.

Cashew nuts
Cashews are excellent with Asian flavours such as soy, sesame, ginger, chilli, garlic, black pepper, coconut, chicken and cucumber.

- **Coriander pesto** This is good made with cashews – see p137 for recipe.
- **Curries** Cashews are also good in these, especially chicken curries.
- **Stir-fries** Cashews are particularly good nuts for stir-fries. Add for just the last few minutes of cooking. See tips on stir-frying on p310.

Hazelnuts – aka cobnuts or filberts
Hazelnuts and chocolate are excellent together, so excellent in fact that this combination, originally known as Gianduia, is now marketed as the hugely successful Nutella – see Chocolate spread! Hazelnuts are also good with coffee, apples and pears, cherries, peaches, plums and caramel.

- **Roasting** This not only enhances the flavour of hazelnuts, it helps make it easier to skin them. When the skins have cracked, pour the hot nuts onto a clean tea towel, wrap them up and leave for a few minutes. Rub the nuts in the towel; the skins should easily flake off onto the towel which is, admittedly, then a bugger to clean!

Dukkah

This Egyptian aromatic nut, seed and spice mixture most commonly contains toasted hazelnuts, coriander, cumin and sesame seeds, salt and pepper plus frequently dried thyme, mint, other nuts, other seeds, other spices. Here is a simple recipe – feel free to fiddle with it. Dukkah is traditionally served with dipping oil and bread and can be advantageously sprinkled on no end of dishes: a salad, soups, dips such as hummus and pilaf, for instance.

60g hazelnuts
2 tbsp sesame seeds
1 tbsp coriander seeds
½ tbsp cumin seeds
1 tsp whole black peppercorns
crunchy sea salt

1. Toast the nuts (as described above) and set aside.
2. Similarly toast all the seeds and spices until fragrant – they won't take as long – and set aside to cool.
3. When everything is cold, grind together with a pestle and mortar or in a designated coffee grinder.
4. Add salt to taste.
5. Store chilled and airtight for up to a month.

Macadamia nuts
Macadamias go well with seafood, coconut, bananas, honey and chocolate.

Peanuts – aka groundnuts – see also Peanut butter
These aren't actually nuts they're legumes, but I still feel they should be here!

> **HANDY HINT**
> Anything you can do with another nut you can do with a macadamia except – **don't give them to your dog** as apparently they find them toxic.

- **Garnish** Sprinkle on appropriate soups such as peanutty sweet potato soup (p197) and spicy chicken soups.
- **Ice cream** Sprinkle coarsely chopped salted or honey roast peanuts over ice cream with a drizzle of honey.

N

- **Peanut Brittle** (p179).
- **Stir-fries** Peanuts are another particularly stir-fry-friendly nut. See tips on stir-frying on p310.

Pecans

These sweet nuts go well with maple syrup, brown sugar, caramel, vanilla, butterscotch and Bourbon.

- **Bread pudding** Pecans are lovely in Bread and No-Butter Pudding (p50) together with maple syrup.
- **Butter-pecan ice cream for cheats** Finely chop pecans and roast until a shade darker and smelling good. Immediately stir in a good pinch of salt and 20g soft butter per 100g of nuts. Allow to cool and absorb the butter, then add to vanilla ice cream.

Pralines

These are not the same as praline! They are a pecan, sugar and cream confection from America's Deep South.

120ml double cream
200g brown sugar
1 tsp vanilla extract
125g toasted pecan halves

1. Line and lightly grease a baking tray and set beside the stove.
2. Mix together the cream and sugar in a heavy pan, stirring together over a medium heat until melted and combined. Stop stirring!
3. Turn up the heat and cook to soft balls stage (115°C) which means that if you drop a little into cold water and then lift out the ball that forms, it will squash between your fingers.
4. Take off the heat, stir in the vanilla and then keep stirring quite vigorously till the mixture is thick and opaque.
5. Add the pecans and drop spoonfuls of the mixture onto the greased tray.
6. Leave to cool completely.

Pine nuts – aka pignolia

- **Pesto** Pine nuts are traditional in Pesto (p137) and go well with tomatoes, chilli and spinach.

Pistachios

- **Garnish** Because of their lovely bright green colour with occasional touches of purple, pistachios make a pretty garnish.

Walnuts

Dark chocolate, coffee, blue cheese in particular and cheeses in general, apples, pears, celery, honey, maple syrup and bananas all go well with walnuts.

- **Cheese scones** Work a few chopped walnuts into the dough (p293).
- **Pasta sauce** Coarsely chopped toasted walnut and roasted garlic (p123–24) are good stirred through hot pasta with blue cheese or Parmesan and a little of the pasta cooking water to form a sauce.

HANDY HINT

Rubbing a scratch in wooden furniture with a walnut should make it less noticeable.

O

Oatmeal – see Porridge

Oats

- **Breakfast (other than porridge)** Make granola or muesli if you have a lot of oats to use up (p301).
- **Coating** Mix with breadcrumbs when coating foods for frying or baking.
- **Crumble** Use the basic recipe (p290) and replace up to one-third of the flour with oats.
- **Happy skin** Oats are very soothing to the skin. Tie some into a piece of cloth, small bag or sock and add to the bath for soft, soothing water. Use the bag of oats like soap to cleanse and soothe the skin.
- **Herring** A traditional way to cook herring is to roll them in seasoned flour, beaten eggs, oats and fry in bacon fat.

Skirlie and Skirlie Mash

Skirlie is a Scottish dish of oatmeal cooked with onions in fat or oil. You'd need quite a lot of leftover oats to serve Skirlie as a separate dish but just a little is delicious and traditional stirred into creamy mash.

90g lard, butter, bacon fat or oil
1 onion, coarsely chopped
50g steel cut or pinhead oatmeal (flaked oats aren't so good for this)
salt and freshly ground black pepper

1. Melt the fat in a frying pan and cook the onion for 5 minutes until tender and browning.
2. Now add the oatmeal and stir-fry until they have absorbed the fat and are crisping. Add more fat or more oats as necessary. Season to taste with salt and pepper.

3. Serve as a side dish, use as stuffing for chicken or turkey or fold into creamy mashed potato just before serving so that the skirlie stays crunchy.

Cranachan

SERVES 3–4

350ml double cream
whisky to taste (within reason!)
2 tbsp oats, toasted in a dry-frying pan until slightly golden
2 tbsp clear honey
250g fresh raspberries, crushed

1. Whisk together the cream and the whisky until thick and softly peaking.
2. Fold in the rest of the ingredients
3. Divide between three or four glasses and chill until needed.

Octopus – see Shellfish

Offal – aka variety meats, organ meats, purtenances and umbles

Offal covers all sorts of bits and pieces of dead animals: eyes, blood, udders, testicles (which are known in polite society as 'fries', although not in our house) and so on, but I'm afraid I am not going into too much detail here.

❋ Use as soon as possible – it doesn't keep well. Fresh offal can be frozen.

● **Haggis** Here are some loose instructions from Gervase Markham in 1615: 'Oat-meale mixed with blood, and the Liver of either Sheepe, Calfe or Swine, maketh that pudding which is called the Haggas or Haggus, of whose goodnesse it is in vaine to boast, because there is hardly to be found a man that doth not affect them.'

O

- **Sonofabitch Stew** A meal reputedly prepared by cowboys in the Wild West, it's a bit boring! Simmer 900g diced lean beef together with half a beef heart and 900g liver in enough water to cover. After a couple of hours, add some salt, pepper, Louisiana hot sauce plus sweetbreads and brains and simmer for another hour.

Giblets – poultry innards

- **Giblet gravy** If your bird still has its giblets, then brown them in a little oil (save the liver for something else as it has rather an intrusive flavour, see p77), add chopped onions, carrot and garlic and sauté for a couple of minutes. Cover with water and simmer whilst the bird is roasting. Strain and use the resulting stock to make gravy. Traditionally giblet gravy is chunky so chop up some of the choicest pieces of giblet and stir into the finished gravy.
- **Rover et al** Cook and feed to your dog.

Heart

- **Pan-fry** Fry thin slices of heart and finish with a little black pepper, brandy and cream.

Kidneys

- **Breakfast** Add to a fry-up or mixed grill.
- **Egg dishes** Chop up cooked kidneys and add to scrambled eggs or omelette.
- **Steak and kidney** Braise kidneys with steak in a slow oven to make steak and kidney (obviously!). Put a crust on to make steak and kidney pie.

> **HANDY HINT**
> If you don't like your kidneys to taste too strong, soak them for 15 minutes in milk before cooking.

Liver – see also Chicken livers

- **Onion gravy** Heat leftover liver through very gently in onion gravy.
- **Pasta** Slice thinly and toss in a cream sauce with pasta – onions, bacon or any sauce associated with the liver will be fine additions.

Tongue

- **Cold meats** Use as with other cold meats, such as ham, or serve as part of a platter.
- **Tongue sandwich** – sorry, sounds a bit rude!

Tripe

I have no idea what to do with this and it serves you right for buying it.

Okra – aka ladies' fingers, bhindi and gumbo

Okra's flavour affinities include chicken, bacon, ham, corn, cornmeal, onions, sweet peppers, tomatoes, basil and filé powder (ground sassafras leaves used in Cajun and Creole cooking), if you happen to have any left over.

❄ Okra keeps well in a bag in the fridge for up to three days and must be blanched or cooked before freezing. Cooked okra chilled in an airtight container is good for three or four days.

- **Deep-fry** Dip clean okra pods in flour, egg and then cornmeal (to be authentic) or breadcrumbs and deep-fry until crisp and golden.
- **Salads** Young okra can be eaten raw in salads, or try marinating just-cooked okra in vinaigrette as part of a cold collation.

HANDY HINT

Eat immediately. Okra does have a well-deserved reputation for sliminess, which can be avoided by eating as soon as it is cooked although this doesn't work well for leftovers.

O

Olives

Olives pair well with garlic, anchovies, capers, chilli, coriander seed, lemon, orange, thyme, rosemary, black pepper, tomatoes and martini.

- **Basic tapenade** For every 10 or so pitted olives you need 1 peeled garlic clove, 1 tbsp capers and an optional anchovy fillet. Pound or process these together to a paste and then work in 1 tbsp olive oil and a squeeze of lemon

> **HANDY HINT**
>
> To pit olives, squash with the flat side of a wide-bladed knife and flick out the pit.

  juice. Taste and season with salt and pepper. Other optional extras include roasted red pepper, tinned tuna and even dried figs. Use tapenade on bruschetta, as a dip, with fish, in salad dressings, sandwiches and so on.
- **Bread** Add to dough, especially crusty, chewy types of bread.
- **Crushed olives** Crush a garlic clove with a pinch of sea salt, add olives and mash into the mixture. Season with herbs (thyme or rosemary are good) and a little orange zest and/or chilli. Serve warm on bruschetta, use to flavour lamb for roasting or stir through hot pasta.
- **Deep-fried olives** Dip olives in seasoned flour, beaten egg and finally breadcrumbs and deep-fry until crunchy. They could be stuffed first with, say, goats' cheese or roasted garlic.
- **Dirty Martini** These are horrible! Mind you I'm not terribly keen on olives or gin. If you do fancy one, mix together five parts gin and one part dry vermouth and then slowly add olive brine until you think it tastes good. Serve in a chilled glass garnished with an olive. (This might be marginally better using vodka instead of gin!)
- **Olive butter** Add coarsely chopped green, black or mixed olives, parsley, a bit of garlic, capers, perhaps even a few anchovies to make a compound butter (p288).
- **Pan bagnat** See p25 for this pressed sandwich recipe.
- **Pizza** Olives are a natural for scattering onto pizza.
- **Roasted olives** Toss black olives with garlic, herbs, orange zest, sea salt and chilli or with lemon, garlic and fennel seed for instance, plus a little olive oil. Roast in a preheated oven at 200°C/gas 6 until they start to soften, 15–20 minutes. Serve at

room temperature as nibbles with cocktail sticks for ease of eating.

- **Salads** Olives are traditional in Salade Niçoise (p118) and Greek Horiatiki salad (p72).

Onions and shallots

❄ Whole onions will be fine in a cool dry place for two to three months. Cut onion will be good in the fridge for two to three days but make sure they are well and truly wrapped or in a sealed container to prevent everything tasting of onion. To freeze, spread sliced or chopped onion on a baking tray and when solid put in a freezer bag. Cooked onion keeps up to five days in the fridge.

- **Garnish** Toss thinly sliced red onion in lemon juice and it will turn a beautiful vivid pink.
- **Onion grass** Thinly, thinly slice raw onion, rinse in cold water, drain and toss in seasoned flour. Deep-fry until crisp and serve with steak or burgers, they are even nicer than onion rings.
- **Onion gravy** Add cooked onions to gravy.
- **Raw onions** These are a basic ingredient in a huge number of dishes but if you can't think what to do with raw onions add them to salad, sandwiches and pizza toppings.
- **Toad in the hole** Stir cooked onions into the batter. See pp284–85.

Oranges – plus clementines, tangerines, mandarins, tangelos and satsumas – see also other citrus fruits and Zest
Oranges are good with almonds, black olives, chocolate, cinnamon, caramel, vanilla, ginger, sweet potatoes, red onion and other citrus fruits.

- **Fish** Serve orange wedges instead of lemon.
- **Jelly** When making orange jelly replace some or all of the water with orange juice.
- **Orange drizzle for cakes** Adapt the drizzle recipe (p159). This is excellent on freshly baked carrot cake.

O

- **Orange Vinaigrette** Use fresh orange juice as the acid component in the basic recipe p312.

Dried Orange Slices

These make pretty and fragrant Christmas decorations. Hang them on the tree, use them to decorate presents or add to potpourri.

1. Preheat the oven to as low as it will go, 110°C/gas ½ ish.
2. Slice oranges crosswise thinly and evenly. Don't use the ends but you could squeeze out the juice or suck them before discarding.
3. Dry slices with a bit of kitchen paper and lay on a baking tray – I line mine with a silicon sheet first.
4. Sift a little icing sugar over the orange slices, turn them over and sift over some more.
5. Bake for 2½ – 3 hours, turning the slices at about half time and then again when nearly ready. They should be leathery dry.
6. Cool – that's an instruction, not a comment!
7. For an even better smell sprinkle with cinnamon before baking, for extra prettiness sprinkle with glitter after baking.

Orzo – see Pasta

Oysters – see Shellfish

Oxtail – see also Beef

- **Hot crusted tails** Roll whole, cooked pieces of oxtail in breadcrumbs and bake in a preheated oven at 180°C/gas 4 until crisp. Serve with mashed potatoes and leftover oxtail gravy.

P

Pancakes and drop scones

I refer here to thick American-style pancakes as opposed to crêpes. For what to do with leftover crêpes see Crêpes! The recipe for these pancakes is on page 283.

❄ Interleave, wrap and chill or freeze until needed.

- **Pancake cake** Layer up several leftover pancakes with something gooey: cream, chocolate sauce, jam, fruit purée, peanut butter, honey, maple syrup, to name but a few, to make a cake and serve in wedges.
- **Reheat** Toast leftover pancakes or, even better, fry in butter.
- **Sandwiches** Use as the outside of a sandwich with an appropriate filling (bananas and peanut butter, for instance) and toast or fry until crisp and hot through.

Pancetta – see Bacon

Panko

These lovely über-crisp Japanese breadcrumbs can be used to add crunch to so much more than deep-fried food, if you have just a spoonful or two left try the following:

- **Crunchy topping** Mix leftover panko with grated cheese to sprinkle on gratins and savoury baked dishes before cooking.
- **French toast** Before frying French toast – see Bread (p51) – dip the soaked bread in panko crumbs. The crumbs will trap the syrup and butter deliciously.
- **Pancakes** A similar effect can be achieved with pancakes; sprinkle panko onto the uncooked side before flipping. See Basic Recipes p283.

P

- **Pastry** When rolling out pastry (scraps) for cheese straws or similar, dust the board with panko crumbs instead of flour for extra crunch.
- **Salad sprinkle** Toast panko crumbs in a dry-frying pan until golden, mix in a little coarse sea salt and sprinkle on salads and similar dishes.

Panettone – see Bread

Papaya – aka pawpaw

Excellent with fresh lime, papayas are also good with other citrus fruits, pineapple, coconut, rum, chilli, black pepper, curry spices, chicken and seafood.

❄ Keep at room temperature until ripe and then in the fridge for two or three days. Once cut press clingfilm against surfaces and store chilled for a couple of days. Freeze diced papaya in freezer bag with the air squeezed out.

- **Caribbean breakfast** A wedge of papaya with a squeeze of fresh lime juice is a traditional start to the day in the islands.
- **Fruit salad** Delicious with papaya.
- **Papaya salsa** Mix diced ripe papaya with complementary ingredients such as red onion, fresh coriander, chilli, lime juice etc. and serve with grilled chicken or seafood.
- **Salads** Papaya is good in chicken or seafood salads.
- **Smoothies** A good smoothie can be made with papaya, coconut milk and rum, perhaps (p308).

Parma ham and other air-dried hams – see Ham

Parsnips

The sweet taste of parsnips is good with roast meats, especially lamb, nuts, honey and nutmeg.

❄ They are good keepers and will be fine in the fridge for three or four weeks. Blanch to freeze. Keep cooked parsnips in an airtight container in the fridge for up to four days, or freeze.

- **Bubble and squeak** Include parsnips in the mixture (p211).
- **Carrot and parsnip purée** Cook with about the same amount of carrots until all the vegetables are tender, then drain and purée with butter and cream for quite a posh side dish.
- **Curried parsnip soup** When you make soup (see p309 for basic recipe), cook a little curry paste in with the onions when they are almost tender. Replace some or all of the potatoes in the basic recipe with raw parsnips OR reduce the quantity of potatoes and add cooked parsnips when they are tender. Coconut is good added at the end of cooking.
- **Fried** Shallow or deep-fry pieces of cooked parsnip until crisp, then sprinkle with crunchy sea salt.
- **Mashed** Parsnips are great mashed with potatoes.
- **Roast** Cook parsnips alone or with other root vegetables; a touch of honey is a good addition. They are also delicious roasted with apples in a little oil with salt, pepper and sage – this goes well with pork.

Partridge – see Game and Chicken

P

Passionfruit and granadilla

Granadilla is a large, golden passionfruit – and is good with other tropical fruits, cream, ice cream and, being quite sharp, it goes very well with meringues.

❄ Keep at room temperature for three or four days and up to a week in the fridge. The older they get, the wrinklier they become (sounds familiar!) and in their case this is an indication of ripeness. Scoop out the flesh and freeze in an ice cube tray.

- **Passionfruit mess** Deliciously messy meringue dessert (see Eton mess p172).
- **Passion vinaigrette** Use passionfruit juice as the acidic ingredient (in the basic recipe on p312).
- **Sparkling passion punch** Strain the pulp into a glass, stir in rum and top up with sparkling water.
- **Topping** Scoop the flesh over ice cream or creamy desserts such as cheesecake or panna cotta.

Pasta – see also Noodles

❄ Fresh pasta can be stored in the fridge, well wrapped, for a couple of days. Cooked pasta, tossed with a smidgen of vegetable oil so that it doesn't clump together, keeps in the fridge for a day or two but is not worth freezing as it tends to be mushy once thawed. Far better to undercook it in the first place but then it wouldn't be a leftover, would it?

- **Frittata di pasta** Reheat the pasta with whatever sauce is clinging to it in a non-stick pan and continue with the frittata recipe (p296).
- **Frittatine di pasta** Make pasta fritters by mixing cooked pasta and any accoutrements into fritter batter (p285–86).
- **Pasta salad** These aren't always successful! Add a bright-tasting dressing and plenty of crunchy vegetables to offset any stodginess.
- **Quasi lasagne** Layer cooked pasta with meat or vegetables,

top with cheese sauce and bake.

- **Reheat** Cooked pasta can be reheated ready for saucing by plunging into boiling water for 30 seconds or so, just to heat through, then draining immediately so that it doesn't cook any further.
- **Soup** Add broken pieces of uncooked pasta to soup shortly before serving for just long enough to cook them.

Pastry

For a simple shortcrust recipe see page 291.

> **HANDY HINT**
> Generally speaking, bake pastry items in a preheated oven at 190°C/gas 5.

❋ Freeze pastry leftovers, well wrapped. Pile puff pastry scraps one on top of another rather than scrunch them into a ball so as to retain and maybe increase the layering.

- **Cheese straws** Roll out pastry scraps, scatter with grated cheese, fold over, roll again and cut into strips to make cheese straws. Give them a twist before baking if you want to be fancy (p69).
- **Crunchy pie topping** Roll out pastry scraps and cut into random or not random (for instance, leaves) shapes, toss with sugar and cinnamon and scatter over the top of a dish of cooked apples (or whatever). Bake until hot and crisp.
- **Nibbles** Spread the rolled-out pastry with something delicious, fold in half and re-roll. Cut into little shapes and bake on a greased baking tray until crisp and golden.

> **COOK'S TREAT**
> Sprinkle pastry trimmings with sugar and cinnamon, as above, on a baking tray and bake until crisp. Make a cup of coffee, have a sit down and eat them.

- **Palmiers** Roll the assembled pastry scraps into a rough, raggedy rectangle. Scatter something delicious over the surface – good combinations would be Cheddar and chopped chilli, pecans and maple sugar, ham and cheese, dried fruit and brown sugar or whatever you have. Roll up from one long edge, moisten the opposite edge and press to seal. You can then place sealed-side down on a greased baking sheet, brush with beaten egg to glaze and sprinkle the top as appropriate. Bake until crisp and golden, then slice into pinwheels. Alternatively, slice before baking and lay cut-side up (and down!) on the baking tray. The second option is good with cheese as it goes all melted and golden.

- **Rustic tarts** Roll pastry scraps into rough rounds and top with your chosen filling, leaving a 1– 1.5cm bare edge. Fold this border up over the filling, leaving the centre uncovered and framed by pastry. Brush with beaten egg and sprinkle with sugar or sea salt depending on the filling. Bake until hot, crisp and golden.
- **Turnovers** Cut squares or circles, put a spoonful of filling on one half, fold in half and seal. Bake or fry in butter.

Pâté

❉ Pâté tends to have a quite limited lifespan in the fridge but freezes well.

- **Beef Wellington** A layer of pâté is traditional in this dish.
- **Dirty rice** Replace the chicken livers with pâté (p77).
- **Enrich sauces** Melt into red wine sauces or gravies to make them even richer.
- **Pâté cake** Bring pâté to room temperature, mix in cooked onions, fresh herbs or spices to taste and enough fresh breadcrumbs to enable the mixture to hold together. Form into little cakes, roll in more breadcrumbs, chill to firm up, then shallow-fry until hot and crisp.
- **Strata** Add pâté to this savoury Bread pudding (p50).

Peaches – see also Fruit

Almonds, honey, brown sugar, Bourbon, vanilla, cinnamon, ginger, cream, cream cheese, cherries, raspberries, blueberries, chicken, duck, ham, and barbecued meats are all good with peaches.

❉ If not quite ripe ('ripen at home'!), keep at room temperature until they are, then transfer to the fridge for a couple of days, cut or otherwise. To freeze, they need to be cooked or in a syrup (see p299 for basic syrup recipe).

- **Amaretti stuffed peaches** (p8).
- **Bellini** This cocktail is particularly useful if you have Champagne or sparkling wine you can't think what to do with (well, it could happen!). Peel stone and purée leftover peach(es) and one-third fill as many glasses as it will stretch to. Top up with chilled Champagne, which is easiest done by stirring in a little and then waiting until the foaming has calmed down before adding the rest. Excellent breakfast drink!
- **Parma ham** Serve sliced ripe peaches with Parma ham, Serrano or similar. I prefer this to the more traditional melon.
- **Peach vinaigrette** Swap peaches for the pears in the recipe on p198 and serve with ham salad.
- **Pizza topping** Try peach slices and Brie.

Peanut butter

Peanut butter goes well with bacon, Asian spicy flavours, cinnamon, bananas, chocolate Nutella, maple syrup, honey and, particularly in America, jelly aka jam.

- **Banana smoothie** Augment a banana smoothie with a spoonful of smooth peanut butter (p308).
- **Nutty hummus** Make this using peanut butter instead of tahini (p301).
- **Pancakes** Stir a couple of spoonfuls of peanut butter into the batter (p283).
- **Peanut butter and cheese patties** Munge together one part each of crunchy peanut butter and cream cheese and two parts each of grated cheese and fresh breadcrumbs. Form into cakes, coat in breadcrumbs or panko and shallow-fry until crisp.
- **Peanutty sweet potato soup** Replace almost all the potatoes with sweet potatoes in the basic recipe (p309) and, when cooked, purée with leftover peanut butter. A bit of chilli heat is good in this and chopped salted peanuts make a fine garnish.

P

- **Popcorn** Melt 2 tbsp peanut butter together with 15g butter and 1 tbsp brown sugar to toss with freshly popped corn.
- **Quick satay sauce type thing** Mix together 3 tbsp crunchy peanut butter, 1 tbsp dark soy sauce, ½ tbsp sweet chilli sauce, then stir in 2 tbsp boiling water. Serve with grilled meat, chicken and fish, south-east Asian dishes, as a dressing for coleslaw (p287) or as a dip.

Pears – see also Fruit

Pears go well with apples, ginger, walnuts, honey, chocolate and blue cheese.

❊ Keep under-ripe pears at room temperature and, when ripe, in the fridge for a few days. Freeze cooked or in a syrup.

- **Locket's savoury** See p269 for this classic pear, blue cheese and watercress dish – it's delicious.
- **Pear and blue cheese pasta** Toss cooked pears with pasta and crumbled blue cheese in creamy Alfredo sauce (p281).
- **Pear and Parmesan salad** Slice fresh ripe pears and toss with tender salad leaves and shavings of Parmesan.

> **HANDY HINT**
>
> It is said that if a pear is almost ripe you should take the day off work and keep close by so as to eat it at the nanosecond of perfection.

- **Pear vinaigrette** This is wonderful with a salad of blue cheese and sugared walnuts (p178). Peel and core a ripe or almost-ripe pear, slice into a small pan and simmer with 160ml cider vinegar until pretty well all the vinegar has gone. Tip the pears into a liquidiser or food processor and add 1 tbsp honey. Purée whilst slowly adding about 200ml of vegetable oil, it should emulsify. Taste and season.
- **Stuff them!** Halve and core a pear, fill the hollows with crumbled blue cheese, sprinkle with a few breadcrumbs and bake or grill until hot, melting and crisp.

P

Peas and green beans

❄ Keep refrigerated for up to five days or blanch and freeze.
Store cooked peas or beans in the fridge for up to five days.

● **Crushed pea bruschetta** Coarsely crush leftover peas with
soft cheese and delicious flavourings such as mint, lemon,
pepper and garlic. Pile onto bruschetta, pop into a hot oven for
just a couple of minutes and serve warm.
● **Fresh pea dip** Purée cooked peas with your choice of lemon
juice, fresh mint, garlic, salt and pepper plus olive oil or crème
fraîche or even tahini until soft and delicious.
● **Last-minute addition** Stir leftovers into soup, pasta sauce,
risotto etc.
● **Pea pods** Treat as broad bean pods (p52).
● **Salads** Add cooked peas and green beans to salads; they are
especially good with a minty dressing.

Pease pudding – see Beans and pulses and also Dhal
This entry is primarily for people living above the invisible pease pudding
line that stretches across Britain at about the level of the Midlands, and
above which pease pudding is readily available in butchers shops and
supermarkets. To make your own pease pudding see the recipe under
Ham (p134) – it's easy, cheap, delicious, nutritious and versatile. It is said
that an oft-heard street cry in Medieval London was 'Pease pudding and a
suck of bacon'. The peddler sold slices of firm pease pudding
accompanied by a brief suck on a piece of bacon on a string. When it was
judged that the purchaser had had a fair suck for his money, the bacon
was yanked from his mouth ready for the next diner. Yummy!

● **Breakfast** Fry slices of cold pease pudding to serve with bacon
and eggs.
● **Fritters** See p99 concerning Dhal.
● **London particular** This is the name give to split pea soup.
The thick fogs that used to occur in London were called 'pea
soupers' after the soup and then the soup was named after the
fog. I wonder what will happen next! Cook a thinly sliced onion
my favourite way (p303), stir in leftover pease pudding, dilute

with ham, chicken or vegetable stock and season to taste.
That's it!

- **Quick spicy dhal** Cook an onion my favourite way (p303) and mix in a little curry powder or paste. Stir in the pease pudding and dilute, if necessary, with stock. Serve with rice, other curries and suitable accoutrements.
- **Sandwiches** Spread pease pudding in sandwiches, particularly those containing ham and made with a stottie cake.

Pea shoots

These pretty leaves taste of peas and grass!

❄ Keep in the fridge and eat within a couple of days. Don't freeze.

- **Garnish** These are very attractive piled on top of appropriate dishes.
- **Last-minute addition** Stir into soups, risotto, stir-fries, pasta, and so on, all at the last minute.
- **Salads and sandwiches** Pea shoots make a welcome addition.
- **Scrambled eggs** Briefly cook pea shoots in butter with a little chopped garlic, then stir into scrambled eggs just before serving.

Peanuts – see Nuts

Pearl barley – see Barley

Peppers – this concerns sweet or bell peppers, see Chilli peppers for hot peppers

Peppers are good with beans, aubergine, anchovies, basil, chillies, fresh coriander, corn, garlic, lemon and orange, olive oil, onions, rice, tomatoes and balsamic vinegar

❄ Whole red and yellow peppers can be stored in the fridge for up to a week and green, being less ripe, a little longer. They all deteriorate rapidly once cut, so use within two days. Freeze sliced or chopped on a baking tray, then store in airtight container or freezer bag.

- **Egg dishes** see basic recipes on p294–98 for ideas.
- **Garnish** Drop thin, thin, thin julienne of red or yellow pepper into iced water where it will go all curly. Drain on kitchen paper and make something look special. Alternatively, very finely diced red and yellow pepper mixed with chopped parsley makes a lovely sprinkle.
- **Hash** Add to potato hash dishes (p211).
- **Pizza** Scatter over pizza before baking.
- **Salads** Dice or slice and toss into salads.
- **Salsa** Finely chopped peppers are tasty and pretty in salsas.
- **Stir-fries** Toss them in with the onions at the start of cooking (see p310).
- **Tomato dishes** Cook chopped peppers in with the onion at the start of making tomato soup or sauce or chilli.

Roasted peppers

Roasted peppers can be frozen or kept in a jar completely covered with olive oil, in which state they will be fine in the fridge for a week or more.

- **Egg dishes** See pages 294–98 for several egg dishes that would benefit from a little roasted pepper.
- **Pizza topping** Roasted peppers add an intense flavour to a pizza.
- **Purée** Stir puréed roasted peppers into dips, sauces, hummus, mayonnaise and so on.
- **Simple roast pepper sauce** Purée roast peppers together with a little olive oil and a small amount of balsamic vinegar to drizzle on things or to mix with hot pasta in Alfredo sauce (p281).

P

Pesto – see also Herbs and p137 for the recipe

- **Baked fish topping** Brush pesto onto fish fillets press on some fresh breadcrumbs or panko and bake.
- **Cheese on toast** Spread pesto onto toast before topping with cheese and grilling to melt.
- **Cooked green veggies** These often take well to a little pesto stirred in just before serving.
- **Pasta** Pesto is traditionally stirred through hot freshly cooked pasta.
- **Pesto butter** Mix a little pesto into soft butter to serve with warm bread, swirl into tomato soup or to make pesto bread like garlic bread (p289).
- **Pesto mayonnaise** Stir pesto into mayonnaise a bit at a time till it tastes good!
- **Soup** Stir leftover pesto into vegetable or bean soups (which will make them similar to the well known Soup Pistou) or drizzle onto potato soups.
- **Vinaigrette** Rinse out an almost empty pesto jar with vinaigrette to make a fine dressing for tomatoes. See p312 for vinaigrette recipe.

Pheasant – see Game

Phyllo – see Filo

Physalis – aka Cape gooseberries – see also Fruit

- **Dunking** They are good dipped in things: melted chocolate, for instance, or cream.
- **Garnish** Physalis are good for decorating posh desserts.

Pigeon – see Game and also Duck

Pine nuts aka pignolia – see Nuts

Pineapple – see also Fruit

Pineapple is good with other tropical fruits, rum, coconut, ham and poultry.

❋ Keep a pineapple at room temperature until ripe and then in the fridge, cut or whole, for up to five days. Cut into pieces to freeze.

- **Kebabs** Thread pineapple cubes between pieces of meat, chicken, fish or shellfish onto skewers for grilling.

- **Pineapple bread pudding** Add pieces of pineapple, a drop or two of rum and a sprinkle of coconut to the basic recipe (p49, 50).

> **HANDY HINT**
> Don't make jelly with fresh pineapple; its enzyme, bromelain, will stop it setting.

- **Pineapple chow** This Caribbean dish is an excellent side for spicy dishes. Toss together the diced flesh of half a pineapple, a little fresh hot red chilli and chopped garlic, a handful of fresh coriander, the juice of ½ lime and a sprinkling of black pepper. Chill until needed. Although neither essential nor traditional, this is extra good sprinkled with sea salt just before serving.

- **Pineapple core** You could just suck or chew this before discarding, but be aware that it is said in the West Indies that this can make you pregnant, or at least help to, especially if you are a girl! A better idea is to cut the core lengthways into sticks to stir rum punch or other cocktails.

- **Pineapple fried rice** Add leftover pineapple to fried rice, especially when serving it with chicken or shellfish dishes.

Pistachios – see Nuts

P

Plums – see also Fruit and Peaches

Plums go well with other stone fruit, oranges, warm spices such as cinnamon, ginger, cardamom, ginger, nutmeg and black pepper, brandy, port and cream.

❄ Keep plums at room temperature until ripe. Refrigerate ripe plums for four or five days. Freeze without their stones in syrup.

Polenta – aka cornmeal mush and all sorts of other things too

- **Fried polenta shapes** Cut cold polenta into different shapes: rounds to use as crostini or dice to use as croûtons, or batons to use as chips, for instance. Coat in seasoned flour or dry cornmeal and deep-fry or shallow-fry in medium-hot oil for about 5 minutes until golden. Drain on kitchen paper and serve immediately. Keep the off-cuts to make polenta hash or gratin.

> **HANDY HINT**
>
> Cooked polenta sets firmly when cold so if intending to cut leftovers into shapes make life easier by spreading it into a dish or onto a board to a useful thickness.

- **Polenta gratin** Toss polenta trimmings with soft, buttery cooked onions or leeks (p303) in a buttered dish. Crumble over some cheese, sprinkle with breadcrumbs and bake in a preheated oven at 190°C/gas 5 for about 15 minutes until hot and bubbling.

- **Polenta hash** Cook finely diced onion in olive oil until tender and golden, then set aside. Wipe out the pan, heat a fresh tbsp of oil and add the leftover polenta pieces. Mash them slightly and cook over a medium heat for about 5 minutes until crisp on the bottom. Turn and cook until the other side is crisp, adding more oil if necessary. When golden, return the onion plus any other cooked leftovers (vegetables, chorizo, roasted tomatoes – all sorts of goodies are suitable) to the pan, toss together and cook until hot through. Serve immediately and may I suggest a fried egg on top?

- **Polenta pie crust** Top a savoury stew with trimmings or slices of cold cooked polenta, cut into pretty shapes if possible, and lay slightly overlapping. Brush with butter or oil and bake in a preheated oven at 200°C/gas 6 for about 25 minutes until hot and crisp.

- **Stuffed polenta fritters** Divide warmish malleable leftover polenta into little cakes, flatten each one and put a piece of cheese in the middle of each. Fold the polenta around the cheese, squeezing the edges together to seal. Form back into neat cakes and chill until needed. Dip in cornmeal and shallow-fry until melting in the middle and crisply golden on the outside. Drain and serve.

Pomegranate – see also Fruit
Pomegranate goes well with orange and walnuts, pheasant, duck and vodka.

※ Pomegranates will be fine at room temperature for a couple of weeks but after that, store in the fridge for up to a month. Once opened, they will keep just two or three days. The seeds can be frozen.

- **Desserts** Add to fruit salads, trifle, sundaes and so on.
- **Garnish** The ruby red jewel-like seeds make sweet and pretty additions to salads, salsas, raita (p279), pilafs and many other dishes.

Popcorn

※ Popped corn stales quickly so keep in a seriously airtight container or freezer bag with the air squeezed out.

- **Garnish** Unsweetened or salty popcorn makes a good topping for soup; for instance creamy corn chowder topped with a handful of popcorn tossed in chilli butter.
- **Peanut butter popcorn balls** For 20g leftover popcorn, melt together 1 tbsp each of honey, sugar and peanut butter with a drop of vanilla extract. Stir in the popcorn and, when cool enough to handle, roll into balls.

Nutty Popcorn Crunch

This is particularly delicious made with salted cashews and a pinch of chilli flakes.

60g popped popcorn
100g nuts
180g soft light brown sugar
120g butter
90g clear honey
½ tsp vanilla extract
½ tsp bicarbonate of soda

1. Preheat the oven to 150°C/gas 2 and grease a roasting pan.
2. Toss together the popcorn and nuts in the prepared pan.
3. Stir together the sugar, butter and honey over a medium heat until the sugar has dissolved then cook, stirring occasionally, for 5 minutes.
4. Remove from the heat, stir in the vanilla and bicarbonate of soda (the mixture may woosh up) and immediately pour over the popcorn.
5. Stir everything together, decant on to the roasting pan and bake in the oven for 20 minutes, stirring halfway through.
6. Turn out onto a piece of lightly buttered greaseproof paper or parchment.
7. Cool, break into manageable pieces, and store in an airtight container.

Poppadoms – aka papadums, pupadoms, pappodums, papads or pappads although some say these last two are thicker and more suitable for grilling

• **Shred them** In the Virgin Islands, I often found that poppadoms served outdoors would waft away on a tropical breeze. I know this sounds very romantic but in reality it was a bit of a nuisance so I took to shredding them, deep-frying and piling on top of suitable dishes. In a temperate climate, this is a good way to use up broken poppadoms.

P

Poppy seeds – see Seeds

Pork – see also Meat
Pork is good with apples, sage, fennel, beans and more pork in the form of bacon, sausages or black pudding.

- **Barbecue wrap** Reheat shredded pork in barbecue sauce and roll in a warm tortilla.
- **Bayou dirty rice** Add some chopped or shredded pork to the dish (p77).
- **Bean dishes** Beans and pork make good partners so add leftover pork to pretty well any bean dish.
- **Crispy shredded pork** Coarsely shred leftover pork and fry in a little fat or oil till crispy. Taste, season if necessary and sprinkle onto soups or salads.
- **Pork rillettes** Make the Duck Rillettes recipe with pork instead (p101).
- **Sandwiches** Make roast pork and apple sauce sandwiches and serve with a little dipping gravy, if possible.

Porridge
In the Highlands and Islands of Scotland, porridge was once left in a designated drawer in the kitchen dresser to set, then sliced and eaten cold for lunch. Apparently babies were often cradled in the drawer above the porridge so that any rising heat would warm the child. Of course, this may be a rural myth, but certainly drawers were used as babies' beds.

I instinctively feel that porridge should be served with brown sugar, Drambuie and, even though I realise it is not Scottish, clotted cream. However, porridge also goes well with honey, maple syrup, golden syrup, jam, fruit and cream.

✳   Porridge can be kept in the fridge for three or four days if you press clingfilm directly onto the surface to cover completely so as to prevent it drying out. To reheat, stir in a little water, milk, cream (or Drambuie) and warm gently in a small pan or the microwave. It freezes well and is easiest to use if frozen in individual portions. Defrost and then reheat as above.

P

- **Binder** Use leftover porridge to bind such things as meatballs and meatloaf.
- **Fritters** Spread warm leftover porridge to about 1.5cm thick, then leave to cool. When cold, cut into squares or wedges and fry in butter until crisp and hot. Serve with fruit or maple syrup or perhaps bacon and eggs. This is fine if you are in a hurry but, with very little effort, it can be finer still, see hotcakes recipe below.

Porridge Hotcakes for Breakfast

SERVES 1

100g cooked porridge
1 tbsp plain flour
½ tsp baking powder
pinch of salt
a little milk

1. Slightly warm the porridge and mix in the flour, baking powder and salt.
2. Stir in enough milk to make a soft dropping consistency.
3. Shallow-fry spoonfuls of this batter in a little hot oil (or leftover bacon fat) turning once, until both sides are crisp and golden.

Porridge Scones

30g soft butter
1 tbsp clear honey
300g cooked porridge, warm
100g flour
1 tsp baking powder
pinch of salt

1. Mix the butter and honey into the slightly warmed porridge.
2. Mix together the dry ingredients and work them into the porridge to make a soft but manageable dough, it will be quite sticky.
3. Knead lightly and roll out on a floured surface to about 1.5cm thick.
4. Cut into rounds, brush with milk and bake in a preheated oven 190°C /gas 5 for 20–25 minutes until cooked, risen and golden.

● **Savoury scones** For savoury scones replace the honey with 75g grated mature Cheddar, season with salt and pepper and continue as above. Sprinkle the tops with more grated cheese and/or crunchy sea salt.

Potatoes

As you've probably noticed, potatoes go with a wide range of other ingredients far too numerous to list here, although I will just mention nutmeg, which you may not have thought of!

Raw potato

❄ Store raw, unwashed, unpeeled, uncut, totally un-interfered with potatoes in a cool, dark, dry place for up to three months. At normal room temperature they should be okay for a couple of weeks. Don't keep in a sealed bag as they need air, and don't put in the fridge as this affects their flavour and colour and not in a good way.

P

- **Crisp potato peelings** Brush clean and dry potato peelings with oil and season to taste. Spread on a baking tray and cook in a preheated oven at 200°C/gas 6 until crispy and golden, which should take about 10 minutes.
- **Soup** Potatoes are the basis for my very flexible soup recipe (p309).

HANDY HINTS

Don't store with onions as they tend to make each other go off!

Rubbing cut potato onto grill racks can help prevent sticking.

Cooked potatoes

❄ Keep in the fridge for three or four days. Creamy mashed potato will freeze well but boiled or baked potatoes will be watery once thawed.

- **Potato salad** Stir leftover cooked potato together with mayonnaise or vinaigrette plus other ingredients of your choice. If you get the chance to plan ahead, dressing the potatoes when warm gives a better result as they absorb some of the dressing.
- **Rich creamed potatoes** Reheat diced cooked potatoes in a little cream, which it will absorb to an extent, until lush. A few chopped spring onions are great cooked in with this.

Bubble and Squeak, Rumbledethumps, Kailkiddy, Colcannon, Clapshot, Punchnep and Hash

These are all regional versions of the same dish, which is typically made from leftover vegetables, primarily cold potatoes and cabbage, crushed together and shallow-fried in butter, oil or bacon fat until crisp. The trick to this is letting the mixture sit over a medium heat, undisturbed, for several minutes allowing a crust to form before turning. These dishes are very amenable to leftovers; meat, fish, grated cheese and so on. Bubble and squeak and its friends and relations also make good toppings for fish pie, cottage pie et al. Sweet potatoes also make good hash mixed with their own flavour-enhancing ingredients.

1. Fry finely chopped onion gently in a little oil, butter or fat for a few minutes until soft.
2. Increase the heat, add the leftover cooked potatoes crushing them slightly and cook until they start to crispen and colour. Add more oil or butter as necessary.
3. Stir in other leftover vegetables and continue to fry and turn until all is hot, crispy in parts and delicious.
4. If adding cooked meat or fish, do so towards the end so as not to overcook it.

- **Deep-fried skins** Cut leftover baked potato skins into strips or halves and fry until crisp, then serve with soured cream.
- **Fried or roast potatoes** Cut into slices, wedges or just random lumps and fry or roast until crisp.
- **Hash brown-ish potatoes** There are many recipes, methods and even finished results of hash browns but, even if this is not authentic, it is certainly both hash brown-*ish* and delicious. Coarsely shred cold jacket potatoes, skin and all if you like, and toss with salt and pepper. Melt together a mixture of oil and butter, just enough to cover the bottom, in a large frying pan, tip in the shredded potato and pack down into a loose cake. Cook until the underside is crisp and brown then flip and cook the other side.

Mrs Beeton's Potato Omelette

This omelette is more interesting than one would first think as it is
not filled with potatoes, it is made of them! According to Mrs
Beeton, this will cost six old pence and feed two people.

SERVES 2

1 leftover baked potato
4 eggs, separated
Seasonings to taste (Mrs B suggests lemon juice, nutmeg, salt and
pepper).
a knob of butter

1. Reheat the potato in the microwave (I made that bit up, Mrs B
   didn't suggest it).
2. Press the hot potato flesh though a fine sieve and allow to cool
   a little.
3. For one medium potato, mix in four egg yolks and season to
   taste with salt and pepper.
4. Whisk the egg whites until stiff, then fold into the mixture.
5. Fry in butter and, as this is a soufflé omelette, once the bottom
   is cooked finish it under a hot grill.

Mashed potatoes – for a few guidelines see Basic Recipes p281

- **Bubble and squeak** Of course (p211).
- **Croquettes** Form mashed potato into cakes or croquettes and
  fry until crisp – add leftover fish, meat, vegetables, cheese and
  so on.
- **Egg dishes** Add to omelette or frittata (p296–97).
- **Pie topping** Pile onto shepherd's, cottage, hunter's or fish pie.
- **Scottish tattie scones** These are known as 'fadge' in Ireland.
  Mix three parts warm well seasoned mashed potato with one
  part melted butter and enough flour to make a soft dough. Roll
  5mm thick, cut into quarters and cook in hot dry pan until
  speckled with gold on both sides. Eat with a fried breakfast or
  butter and jam.
- **Soup** Stir leftover mashed potato into soup to add body and

flavour or, even better, stir soup into leftover mashed potato as it's easier that way.

- **Taquitos de papa** Roll mashed potato in a wrap or tortilla together with grated cheese. Shallow-fry until crisp and golden all over and serve with soured cream, salsa and guacamole.

Gnocchi and Krumplinudli

The latter is Hungarian for potato noodles, which they say so much more enticingly than we do.

SERVES 2

1 egg
150g leftover mashed potato
120g flour
butter and fresh breadcrumbs for the krumplinudli

1. Mix the egg into the mashed potato and then enough flour to give a soft, workable dough. Add more flour until such a situation is achieved.
2. On a floured surface, roll the dough into snakes and cut into short lengths for gnocchi or longer ones, about 10cm, for *nudli*.
3. Leave uncovered on the floured surface to dry for an hour.
4. Bring a large pan of salted water to the boil, add the gnocchi or *nudli* and cook for 1–2 minutes – they are ready when they float to the surface. Scoop out with a slotted spoon and drain in a colander.
5. For gnocchi serve immediately with butter and cheese or a sauce.
6. For *krumbplinudli* it is necessary at this point to have ready a preheated oven at 190°C/gas 5.
7. Toss the drained *nudli* in a little melted butter and then fresh breadcrumbs (or panko for Hungarian-Japanese fusion) and bake until crisp and golden.
8. Serve *krumplinudli* as a side dish to a main meal.

Mashed Potato Bread

MAKES ONE MEDIUM LOAF

1 sachet dried yeast
1 scant tsp sugar
300ml warm water
150g mashed potato, at room temperature
300–400g plain flour
a little salt, depending on the mashed potato
1 tbsp olive oil

1. Stir the sugar into the warm water then sprinkle with the yeast and wait a few minutes until it starts to bubble.
2. Stir into the mashed potato and mix in enough flour, together with the salt and oil, to make a soft, sticky but workable dough.
3. Knead until smooth and elastic, adding a little more flour if necessary.
4. Put into a lightly oiled bowl, cover with a clean cloth and put in a warm place until risen to twice its size; an hour or so.
5. Knock down the dough and knead briefly.
6. Shape into a loaf or loaves and put in a warm place until risen again which will take about 30–40 minutes.
7. Meanwhile preheat the oven to 220°C/gas 7.
8. When risen, do with it what you will in the way of oiling, flouring, seasoning, decorating etc. and bake in the oven for about 25–30 minutes until risen (again!), golden and the bottom sounds hollow if you rap it with your knuckles.
9. Cool on a rack.

Praline – see recipe for Praline on p179

- **Creamy desserts** Sprinkle over or fold through creamy desserts and ice cream.
- **Pâté** Oddly enough, praline is good sprinkled over chicken liver or other rich pâté; the lush creaminess being perfectly offset by the sweet crunchiness.
- **Praline bread pudding** Fold some praline through the dish

just before baking and sprinkle a little more on top for the last few minutes of cooking (p49).

Prawns – see Shellfish

Prunes – see also Dried Fruit

Prunes have an affinity with Armagnac and Cognac, chocolate, oranges, cinnamon, rabbit and chicken.

- **Baked goods** Add chopped ready-to-eat prunes to cakes and puddings, especially those of the chocolate persuasion.
- **Cock-a-leekie soup** This traditionally includes shredded prunes.
- **Prunes in Armagnac** A lovely flavour combination, soak prunes in the liquor. Cognac is good too.
- **Stuffed prunes** Like dates, prunes can be filled with nuts or marzipan or even cheese.

Pumpkin – see also pumpkin's close relation Squash

Pumpkin goes well with cinnamon, nutmeg, allspice and ginger, with maple syrup, coconut, nuts, caramelised onions, apple and sage.

❄ A whole uncut pumpkin will keep a couple of months in a cool pantry but not so long at room temperature. Once cut, keep wrapped in the fridge for three or four days. Cooked pumpkin should be stored in an airtight container for up to four days and freezes successfully.

- **Bread pudding** Add cooked pumpkin to bread and no-butter pudding (p50), use soft light brown sugar, add cinnamon and maybe pecans or walnuts.
- **Crisply fried pumpkin** Coat slices in seasoned flour and fry until crisp and tender.
- **Mashed pumpkin and potatoes** Either cook pumpkin in with the potato or cook and mash the two separately and partially fold together for a marbled effect.

P

- **Pumpkin soup** Replace most of the potato in the basic recipe on p309 with pumpkin. That's it for a simple pumpkin soup but try adding apple with the pumpkin or stir Thai red chilli paste in with the onions. Substitute all the potato with pumpkin, purée with coconut milk and stir in fresh coriander for a south-east Asian version.

Pumpkin seeds – see Seeds

Q

Quail – see Game

Quail eggs – see Eggs

Quark – see Cheese (rather than the building blocks of matter!)

Quince

Some say that the fruit from the Tree of Knowledge that caused Adam and Eve so much bother was probably a quince. On the other hand, some people say it was a banana which, to my mind, seems more believable!

Quinces (I feel the plural should be quince but have researched it), are an old-fashioned fruit, if such a thing is possible, related to apples and pears. Their flavour is enhanced by honey, vanilla, warm spices such as nutmeg, ginger, cinnamon and clove, almonds, apples and pears.

❄ Store in a cool, dark place, not necessarily the fridge, for up to two weeks. Cook before freezing.

● **Apples and pears** Cook quinces according to most apple and pear recipes or add to apple or pear dishes to extend and augment.
● **Sniff it!** Sit in a comfy chair, close your eyes and enjoy its aroma!

> **HANDY HINT**
> Don't try eating raw quince because uncooked it is yuk or, to go into more detail, hard and astringent.

Q

Quinoa

Quinoa (pronounced keenwah) is a seed but with a very grain-like attitude. Its nutty taste is good with spices and caramelised onion.

- **Breakfast** Heat leftover quinoa gently in cream with sugar, nuts and fruits to taste and eat for breakfast.
- **Quinoa arancini** See the recipe under Risotto on p306.
- **Quinoa tabbouleh** Mix with lots of parsley, lemon juice, black pepper and a little olive oil to make a refreshing salad in the style of Tabbouleh (p55).
- **Stir-fry** Cook as leftover rice (p310).

Quorn

This is a vegetarian meat substitute made from mycoprotein which is used to make vegetarian sausages, mince, 'steaks' etc. Treat as you would the real meat version.

R

Rabbit – see Game and also Chicken, many ideas for which are fine for rabbit.

Radicchio – see also Lettuce

Radicchio, being an endive with a typical endivey bitter taste, goes with blue cheese, air-dried ham, black pepper, garlic, mustardy or sweet vinaigrettes, orange and onion.

- **Garnish** Finely shredded radicchio makes a pretty garnish.
- **Last-minute addition** Stir shredded radicchio into risotto, creamy pasta dishes or soups when almost ready.
- **Pizza** Sprinkle over blue cheese pizza for the last couple of minutes of cooking.
- **Salads** Add to salads and coleslaw (p287); tasty and pretty.
- **Serving containers!** Use radicchio leaves as little bowls or scoops for salads or dips.

Radish

The strong and distinctive flavour of radish can be enjoyed simply with good bread, sweet butter and salt but also has affinities with lettuce, spring onions, fennel, some of the sweeter vinegars such as sherry and balsamic, parsley, smoked fish, cheese and soured cream.

❄ Keep radishes loosely wrapped in the fridge for up to two weeks. They don't freeze well.

- **Coleslaw** Coarsely grate or slice into coleslaw (p287).
- **Cooking radishes** Whilst they are at their best raw they are good added to stir-fries or roasted along with other veggies.

> **HANDY HINT**
> Crisp up radishes by submerging in iced water for an hour or so.

- **Crudités** Serve as part of a selection of vegetables with a dip.

R

- **Don't peel** Their vibrant colour is part of their charm.
- **Garnish** Carve into roses and use to decorate nostalgic dishes from the 1920s!
- **Potato salad** Add thinly sliced radish to potato salads for colour and heat.
- **Radish butter** Mix grated skin-on radish into soft butter adding crunchy sea salt and black pepper to make a pretty butter. This is good on hot bread or melted over steak or fish. See Compound butters on p288.
- **Raita** Use grated radish with or instead of cucumber in raita (p279).
- **Salads** Toss finely shaved radish into leafy salads with balsamic vinaigrette and sea salt. Young radish leaves are also good in salad.

Raspberries – see also Berries
Raspberries are good with white chocolate, cream, yoghurt, peaches and other soft summer fruits, almonds, hazelnuts and vanilla.

❄ Soft and fragile, raspberries tend to go mouldy quickly so don't keep for long. They can be frozen but will be squidgy when thawed.

- **Raspberry coulis** Delicious (p300).
- **Raspberry vodka** After making coulis, add the strained out seeds and any adhering pulp to a bottle of vodka. Give it a good shake, put the lid on and store in a cool dark place for a few weeks.
- **Spritzer** If you strain out the raspberry seeds after making coulis top them up with fizzy water, let it sit a while in the fridge, strain and drink.

Raspberry Vinegar

500g 'leftover' or 'surplus' raspberries
500ml white wine vinegar
100g white sugar

1. In a non-reactive bowl, crush together the fruit and the vinegar. Cover and steep for 2 or 3 days in a cool place.
2. Strain gently and slowly through cheesecloth or muslin.
3. To the resulting juices, add 100g white sugar and bring to the boil in a stainless steel pan (this is essential, aluminium will ruin everything), stirring until the sugar has melted.
4. Skim off any scum, turn down the heat and simmer gently for 10 minutes.
5. Cool, then pour into sterilised bottles.
6. This will keep in the fridge for up to a year and can be used as a drink topped up with sparkling wine or water; in vinaigrette; over ice cream or to deglaze pans after cooking pigeon or chicken or calves' liver etc. You can also add a spoonful to summery fruit salads.

Ravioli

- **Buttered ravioli** Toss in a suitably flavoured butter (lots of ideas throughout this book!) until hot through.
- **Deep-fried** Lightly coat cold ravioli in flour then beaten egg and finally breadcrumbs and fry until crisp.
- **Gratin** Whatever your leftover ravioli are filled with, they will probably work well reheated in a creamy sauce, sprinkled with breadcrumbs and grated Parmesan and baked until hot and crisp.
- **Ravioli 'in restes'** Heat through in a little leftover meat stew or gravy and serve sprinkled with crunchy breadcrumbs (p44).

Red cabbage – see Cabbage

R

Redcurrants – see Berries

Redcurrant jelly – see Jam
I would just say that a little stirred into gravy for roast lamb is very good.

Rhubarb – see also Fruit
Strawberries, ginger, orange, vanilla, cream, crumble and custard all go well with rhubarb as do pork, game and oily fish.

❋ Rhubarb is good in the fridge for about a week and can be frozen raw (wash, dry, slice, and pack into freezer bags) although is better frozen after cooking. Cooked rhubarb will be okay in the fridge for up to four days.

> **COOK'S TREAT**
> Dip young raw rhubarb in sugar or salt or both and nibble on them.

- **Pink drink** Top up rhubarb juice left over after cooking with fizzy water for a pleasant pink drink.
- **Rhubarb cranachan** (p185).
- **Rhubarb mess** Mix with crushed meringues and whipped cream (p172).
- **Rhubarb sorbet** Use puréed rhubarb with orange zest or finely chopped stem ginger in the basic sorbet recipe (p299).

> **COOK'S TREAT**
> Just one stalk left? Wrap it in pastry, cut a few slits in to let the steam out, sprinkle with sugar and bake yourself a personal pie.

- **Sauce for mackerel** Cooked rhubarb (not too sweet) with a squeeze of lemon or orange and a little black pepper makes a good sauce for mackerel.
- **Sweet addition** Stir cooked rhubarb into yoghurt, rice pudding or porridge.

Rice

This section mainly concerns leftover cooked rice.

❄ Cooked rice, in an airtight container, will keep for a couple of days in the fridge and freezes well.

- **Rice pudding from leftovers** Over low heat, stir together approximately equal quantities of cooked rice and milk together with sugar to taste and a drop of vanilla. Cover and simmer until thick and stir in a spoonful of cream to serve.

HANDY HINT

It is important to cool rice quickly, store properly in the fridge and to reheat thoroughly to avoid food poisoning: bacillus cereus to be precise.

- **Soup** Add a handful of rice to broths or lentil soups.
- **Stir-fry it** You can mix rice with all sorts of leftovers. See tips on stir-frying on p310.
- **Stuffed peppers** Cut lids from the tops of bell peppers, scoop and fill with leftover rice mixed with other ingredients of your choice; garlic, basil and cheese, for instance. Put the lids on, drizzle with oil and cook in a preheated oven at 180°C/gas 4 for 20– 30 minutes until tender.

West Indian Rice 'n' Peas

A Caribbean side dish which is also delicious eaten with just a little hot sauce!

SERVES 2–3

1 onion, finely chopped
½ tbsp vegetable oil
a little minced garlic
a little minced hot chilli
100ml unsweetened coconut milk
1–2 fresh thyme sprigs
200g cooked or canned dried beans, drained (gungo or pigeon peas are traditional but any dried pea or bean will work)
225g leftover rice
salt and freshly ground black pepper to taste

1. Cook the onion in the oil, stirring, until starting to turn golden, then add the garlic and chilli and cook for a further few seconds.
2. Stir in the coconut milk and thyme. Bring to the boil and simmer until the coconut milk has reduced by half.
3. Stir in the beans. Remove from the heat, stir in the rice, cover and set aside for a few minutes to absorb the coconut milk.
4. Taste and season.

Risotto rice – see Risotto below

Uncooked rice
If you have a little bit of uncooked rice you don't know what to do with here are a couple of ideas.

- **Keep salt dry** Add a few grains to salt shakers to stop the salt becoming damp – there is some argument as to whether this works but all I can say is it has worked for me when living in humid climates.
- **Pastry weights** Use instead of baking beans to weigh down a pastry case when baking blind.

Rice pudding

- **Brulée** Divide chilled rice pudding between ramekins or small heatproof dishes, sprinkle with sugar and caramelise as with crème brulée. If the rice pudding is very thick, stir in a little cream first.

Risotto

Risotto is itself a great way of using up delicious odds and ends so there are guidelines for making it on page 307. Although risotto is supposed to be stirred constantly whilst cooking and served immediately, and I have no argument with this, it can, with care, be reheated successfully. Heat a little appropriate stock, gently stir in the leftover risotto together with any additions and keep stirring over low heat until hot through. Add a knob of butter, more Parmesan or a little cream just before serving. If you then have leftover risotto, here's what to do with it.

- **Arancini** A classic way to use leftover risotto. Form cold leftover risotto into balls using about 2 tbsp for each one. Insert a small piece of mozzarella (traditional) or other cheese (creative). Roll the balls in seasoned flour then beaten egg and finally fresh breadcrumbs. Deep-fry until golden and serve hot, maybe with some leftover tomato sauce.
- **Riso el salto** Another classic way to serve leftover risotto. Melt butter in a cast iron or non-stick pan and when hot, press leftover risotto into pancakes about 1cm thick. Fry until crisp, turn, do the other side and serve sprinkled with grated Parmesan.

Rocket – aka arugula, ruccola and roquette

The peppery taste of rocket (the larger the leaf the stronger the flavour) is good with goats' cheese and Parmesan, white beans, tomatoes, peppers, bacon and chicken.

- ❄ Store in a damp kitchen paper in a plastic bag in the fridge for up to three days. Wash carefully – see Leeks (p156) for a good method. Don't freeze except as part of a cooked dish.

R

- **Pasta** Stir through creamy pasta dishes.
- **Pizza** Sprinkle onto just out the oven pizza where it will wilt and exude its flavours.
- **Rocket pesto** In the basic recipe on p137, replace basil with rocket; pine nuts are fine although walnuts make a good alternative here.
- **Rocket soup** Purée fresh rocket leaves into the finished basic soup (p309), keeping a few back to garnish or add to brothy soups just before serving.
- **Salads** Add to green or potato salad.
- **Tuna and white bean salad** This salad on p118 benefits from a little rocket.

Rollmops – see also Fish

These raw pickled herring are good with horseradish, soured cream, raw onion, dill, black pepper, brown bread, Aquavit and vodka.

❄ Keep in the fridge in accordance with best-before date or, if homemade, for a week or so.

- **Bruschetta** Serve on bruschetta or black bread topped with soured cream and the almost obligatory horseradish and dill.
- **Potato salad** Add leftover rollmops, also with a little horseradish and fresh dill.

Romanesco – see Cauliflower

Runner beans – see Peas and Green beans

Rutabaga – see Swede

S

Salad

❄ Undressed salad can be kept in a plastic bag with a damp piece of kitchen paper and served the next day. Dressed salad is not a good keeper, you could try the following but results can be variable so I am not exactly recommending it!

● **Leftover salad soup** The basic method is to put the leftover salad, dressed or otherwise, into a liquidiser or food processor together with some appropriate liquid and purée it. For instance with a tomatoey, oniony, peppery salad I would add tomato juice (and possibly call it Gazpacho depending how pleased I was with it) but with a cucumber and lettuce salad perhaps vegetable stock and then finish with cream, soured cream or yoghurt. Adjust seasoning with whatever tastes good and serve chilled.

Salad dressing – see Vinaigrette or Mayonnaise

Salami

There are quite a few varieties of salami but the one I refer to here is the familiar cured, salted or air-dried salami which is hard and dry and tastes good with cheese, tomatoes and red wine.

❄ Check the labelling for storage – some can be kept for months even at room temperature but if unsure store in the fridge for up to six months. Salami does freeze but not for long; two or three months max, and quite honestly if you haven't eaten it in the last six months you probably don't want it! Once sliced salami should be kept chilled and used within a couple of weeks.

● **Cold collation** Serve as part of a selection of cold meats, cheeses, good bread etc. and hopefully red wine.

S

- **Crisp garnish** Shred, fry until crisp (it will only need a little oil, if any) and sprinkle on things.
- **Egg dishes** Plenty of options here in the Basic Recipes section.
- **Substitute** Salami can be substituted for ham, bacon or chorizo in many recipes.
- **Tomato sauce** Fry a little chopped salami in with the onions when making tomato sauce.
- **Useful addition** Add to sandwiches, salads, pasta and pizza.

Salsa

- **Mayonnaise** Spice up some mayo by simply stirring in leftover salsa.
- **Sauces** Stir appropriately flavoured salsa through pasta with cream or a creamy sauce.
- **Soup garnish** Swirl into soups to brighten both the taste and the look of the dish.
- **Spicy scrambled eggs** Cook salsa in with the eggs and hopefully add some fresh coriander.

Salsify – and scorzonera – both also known as oyster plant

Salsify gets on very well with the onion family plus parsley, celery, spinach, potatoes, air-dried ham, cream and butter.

❊ Keep in the fridge for up to a week. Don't bother freezing it.

> **HANDY HINT**
> It is easiest to peel salsify once cooked not least because when raw it releases a sticky goo that feels uncomfortable on the hands and can stain them.

- **Root vegetables** Use salsify pretty well as any other leftover root vegetable – mash, cakes, fritters, sautés, gratins, roast, and so on.
- **Salads** Grate cooked salsify into salads and coleslaw (p287).
- **Salsify salad** Dress cooked salsify with mustardy vinaigrette.

- **Salsify soup** Replace some or all of the potato in the basic recipe on p271 with sliced salsify and add a good dose of parsley at the end of cooking.

HANDY HINT
Drop pieces of salsify into acidulated water (p281) whilst preparing as cut surfaces tend to discolour.

Samphire – aka glasswort

The salty sea taste of samphire is a natural partner to fish and is also good with butter. Steam or cook in unsalted water for just a few minutes until *al dente*.

❊ Samphire is best as fresh as possible but if necessary will be okay for a day or two wrapped in the fridge. No freezing allowed.

HANDY HINT
Wash well under cold running water.

- **Pasta** Drop a few stalks into the water when cooking pasta for the last few minutes. Drain and toss with cooked seafood, butter and lemon juice.
- **Risotto** Add cooked samphire to seafood risotto at the end of cooking (p307).
- **Salads** Add raw samphire to salads.
- **Serving suggestion** Serve fish on a bed of just cooked samphire to look impressive.

Sandwiches

- **Bread and butter pudding or strata** The more interesting the sarnie, the more interesting the dish (p50).
- **French toast sandwiches** Why not? (p51).
- **Mrs Beeton's bread and butter fritters** Mrs B. suggests making jam sandwiches, pressing firmly together, dipping in batter and cooking in 'boiling lard'.

S

Sashimi

As Sashimi is in essence just raw fish, see Fish or Shellfish for what to do with leftovers.

Satsumas – see Oranges

Sausages – as in fresh sausages and sausage meat; for dried sausages see separate entries for Salami and Chorizo

'How long will dinner be?' ...'4 inches – it's a sausage!' *Morecambe & Wise*

Raw sausage meat
This includes sausages released from their skins.

- **Sausage meat patties** Serve these with a fry up; this is a good way to serve three sausages to four people.
- **Sausage meatballs** Roll into little balls, coat in flour and fry until hot. Serve atop pasta or in soup.
- **Scotch eggs** (p105).
- **Stuffing** Sausage meat makes a great addition to bread stuffing (p45).

Cooked sausages

- **Bean dishes** Add sliced sausage to bean dishes including baked beans and warm through.
- **Pizza** Add to pizza topping.
- **Sausage sarnies** Add tomato ketchup, mustard or pickle to taste.
- **Soup** Stir coarsely chopped sausages into sausage-friendly soup.

Scallion – see Spring onion

Scallops – see Shellfish

Scampi – see Shellfish

Scorzonera – aka black salsify – see Salsify

Seeds

The seeds listed here are not whole spices, such as cardamom or cumin, because I see those more as storecupboard items than leftovers.

❄ Store in a cool, dry, dark place.

> **COOK'S TREAT**
> Nibble on them.

● **Baked goods** Add seeds into the mix when you are baking or sprinkle on top before you put the bake in the oven.
● **Breakfast** Sprinkle onto cereals, or add to granola, muesli or trail mix.
● **Crumble** Add seeds to the crumble recipe (p290).
● **Crunchy butter** Try a butter made with sunflower seeds and honey, or sesame, green onion and ginger (p288).
● **Salads and stir-fries** Seeds make a great addition.
● **Seedy brittle and praline** Use seeds with or instead of the nuts in the recipe on p179.

Caraway seeds

Caraway is popular in German and Eastern European cooking and tastes well with apples, potatoes, cabbage and in rye bread.

● **Potato salad** This could benefit from a few caraway seeds.
● **Rye bread** If you are making rye bread add a handful of caraway seeds as is traditional.

> **HANDY HINT**
> Caraway seeds are not only good in cabbage dishes but are said to help with digesting it!

S

Flax seeds – aka Linseed

- **Tasty addition** Golden Flax seeds have a nutty taste but darker ones are bitter. Add them to cereals, salads and bread dough.

Poppy seeds

- **Bagels** Poppy seeds are traditionally sprinkled on bagels and are also good on other breads and baked goods.
- **Butter** Roll logs of appropriately flavoured compound butter in poppy seeds for attractive slices (p288).
- **Lemon affinity** Poppy seeds seem to be inextricably linked to lemon in our minds, or at least in mine. Add them to lemon vinaigrette, lemon sauce on pasta, muffins, scones, cheesecake and so on.
- **Orange** They are also good in orange poppy seed cake!

Pumpkin seeds – aka pepitas

Pumpkin seeds are good with pumpkin and squash, soy, sage, caramelised onions and are popular in Mexican cooking. Toasted or roasted pumpkin seeds have a taste reminiscent of bacon.

- **Pesto** Use to replace pine nuts in fresh coriander pesto (pp137, 139).
- **Soup** Sprinkle over pumpkin soup.

Roasted Pumpkin Seeds

If you have leftover seeds after preparing a pumpkin, they are worth roasting.

1. Put the seeds plus any attached flesh in a sieve and run cold water through them, separating the seeds from the rest of the detritus.
2. Dry the seeds with kitchen paper.
3. Stir in a little oil and whatever seasonings you favour – salt and pepper and who knows? Chilli powder is good.

4. Preheat the oven to 160°C/gas 3.
5. Spread the seasoned seeds on a baking tray and roast until golden brown – start checking after about 10 minutes as they will become bitter if too dark. Remove any that look done.
6. Cool and store in an airtight container in the fridge for up to a month.

Sesame seeds
These are good with Asian flavours and with spring onions, broccoli and chickpeas.

- **Asian dishes** Add sesame seeds to noodle dishes, stir-fries, and *tsung yu ping* (see p271 for recipe).
- **Burger buns** Sprinkle on homemade burger buns as is traditional for some reason.
- **Tuna** Coat prime pieces of tuna with sesame seeds before searing briefly and serving rare with the usual accoutrements: soy, wasabi and ginger.

Sunflower seeds
These are particularly good with honey.

- **Baking** Add to baked goods especially honey flavoured.
- **Salads** Many salads can be enhanced by a sunflower seed sprinkle.

Serrano – see either Ham or Chilli

Sesame seeds – see Seeds

Shallots – see Onions

S

Shellfish – see also Fish

Generally speaking, exoskeleton-bearing aquatic invertebrates taste good with citrus, mayonnaise, white wine and Champagne but all have their own characteristics too.

Note that I specifically refer here only to cooked leftovers of mussels, clams, oysters, lobster and crab, which are all cooked alive; the idea of having a living leftover is bizarre!

❊ Eat all shellfish as soon as possible and in the case of raw shellfish, the fresher the better. Cooked, it will keep one or two days in the fridge and can be frozen if well wrapped. Thaw slowly in the fridge rather than at room temperature and reheat very gently or the flesh will toughen.

- **Avocado filling** Mix with mayonnaise to fill avocado halves.
- **Delicious addition** Add shellfish to salads and sandwiches or mix with mayonnaise and use to top bruschetta and crostini.
- **Precious juices** If a dish is to be served immediately add any delicious juices that have exuded from the shellfish whilst cooking, reduced if necessary, to whatever sauce, mayonnaise or vinaigrette you intend serving with it.
- **Seafood chowder** Add raw or cooked shellfish to seafood chowder (p114).
- **Seafood pasta** Toss leftovers of these creatures over medium heat together with freshly cooked tagliatelle or similar. Flavour with finely grated lemon zest, parsley, black pepper and a generous amount of butter or with chilli, parsley, orange zest and olive oil.
- **Soup garnish** To share around just a little shellfish, warm it in butter, cream or flavoured oil and serve a spoonful in the middle of a complementary soup.

Shellfish Stock

Store shells tightly wrapped in the freezer until there are enough to
make stock to use in soups, chowders and sauces.

500g shells
3 tbsp oil
250ml dry white wine
1 tbsp tomato purée
1 small onion, chopped
1–2 garlic cloves, crushed
a few parsley stalks
a few black peppercorns
salt and freshly ground black pepper

1. Crush the shells; use a processor for softer shells but not, of
   course, for crab or lobster. Wrap these in a tea towel to stop
   bits going all over the place and bash with a mallet or similar.
2. Add the shells to a little hot oil and cook for 1–2 minutes,
   stirring all the time.
3. Add the wine and then enough cold water to cover. Bring to
   the boil, then skim.
4. Add the tomato purée, onion, garlic, parsley and peppercorns
   and simmer for 30–40 minutes.
5. Strain, taste and season with salt and pepper.
6. Chill or freeze until needed.

S

Crustaceans – including crab, crawfish, crayfish, crevettes, Dublin Bay prawns, langoustine, lobster, prawns, scampi, shrimp. The sweet flesh of these chaps is excellent with orange, lemon, lime, mango, chilli, ginger, coriander, leek, fennel, avocado, butter, mayonnaise, brandy and white wine.

- **Crab rarebit** Spread crab, especially brown crab, onto toast, top with cheese and grill or bake until hot.
- **Crab in filo** Add a little fresh ginger and lime zest to the crab. Make individual filo-wrapped parcels, brush with butter and bake in a preheated oven at 200°C/gas 4 for about 10 minutes until crisp.
- **Creamy filling or topping** Mix with cream cheese or whipped cream plus 1 tsp of brandy and some black pepper to pile onto little toasts as an impressive nibble. Use the same mixture to fill beignets, tart cases, vol au vents and so on and so forth.
- **Egg dishes** Lots of choices to try in the Basic Recipe section.
- **Little crab pasties** Fold leftover crab in leftover pastry, brush with milk or cream or egg, make a slit in the top, maybe sprinkle with crunchy sea salt and bake on a greased baking sheet in a preheated oven at 190°C/gas 5 to hot and crisp and golden.
- **Lobster roe butter** Make a rich finishing butter to enhance chowders and sauces (p288).
- **Sauce** Warm in cream with a splash of dry sherry or brandy to sauce a more boring fish.
- **Shellfish butter** Make a savoury butter and use to top fish, or stir into soups and sauces, seasoning accordingly (p288).
- **Sweet potatoes** Shellfish go very well with sweet potatoes. Add to potato cakes (p212) or hash (p211) or use to fill a baked sweet potato.

Easy Peasy She-crab Soup

She-crab Soup is a traditional dish from South Carolina and this is what I have written in my perpetual recipe file: 'Roux sce, milk and cream, crabmeat, bit worcs, dash hot sce, s & p and sherry. Doddle!' In more detail ...

1 small onion, finely chopped
30g butter
30g flour
240ml milk
120g double cream
crabmeat, whatever you have available
salt and freshly ground black pepper
cayenne
Worcestershire sauce
dry sherry

1. Cook the onion gently in the butter until tender.
2. Stir in the flour and cook for 1– 2 minutes.
3. Whisk in the milk and bring to the boil, whisking until thick and smooth.
4. Add the cream and return to the boil.
5. Turn the heat down to very low.
6. Add the crabmeat, taste and season as you like it with some or all of the other ingredients.

Molluscs – aka mollusks including scallops, mussels, clams, oysters, cockles, whelks and also octopus and squid aka calamari
Mussels and clams are good with white wine, Belgian beer and chorizo, scallops are at their best with cream, butter, asparagus, leeks, bacon and black pudding, saffron, white wine and vermouth. Squid and octopus go well with tomato, garlic and saffron.

❋ Scallops are delicate and expensive; keep them cold, eat them soon and whatever you do don't overcook them!

S

❄ Raw squid should be wrapped well and kept in the fridge for no more than a couple of days; it really takes well to freezing. Exactly the same instructions for cooked!

❄ Mussels, clams and cockles are best frozen in their own cooking liquid. Leftover broth is well worth keeping to add to sauces, soups and stews. Strain carefully and freeze in cubes.

- **Baked on the half shell** Stuff mussels or oysters on the half shell with fresh breadcrumbs tossed in garlicky olive oil and bake in a preheated oven at 190°C/gas 5 for about 10 minutes until crisp.

> **COOK'S TREAT**
> Wrap individual mussels in pastry and bake or fry to make tiny turnovers.

- **Bean soup** Add to white bean soup together with chorizo, if possible.
- **Sauce for fish** Coarsely chop a few leftover molluscs and heat in olive oil with 1–2 chopped tomatoes, chopped parsley and some lemon juice as an interesting sauce for fish.
- **Scallop and leek pasta** Leftover cooked scallops are great tossed with hot pasta in a creamy leek Alfredo sauce (p281). Stir them in just as you take the dish off the heat.
- **Soup garnish** Top asparagus, pea or leek soup with a few slices of leftover scallop.
- **Squid fritters** Slice raw leftover squid and octopus into strips, rings or tentacles, coat in batter or breadcrumbs and deep-fry.

Shrimp – see Shellfish

Sloppy peas – see Mushy peas

Smoothies – instructions in basic recipe section, p308

Depending on the constituents of the smoothie, try making ice lollies or freezing ice cubes to add to future smoothies.

- **Smoothie cocktails** Make leftover smoothie go further with a measure of appropriate spirit or liqueur and/or top up with sparkling water.

Snails – if you really, honestly have leftover snails see Shellfish as they are classified as molluscs.

Sorbet

- **Champagne** Stretch too little to go round by serving in small glasses topped up with Champers.
- **Cooler** Use instead of ice in drinks.
- **Just drink it** Thaw and drink or use as the basis of a cocktail.
- **Seafood!** A scoop of not-too-sweet-lemon sorbet is good served with oysters or smoked salmon.
- **Smoothies** Add a scoop of sorbet when blending (p308).

Soufflé

As everyone knows, soufflés should be served as soon as they are cooked so the very idea of using leftovers is anathema. Having said that, I have had some success reheating soufflé. In my experience the soufflé re-puffs slightly and whilst not as wonderful as the first time round is still quite capable of being enjoyed.

1. Preheat the oven to 200°C/gas 6.
2. Carefully pour a little cream over the top of the leftover soufflé to cover completely. If sweet dust, with sugar, if savoury maybe Parmesan.
3. Bake for 10–12 minutes.

S

Soup

I think the most surprising thing I ever did with leftover soup was make fritters! One very busy lunchtime, a group of regulars decided they needed a celebratory party, with delicious finger foods, immediately! I calmly-ish added handfuls of fresh breadcrumbs to the last couple of portions of seafood chowder (p114), chilled it briefly in the freezer and shallow-fried it by the spoonful until crisp. People asked for the recipe, as is often the case when it is almost impossible to give one.

Of course different soups have different potentials but here are some suggestions.

- **Cook-in sauce** Pan-sear chicken, meat or fish, pour over hot appropriately flavoured leftover soup and bake till tender.
- **Mix with more soup** This can lead to some delightful flavour combinations that you might not otherwise have tried.
- **Pancakes** Some soups can be used as part of the liquid when making pancakes (p283).
- **Pasta sauce** Use as some or all of the sauce with pasta.

Soured cream

Pair soured cream with chives, dill, parsley, mustard, smoked fish, bacon, spinach, cucumber and hot spicy flavours.

- **Baked potatoes** Soured cream, perhaps with chopped chives or spring onions, is excellent in baked potatoes instead of butter.
- **Berries** Serve with sour cream sweetened with sugar or honey.
- **Cheesecake topping** Spread a layer of sweetened soured cream onto a baked cheesecake and return to the oven for the last few minutes of cooking.
- **Chocolate soured cream frosting** Melt together equal quantities of dark chocolate and soured cream, taste and add sugar, vanilla extract or a drip or two of liqueur. Cool, then whisk to thick.
- **Cucumber dressing** Mix with fresh dill and a little white vinegar and sugar to dress sliced cucumber.
- **Enrich sauces** Stir into pan sauces at the last minute, just before serving.

S

- **Fish pâté** Follow the guidelines on p117 and add a spoonful of soured cream.
- **Garnish soup** Put a spoonful of soured cream in the centre of a bowl of soup.
- **Mashed potatoes** Replace milk or cream in mashed potatoes.
- **Sauce for pork chops** Stir together soured cream, caramelised onions and coarsely chopped cooked smoky bacon. Either heat gently and pour over the cooked chops or spoon on top of the chops halfway through cooking and finish in the oven.
- **Soured cream dip** Mix in pretty well anything you like within reason: herbs, spices, citrus, mayonnaise, crumbled cheese, cream cheese, fresh chilli, garlic, raw onion, cooked onion and so on and so forth, tasting as you go until it is delicious! Remember to serve with something to dip into it.
- **Soured cream dressing** Whisk leftover soured cream into your favourite vinaigrette.
- **Tex Mex** Soured cream is a traditional side dish with nachos, spicy bean dishes and other hot Mexican style foods.

Soya milk – see Milk

Spinach
Cream, nutmeg, black pepper, garlic, bacon, lentils, most cheese, beans and pulses all complement spinach.

❄ Keep fresh spinach in the fridge for up to five days and the same for cooked. It must be blanched or cooked to freeze.

- **Bubble and squeak** Add to your bubble (p211).
- **Dhal saag** Stir cooked spinach into spicy dhal, or vice versa!
- **Hummus** Purée leftover cooked spinach into bean dips such as hummus (p301).
- **Last-minute addition** Stir through hot dishes such as beans, rice or roasted squash just before serving, where it will wilt deliciously.
- **Raita** Replace the cucumber in the basic recipe with shredded

baby spinach or cooked spinach, squeezed dry and chopped (p279).

- **Saag aloo** This Punjabi potato and spinach curry is easy to rustle up with some leftovers and curry spices.
- **Salad** Toss baby spinach leaves into salad.
- **Soup** Stir leaves into soup at the last minute for them to wilt.
- **Spinach dip** Sauté a little garlic in oil to fragrant, add spinach and, if raw, cook to wilt. Cool slightly before puréeing with a few spring onions. Fold into soured cream, taste and season.
- **Spinach pesto** Use fresh baby spinach instead of basil in the basic recipe (p137).

Spirits and liqueurs

Four important points:

- **Exercise caution** Spirits and liqueurs are strong stuff both in flavour and alcohol so do err on the side of caution; you can always add more if you have it.
- **Warn diners** I think it is only fair to warn diners that a dish contains alcohol in case anyone can't have it for health reasons.
- **Storage** Spirits and liqueurs should be stored somewhere cool and dark where they will keep approximately forever – if you don't drink them!
- **Very important** Do not pour spirits from the bottle straight into a pan over an open flame or you could have a very nasty accident; the whole stream of liquid could catch fire and make the bottle explode in your hand.

Firstly here's a list of all the ideas I can think of that apply generally to spirits and liqueurs.

- **Boozy cream** Add 1–2 tsp of your chosen liqueur into cream whilst whisking.
- **Christmas cake** Pour a spoonful into its bottom, repeating every few days till Christmas.
- **Custards** Add a few spoonfuls to custard based desserts such as bread pudding or French toast (see p50 and 51).

S

- **Drizzle** Pour abstemiously over creamy desserts and ice cream.
- **Enhance an Affogato** (p150).
- **Glaze** Warm together jam and a little appropriately flavoured beverage as a glaze for tarts and cakes.
- **Hot drinks** Stir a little into coffee or hot chocolate.
- **Ice cream** Use a tot when making ice cream but not too much or it won't freeze.
- **Macerate fruit** see Dried fruit p100.
- **Mulled wine** Add a glug of your chosen spirit when just about to serve so as not to evaporate the alcohol.
- **Pan sauce** Use spirits to deglaze a pan after searing meat (do this carefully, see above). Cook for 1–2 minutes, stirring and melting any cooked meaty juices into the liquor. Add a knob of butter and/or a little cream. Taste and season before pouring over the meat.
- **Smoothies, milkshakes and eggnog** Add a splash of liqueur to the basic recipes on p103 and 308.
- **Sticky toffee sauce** Add a little spirit for an even more wickedly indulgent treat (p56).
- **Trifle** Drizzle over the cake in a trifle before adding fruits etc.

Bourbon
This is American Rye whiskey but it tastes so different to 'normal' whisky that it deserves its own entry. It is particularly good with pecans, sweetcorn and brown sugar.

- **Bourbon cream** Whip a spoonful with cream to serve with pecan pie.
- **Mint julep** Put 1 tsp each of water and icing sugar in a whiskey tumbler. Add 3–4 sprigs of fresh mint and muddle everything together with a teaspoon until the sugar has dissolved and the mint leaves are crushed. Fill the glass with ice and top up with Bourbon.

Brandy – including Cognac, Armagnac, Spanish and Mexican
Brandy is lovely on its own but also good with coffee, chocolate, vanilla, fruit especially stone fruits, dried fruits, cream, cheese, black pepper, shellfish, and balsamic vinegar. Rich foods can carry a shot of brandy far better than lighter dishes.

S

- **Brandied black pepper butter** Make a compound butter using black pepper, a little brandy and salt to taste (p288). This is great on steak and also on new potatoes to name just two of its myriad uses.
- **Brandy butter** This is traditionally served with Christmas pudding and mince pies but is also great on toast! Cream together equal quantities of butter and icing sugar (classic) or light brown sugar (delicious too) then beat in a few spoonfuls of brandy to taste but not too much or the mixture will curdle. If this does happen, add more sugar. Put in a pretty Christmassy container and chill until needed.
- **Cheese** Add a spoonful to potted cheese or *fromage fort* (p65).
- **Mushroom sauce** Add a dash of brandy when making a creamy mushroom sauce.
- **Pâté** Incorporate a little brandy when making chicken liver or any meat pâté.
- **Peppercorn sauce for steak** Follow the recipe for peppered steak salad (p35).
- **Prunes** Add a spoonful to prunes when soaking or to dishes containing prunes; Armagnac is particularly suited for this.
- **Soup** Put a spoonful into the bowl before ladling in French onion soup (or seafood chowder, mushroom soup ...).

Calvados
Being distilled cider Calvados goes well with apple dishes and things that go well with apples such as pork and bacon.

- **Apple sauce** Add a spoonful of Calvados to the recipe (p15).
- **Pâté** Mix a spoonful into homemade pork-based pâté.
- **Pork gravy** After cooking pork, deglaze the pan (carefully – see 129) with Calvados or add a little to pork gravy.

Gin
The distinctive flavour of gin is good with tonic, lemon and other citrus fruits and juniper-friendly foods such as salmon, cured meats and game.

- **Red cabbage** Add a spoonful when braising red cabbage.

> **HANDY HINT**
> Soak 'leftover' diamond jewellery in gin to clean it – although this is probably a waste of gin.

Rum

'... it's not just for breakfast' *Ministry of Rum*

- **Buttered rum** Put ½ tbsp butter and 1 tsp soft light brown sugar into a mug or heatproof glass. Stir in a generous shot of rum and top up slowly with hot apple juice or water, stirring constantly (with a cinnamon stick, perhaps) to emulsify the mixture. Serve immediately topped with a little grated nutmeg.
- **Fruit salad** It seems only right to add a spoonful of rum to tropical fruit salads.
- **Moose milk** See p91 for this rum based drink.
- **Rum punches and cocktails** Rum is the basis of many cocktails: daiquiri, tropical punch and mojito to name but a few. See 'ti punch for my favourite (p127).

Vodka

Vodka is good with fish, especially cured and smoked, tomatoes, lemon and takes up other flavours very well.

❄ As vodka is best served chilled you might as well keep it in the freezer.

- **Bloody Mary** Fill a tall glass with ice and add a measure or glug of vodka. Top up with tomato juice and season to taste with Tabasco, Worcestershire sauce, celery salt, lemon juice, black pepper and maybe horseradish. Stir with a stick of celery.
- **Fruit sorbet** A little vodka added to fruit sorbets will help keep them soft without affecting the flavour very much. Just a little, mind.
- **Iced vodka** is a lovely accompaniment to smoked and cured fish.
- **Marinate tomatoes** Prick holes in cherry tomatoes and marinate in vodka for an hour or so, tossing from time to time. Serve with a little bowl of black pepper or lemon, pepper and sea salt to dip the tomatoes in and some cocktail sticks to facilitate such dipping.
- **Peppered vodka** Just add a few dried chillies to a bottle of vodka and leave to infuse for a couple of weeks or more.
- **Tomato sauce** Add a splash of peppered vodka to creamy tomato sauces, especially for pasta.

S

Whisky – aka Scotch and Irish whiskey
Whisky is nice with smoked fish, bacon, haggis, dark chocolate and fruit cake and so is whiskey.

- **Cranachan** A creamy raspberry, oat and whisky dessert (p185).
- **Haggis** Pour a nip over haggis on Burns Night.
- **Medicinal use** If you have a cold, or even think you might possibly be going to have one sometime, mix together the juice of $\frac{1}{2}$ lemon plus honey to taste, top up with hot water and stir in a spoonful of whisky.
- **Tipsy laird** A Scottish version of trifle (p119) made with raspberries, cream and a wee dram of whisky.

Spring onions – aka scallions and green onions
These mild, young onions are good with Asian dishes, fish, chicken, potatoes and cream.

❄ Store in the fridge, loosely wrapped so as not to taint other residents, for four to five days, chop to freeze.

- **Asian dishes** Add to stir-fries steamed fish, noodle dishes and other Asian recipes.
- **Egg dishes** Sprinkle chopped into omelettes and scrambled eggs (see p296– 98).
- **Garnish** Thinly slice spring onions on a sharp diagonal for a pretty garnish.
- **Potato salad dressing** A delicious potato salad can be made by simply puréeing spring onions with mayonnaise and dressing freshly cooked potatoes.
- **Re-grow them!** If you have used most of your spring onions but have the root ends left put them root down in a glass of water, wait a few days *et voilà*.
- **Spring onion pesto** Replace the basil in the main recipe on p137, with spring onions and maybe the pine nuts with cashews or peanuts.

Chinese Spring Onion Pancakes

Also called *tsung yu ping*, these are really more panbreads than pancakes.

MAKES 8 PANCAKES

200g plain flour
salt and freshly ground black pepper
125ml boiling water
2 tsp sesame oil
a bunch of spring onions, coarsely chopped
crunchy sea salt
oil for frying

1. Sift the flour and season lightly with salt and pepper.
2. Gradually mix in the hot water and knead until you have a soft dough but one that is no longer sticky. As the dough is hot, this is much easier done in a mixer.
3. Cover with a damp cloth and leave for 40 minutes.
4. Divide into eight balls and roll each ball into a thin disc.
5. Brush each pancake with sesame oil and sprinkle with spring onions and a pinch of sea salt then roll from one edge to form eight little snakes.
6. Coil up each snake and re-roll into pancakes thus creating layers.
7. Heat about 1cm depth of oil in a frying pan and fry the pancakes until crisp and golden on each side.
8. Drain on kitchen paper and eat!
9. Leftover *tsung yu ping* heat up nicely if popped in a preheated oven at 200°C/gas 6 for a few minutes.

Irish Champ

Delicious buttery mashed potatoes.

SERVES 2–3

500g potatoes
½ bunch spring onions, coarsely chopped
75ml milk
30g butter
salt and freshly ground black pepper

1. Boil the potatoes for mashing in the usual way.
2. Meanwhile, simmer the spring onions in the milk for 5 minutes.
3. Drain the potatoes and mash with the milk and spring onion mixture and half of the butter.
4. Taste and season.
5. Serve in a mound, make a well in the top and put the rest of the butter in it.
6. Eat the champ from the edge, dipping into the melting butter as you go.

Spring greens – these are early cabbages so see Cabbage for other ideas

❋ Being so young and tender, spring greens don't keep very well. Store in the fridge and use within a couple of days.

● **Last-minute addition** Shred and add during the last minute of a stir-fry, a risotto or soup.

Squash – see also Pumpkin

This entry concerns butternut squash and its winter squash relatives such as acorn, hubbard, turban etc. Pumpkin is also part of the family but being the Daddy has its own entry. For summer squash see Courgettes.

These sweet squash go with nuts, amaretti, leeks, caramelised onion, sage, chilli, roast meats, sweetcorn, balsamic vinegar and many other things.

Roasting is to my mind the very best way of cooking squash, producing a lovely sweet flavour, and leftovers can be used in so many ways.

❊ A whole uncut squash will keep for several months in a cool, dry, airy place. In fact, they keep less well in the fridge but will be okay for a couple of weeks. Once cut, refrigerate with clingfilm on the cut surface to stop it drying out, and it will keep another week (officially) or a fair bit longer.

- **Add to succotash** (p252).
- **Corn and squash chowder** If you have leftover squash add it to corn chowder, if on the other hand you have too much corn add it to squash soup, the flavours marry very well.
- **Hummus** Fold chopped, crushed or puréed roast squash into hummus and other bean dips (p301 and 31).
- **Mayonnaise** Leftover roast squash makes a deliciously different salad dressing or dip by simply puréeing leftovers with mayonnaise. Any onion, spices etc. roasted with the squash so much the better, bung the lot in!
- **Risotto** Add to risotto (p307) for the last few minutes of cooking time, just to heat through. Caramelised onions and/or toasted nuts would be good additions (p176).
- **Roast** Add raw squash to other vegetables whilst roasting.
- **Roasted squash and garlic bisque** Using the basic soup recipe on page 309, reduce the potato somewhat in the original recipe and, when fully cooked, add roasted squash and a few pieces of roasted garlic. Use a liquidiser if possible to produce the smoothest most luxurious soup possible. Purée in the cream.
- **Salad** Toss roasted butternut squash into salad with nuts and a balsamic dressing.
- **Squash gratin** Mix leftover squash and caramelised onions together with sage if you have it. Put into an ovenproof dish and pour over a little cream. Mix together fresh breadcrumbs and melted butter and sprinkle over. Bake in a medium oven for 30–40 minutes until hot and crusty.
- **Squash soup** Add raw squash to the basic recipe when the potatoes have come to a boil and reduce the amount of potato accordingly (p309).

S

Squid – aka calamari – see Shellfish (oddly enough!)

Steak – see Beef

Stock

❄ Simmer until reduced and concentrated and freeze as your own stock cubes to use in soups, sauces, gravies, casseroles and braises.

● **Baking** Replace some of the liquid in savoury scone and pancake recipes with cold stock.
● **Boulangère potatoes** Use instead of cream in scalloped potatoes, add some thinly sliced or cooked onion to the layers and call it by a new name (p305).
● **Cooking liquor** Stock can be part or all of the liquid when cooking rice, pasta, couscous, quinoa, or polenta or cook vegetables in it.

Stollen – see Bread and also Cake

There is, however, one quick, easy and so utterly delicious way to use leftover stollen that I want to make a point and mention here. Dice, slice, coarsely chop or crumble the stollen into a buttered dish, pour over double cream and bake in a preheated oven 180°C/gas 4 or thereabouts for about 15 minutes. Eat warm or hot.

Strawberries – see also Berries

Strawberries are excellent with black pepper, balsamic vinegar, orange, rhubarb, other soft summer fruits, cream, sugar and chocolate, especially white.

> **COOK'S TREAT**
> Dip in something:
> cream and sugar or
> melted chocolate
> and eat.

● **Add to scones** If you don't have enough strawberries to go round, coarsely chop and stir them into scone dough for an alternative cream tea (p293).

- **Eton mess** This classic dish is simply strawberries (maybe lightly crushed) and crumbled meringues folded into whipped cream.
- **Fruit salad** Strawberries are always welcome here.
- **Strawberry smoothie** One of the best (p308).

Sunflower seeds – see Seeds

Stuffing – see Christmas.

Sushi

- **Deep-fry** The only really viable thing I can suggest for leftover but still fresh sushi is to dip it in batter and deep-fry.

Swede – aka Rutabaga; see also Turnips

These can be cooked in much the same way (and the names are used the other way round in some areas).

Swede tastes good with sweet warm spices such as nutmeg, cinnamon and allspice.

❋ Keep raw swede in the fridge for a couple of weeks, cooked for four or five days. Only freeze when cooked.

- **Coleslaw** If you have a nice swede, try grating it into coleslaw (p287).
- **Mash** Mix hot cooked swede in with potatoes when mashing.

Sweetcorn

Butter, beans, squash, bacon, tomato and avocado are all good matches for sweetcorn as are cream and brown sugar.

> **HANDY HINT**
> Simmer stripped cobs in water for 15 minutes to make corn stock.

S

- **Corn fritters** Together with sweetcorn, add such things as spring onions or chives, fresh coriander and cayenne or chilli to the basic recipe (p285– 86).
- **Salads** Add kernels to mixed salads.
- **Succotash** A Native American dish of corn cooked in butter with shelled beans (often lima beans in America, soya beans – edamame – make a good substitute) until tender. Whilst this is happening in a separate pan cook peeled and chopped tomatoes in more butter with a pinch of sugar until tender. Stir everything together and simmer for a few minutes. Recipes often include squash and sometimes bacon and cream.

Sweet potatoes – aka sometimes, incorrectly, yam

There are two types of sweet potato: white-fleshed, which is dry and not very sweet when cooked, and the much more readily available, lovely soft, sweet orange-fleshed variety, also known as kumara, which is best for the ideas below. Neither of these is related either to the yam or the potato but both can be cooked the same way as potatoes.

Sweet potatoes go with salmon, shellfish, mango, orange, coconut, cinnamon, cardamom, chilli, pecans, brown sugar, honey, rum and Bourbon.

❄ Store in a cool, dark, dry and airy place but not the fridge. Use within a couple of weeks.

- **Fish cakes** Use mashed sweet potato in fish cakes (p114) – salmon or shrimp in particular.
- **Frazzled sweet potato** Peel a sweet potato and keep peeling until you have a pile of ribbons. Rub with a little cornflour (the white cornflour kind, not cornmeal) and deep-fry briefly until slightly darker. Drain well on kitchen paper and they will crispen. Season, a pinch of chilli powder would not go amiss, and serve as a nibble or a lovely crunchy garnish.
- **Peanutty sweet potato soup** (p197).
- **Potatoes** Anything you can do with a leftover potato you can do with a leftover sweet potato (see Potatoes).
- **Slaw** Add coarsely grated raw sweet potato to coleslaw (p287) or make sweet potato slaw with red onion, nuts and seeds in a spicy dressing.

• **Sweet potato crisps** Preheat the oven to 160° C/gas 3 and grease a baking tray. Slice raw sweet potato into rounds, as thinly as you can. Lay them on the tray, brush with oil and sprinkle with sea salt and black pepper or chilli powder. Bake for about 30 minutes, keeping an eye on them, until the edges have curled and the middles are shade darker. Cool on a rack to crisp.

Fartes de Batatas

This snippet of Portuguese means something like Potatoes that Satiate – what did you think it meant? These little cakes or candies are very sweet and gooey.

170g caster sugar, plus more for sprinkling
1 egg
15g soft butter
170g cooked, mashed and cooled sweet potato
70g ground almonds
finely grated zest of 1 orange
squeeze of lemon or orange juice
1 egg white, lightly beaten with a pinch of salt

1. Whisk together the sugar, egg and butter very well indeed until light and fluffy.
2. Stir in the mashed sweet potatoes, ground almonds, citrus zest and juice.
3. Scrape the mixture into a pan and stir over medium heat to dry out; when the texture of stiff mashed potato, spread onto a floured board to cool.
4. Preheat the oven to 200°C/gas 6.
5. Roll the potato into walnut-sized balls, then flatten into little cakes.
6. Place on a greased baking tray, brush with the beaten egg white and sprinkle with caster sugar.
7. Bake for about 20 minutes until slightly puffed up, golden and fragrant.
8. Cool on a rack and serve with coffee.

Kamote or Camote Cue

These caramelised sweet potato fritters, traditional Filipino street
food, are normally served on sticks. Bananas can be treated the
same way.

SERVES 1–2

250ml vegetable
200g soft light brown sugar
1 sweet potato, cut into 1cm slices

1. Heat the oil in a small pan and, when hot, sprinkle in the sugar.
   Cook together for 1–2 minutes, during which time the sugar
   will rise to the surface and form a bubbly crust.
2. Carefully add the potato slices and cook over a medium-high
   heat, turning occasionally for 7–8 minutes until tender and
   speckled with caramel. Lift out and drain on kitchen paper.
   Cook in small batches.
3. Eat whilst hot.

Swiss chard – aka Chard, see also Spinach

Chard is good with garlic, lemon, olive oil, olives, chilli and capers. It is
pretty well interchangeable with spinach, although it may need a little
longer cooking. Chard's stalks cook at a seriously different rate so should
be removed from the leaves before cooking. You will then have leftover
chard stalks or ribs; no worries ...

- **Chard stalks** Cut the stalks into equal-ish pieces and simmer
  in salted water for about 5 minutes until tender. Serve hot with
  butter or toss in a vinaigrette and serve chilled. Alternatively
  sauté in olive oil with garlic, lemon and parsley.

T

Tangelos and tangerines – see Oranges

Tapenade – see Olives

Tea

'If this is coffee, then please bring me some tea, but if this is tea, please bring me some coffee.' *Abraham Lincoln*

These ideas are for leftover tea with no milk and sugar.

- **Compost** Put tea leaves on the compost or scatter them on the garden to nourish roots.
- **Eyes** Put cold used teabags on tired or sore eyes to soothe them and also to reduce puffiness and dark circles.
- **House plants** quite like to be 'watered' with cold tea.
- **Ice cubes** If you have truly outstanding tea left over, then it is worth freezing in cubes. Make them extra special by adding an edible flower, a mint leaf, a twist of zest or a slice of fruit. Use in iced tea, of course, or punch, lemonade and so on.
- **Iced tea** I realise that aficionados would be aghast at using leftovers for iced tea but if it's a good brew why not? Sweeten with syrup or honey, add a slice of lemon or orange, a sprig of mint or some pretty tea-flavoured ice cubes.
- **Tea bread** There are lots of recipes around, here is my favourite.

T

Orange Fruit Tea Bread

MAKES A 900G LOAF

300g mixed dried fruit of your choice (dried cranberries are good in this)
150g dark brown sugar
grated zest of 2 oranges
300ml leftover tea, reheated if cold
1 egg, lightly beaten
300g self raising flour
pinch of salt

1. Mix together the dried fruit, sugar, orange zest and hot tea, cover and leave overnight.
2. The next day, all bright and sunny in the morning, preheat the oven to 150°C/gas 2 and grease a 900g loaf tin.
3. Stir the egg into the fruit mix, then fold in the flour and salt.
4. Scrape the mixture into the prepared loaf tin and bake for about 1 ½ hours until risen and firm and a toothpick or similar inserted into the centre comes out clean.
5. Turn out and cool on a rack
6. Leftovers of this cake are gorgeous toasted and buttered, possibly for breakfast.

Toast – see Bread

Toffees – chocolate-covered or otherwise

- **Creamy desserts** Add chopped toffees to sundaes, trifles and similar.
- **Crumble** Add coarsely chopped toffees to crumble mix remembering to sprinkle a little extra crumble over the top to protect it whilst baking (p290).
- **Toffee ganache** Melt toffees very gently in two parts cream to one part milk (a rough guideline is 60ml cream and 30ml milk per 75g toffees), stirring until smooth, and use as a sauce on ice cream, banana splits or similar. Add more milk to make a

delicious hot toffee drink or pour into little cups and chill to serve with crisp biscuits as a dessert. Or chill and whisk until thick and use as a toffee frosting.

Tofu – aka soyabean curd or just bean curd

Tofu, being fairly bland, goes well with a huge range of flavours. Actually my sister once bought a book about tofu which said in the introduction that the writer had tried everything but still couldn't really like the stuff!

❄ Keep it in the fridge and use within five days.

● **Marinate** Tofu takes up flavours very well so take advantage of this by marinating it before adding to a dish.
● **Stir-fry** Cube it and add it at the end of stir-frying. See tips on stir-frying on p310.

Tomatoes – including green tomatoes

Tomatoes taste great with onions, garlic, peppers, aubergines, cheese, vinaigrette and famously well with basil but also with oregano and thyme.

❄ Don't refrigerate tomatoes until fully ripe as this will inhibit ripening and damage both texture and flavour. Keep ripe tomatoes in the fridge but use as soon as possible to enjoy at their best. Cut tomatoes can be kept covered in the fridge for a couple of days. Raw tomatoes whole or otherwise can be frozen but will be mushy and only good for cooking with once thawed.

● **Mexican salsa cruda** Simply ripe tomatoes, peeled, seeded, diced and mixed with onion, garlic, salt and fresh coriander, if possible.
● **Roasted tomatoes** Pop some in the oven (at whatever temperature you are already using) until collapsed and tender, they will be delicious on toast or added to all sorts of things.
● **Salads and sandwiches** These can often benefit from a few tomatoes.

T

Green tomatoes

❊ You could wait until they ripen which they will do best at room temperature. If you don't want them to ripen, keep them in the fridge and use a soon as possible.

● **Fried green tomatoes** Someone complained when I had these on the menu, feeling it implied that we killed and cooked our customers, which we hardly ever did. Thickly slice green tomatoes, dip in seasoned flour and shallow-fry until crisp. Whilst often served as a side dish, I prefer them as the centre of attention, sprinkled with crumbled goats' cheese or feta with a drizzle of balsamic.

● **Salsa** Make sure to add some sweet ingredients to green tomato salsa to balance out the flavours.

● **Substitute** Use green tomatoes in place of red tomatoes but remember they are sharper so taste and season accordingly.

Sun-dried tomatoes

● **Egg dishes** Add to omelette or frittata (p296– 97).

● **Pasta and Risotto** Add to both these dishes. See basic risotto recipe on p307.

● **Salad dressings** Purée sun-dried tomatoes into mayonnaise or vinaigrette (p312).

● **Sun-dried tomato butter** Add garlic, parsley and maybe chilli, olives or Parmesan to make a compound butter (p288).

Tinned tomatoes

❊ Store in an airtight container in the fridge for up to a week.

● **Tomato juice** Freeze leftover juice from the tin to add to stocks, sauces or soups later.

● **Useful addition** Tinned tomatoes can usefully be added to soups, stews, chillies, casseroles and sauces.

Tomato paste

❄ Tomato paste freezes very well and can be used from frozen; just scrape off what you need. That's all I have to say.

Tongue – see Offal

Tortillas and wraps

- **Garnish** Shred broken or leftover wraps and fry until crisp to sprinkle on things.
- **Mexican migas** As distinct from Spanish migas, this is a dish of scrambled eggs (p298) with onions, tomatoes, hot and sweet peppers and Monterey Jack (or Cheddar) with crisply fried pieces of corn tortilla folded in at the end.
- **Quesadillas** A kind of fried sandwich made with tortillas. Traditional fillings include such things as chilli, chicken and cheese and they are normally served with soured cream and salsa. Try also **Chocolate quesadilla** A sudden inspiration! Coarsely chop chocolate (dark chocolate with chilli is particularly suitable) and sprinkle over a plain wrap. Put a second wrap on top and press firmly so that no chocky can escape. Melt a knob of butter in a non-stick pan and fry the quesadilla to crisp and golden on both sides and gooey in the middle. Eat immediately with some good coffee.
- **Wedges** Brush leftover wraps with oil or butter, cut into wedges and sprinkle with seasonings such as chilli powder and cumin, or salt and pepper, bake in a preheated oven at 180°C/gas 4 until crisp and golden. For a sweet version sprinkle with sugar and cinnamon to serve with ice cream, or nibble with coffee.

T

Trail mix – and similar fruity nutty concoctions

Trail mix is sometimes called gorp which some say stands for Good Old Raisins and Peanuts and some say doesn't.

- **Balls!** Weigh the leftover trail mix. Take a quarter of that weight in peanut butter and the same weight of honey and warm together, stirring gently. When completely mixed, stir in the trail mix and a quarter of its weight in dried oats. Cool until you can handle the mixture, then roll into balls and cool completely.
- **Flapjacks and crumbles** Both can benefit from a handful of leftover trail mix.
- **Pilau** If the mix is not too sweet, stir into Indian-style rice dishes.
- **Sprinkle** Create a crunchy contrast by sprinkling on creamy desserts.

Truffles – the fungi type

Truffles are great with eggs, and with pasta, risotto, potatoes, mushrooms, Brie and Camembert.

> **HANDY HINT**
> Stand a truffle on a piece of kitchen paper to absorb any moisture so it won't rot.

- ❄ Store in a sealed container in the fridge and use within ten days to two weeks.

- **Cheese** Shave a little truffle over perfectly ripe Brie or Camembert.
- **Egg** These go really well with truffles so store some whole raw eggs in the truffle container and they will become infused with truffliness. This is not, I agree, a perfect solution as you still have the truffle to get rid of! Scramble the eggs or make an omelette (p297).
- **Luxurious addition** Add to creamy pasta dishes or risotto.
- **Truffle butter** This is a good way of using every trimming and scrap (p288).

Turkey

Turkey is possibly the most talked about leftover in the history of cooking and the internet is rife with recipes for it so I'm not going to go over old ground; see Chicken and Christmas for ideas.

Turnips – see also Swede

Pair turnips with cream, butter, potatoes, onion, lemon, pork, duck, lamb, curry, black pepper, marjoram, thyme and, once bashed, haggis.

❄ Store raw in a cool dry place for up to a week or up to a month in the fridge. Cooked turnip will be good in the fridge, covered, for four to five days and can be frozen.

- **Bubble and squeak** (p211).
- **Mash** Make turnip mash or add to mashed potatoes. Turnips absorb fat readily, which can be a bad thing health-wise but good if you want something rich and tasty!
- **Roast** Cook alongside potatoes.
- **Stovies** Add to this baked meat and potato dish (p170).
- **Turnip soup** Replace some or all of the potatoes in the basic recipe with turnips. Be generous with the black pepper or float a slice of black pepper butter on each serving (p309).

U

The letter U has been quite a challenge so I've decided to cheat a bit!

Under-ripe fruit – see also
individual fruits

Ugli fruit – see Grapefruit

Umeboshi plums
If you have some of these intense, pungent salted and dried Japanese apricots, as it happens, then I presume you know better than I what to do with them!

HANDY HINT

Some ripe fruits – such as apples and bananas – release a gas called ethylene which hastens the ripening of other fruits, so to speed things up put a ripe apple or banana in a brown paper bag together with whatever under-ripe fruit you are trying to deal with.

- **Hangover** I have heard they can help with a hangover and understand it is best to soak your umeboshi in hot water for 5 minutes then both eat the plum and drink the water. Good luck to you!

Urad dhal – see Dhal and also Beans and pulses

Unleavened bread – see Bread

V

Vanilla pods

Vanilla's exotic flavour is lovely with chocolate, coffee, cream, soft summer fruits, eggs, sugar, milk, brandy, coconut and shellfish. A vanilla pod left over after flavouring a custard, for instance, even if the seeds have been scraped out, should never, ever be discarded; there is so much more flavour in it. Rinse in cold running water to remove any cream or custard adhering to it, dry thoroughly and use in one of the following ways.

- **Homemade vanilla extract** Add leftover vanilla pods to a bottle of spirit – brandy is my favourite but rum and vodka work well too – wait quite a while (we're talking at least 8 weeks) and then enjoy.

- **Vanilla honey** Snip the pod into manageable pieces and stir into a jar of honey. After a week or so, the honey will be infused with its wonderfulness.

> **COOK'S TREAT**
> Spread butter right out to the edges of fresh toast, sprinkle fairly generously with vanilla sugar and pop under the grill until bubbling and golden.

- **Vanilla salt** Dry the washed pod *very carefully indeed* and add to a container of coarse sea salt, then leave as long as you like till needed. This is great lightly sprinkled on popcorn, caramel dishes and seafood, especially lobster.

- **Vanilla sugar** Do exactly the same as with vanilla salt but using sugar. Over time, the sugar will become more and more delicious – perfect for sprinkling on cakes or fruit or to make any recipes that will benefit from vanilla flavour.

V

Vanilla Syrup

This is a delicious addition to coffee, fruit salads, whipped cream, poured over ice cream, used to glaze cakes and probably lots of other things too.

MAKES ABOUT 150ML

100ml water
200g sugar
1 leftover vanilla pod

1. Stir the water and sugar together over a medium-low heat until the sugar has dissolved, brushing down the sides of the pan with a damp brush to keep all the sugar under water.
2. When the liquid is clear, turn up the heat until it boils, add the vanilla pod, turn down the heat and simmer to a syrup, which takes about 5 minutes. During this stage of the proceedings, don't stir it but do pay attention.
3. It is ready when the syrup forms a thread when dripped off the spoon. If you have a sugar thermometer you are aiming for 106–112°C. I like to stop cooking at the lower temperature so that the syrup is still a bit runny when chilled.
4. When cool, decant into an appropriate container, leave the vanilla pod in but make sure it is entirely covered by syrup. Cut it into pieces, if necessary, or it might go mouldy.

> **COOK'S TREAT**
>
> The best way to clean up is to add a little water to the pan, bring to the boil, stirring to dissolve any residual syrup, and make yourself a cup of coffee with the resulting sweet, vanilla-flavoured water.

Various bits and pieces

If you have a collection of diverse leftovers here are some ideas to use them all up in one go.

Savoury leftovers

- **Hash** All sorts of meats, fish, vegetables and even fruits can be used in a hash (p211). How about, just off the top of my head, sweet potato hash with salmon and mango?
- **Omelette** I used to occasionally partake of breakfast at a beach bar called De Loose Mongoose, just a few watery yards from our boat, where they served Trash Omelette, cunningly made out of whatever they had left over from the night before. It was sometimes surprising but always good.
- **Soup** Add suitable bits and pieces to the basic soup recipe (p309).

Sweet leftovers

- **Ice cream** Mix into, layer up with or sprinkle over ice cream dishes and sundaes.
- **Trifle** If appropriate, use in a trifle (p119).

Veal – see Meat

Vegetables – see also individual veggies

Raw vegetables

- **Hash** Add to bubble and squeak or its variations (p211).
- **Pizza topping** Some vegetables (tomatoes and thinly sliced onion, mushrooms, courgettes, aubergine) are good added to pizza before cooking.
- **Vegetable soup** To the basic soup recipe (p309), add carrot, celery, fennel and garlic with the onions, starchy vegetables with the potatoes, and green and leafy vegetables towards the end of cooking.

V

Vegetable stock

Put a load of vegetables in a large pot, cover with cold water, season with salt and pepper, bring to the boil, turn down the heat and simmer for about an hour. Cool, strain and keep in the fridge or freeze in small usable portions. Here are some details.

As long as the vegetables are clean there is, in most cases, no need to peel them. You can use them whole, in chunks or coarsely chopped.

Almost all vegetables are suitable, but onions and carrots are pretty well *de rigueur* and celery is a valuable addition.

- **Fry first** For a more robust flavour, sweat the vegetables in a little olive oil until taking colour before adding the cold water.
- **Herbs and spices** Add fresh herbs, garlic, ginger and so on according to taste and what you intend using the stock for.
- **Mushrooms** These will make a darker broth.
- **Tomatoes** Make for a prettier broth.
- **Trimmings** Use trimmings, stalks and clean peelings.
- **Wine or soy sauce** Pour in a sloosh of wine or a couple of spoonfuls of soy sauce towards the end of cooking.

Cooked vegetables

- **Egg dishes** Add to omelettes, scrambled eggs, frittatas. See recipes on pp294–98.
- **Hash** Add to Bubble and squeak et al (p211).
- **Pizza toppings** Sprinkle onto appropriate pizzas.
- **Russian salad** Similar to potato salad, this is a mixture of vegetables usually including potatoes, carrots, peas and often green beans, cauliflower and beetroot. Sometimes boiled eggs and gherkins are added and everything is tossed together in mayonnaise.
- **Vegetable gratin** Put them in an ovenproof dish, pour over a lovely cheese sauce (p66), sprinkle with fresh breadcrumbs and grated cheese and bake in a preheated oven at 180°C/gas 4 for about 30 minutes until hot, bubbling, crisp and golden.

Venison – see Game and also Beef for which it can be substituted Port, red wine, redcurrant, rosemary, juniper and therefore gin enhance venison.

Vinaigrette

There's more information on p312.

- **Calves' liver** Sweetish vinaigrettes such as balsamic, sherry vinegar or those with a touch of honey are good drizzled over calves' liver.
- **Dress hot vegetables** Toss hot just cooked summery green vegetables (peas, beans, asparagus; that sort of thing) in a little citrus or mint vinaigrette immediately before serving;
- **Drizzle** Hummus (p301) or other bean dips are good served with a drizzle of vinaigrette.
- **Hot potato salad** Toss just cooked new potatoes in vinaigrette and serve straight away.
- **Marinade** Marinate meat, poultry or seafood in leftover vinaigrette to both tenderise and add flavour.
- **Sauce** Use to sauce grilled meat, poultry and seafood.

> **COOK'S TREAT**
>
> When making dressing/vinaigrette in a food processor or similar, wipe out the bowl with salad leaves and eat them!

W

Waffles

- **Reheat** In a toaster, under the grill or for a couple of minutes in a preheated oven at 200°C/gas 6 – microwaving will make them flabby. Use as a base for savoury as well as sweet toppings.

Walnuts – see Nuts

Wasabi – aka Japanese horseradish – I am talking about leftover wasabi paste or powder here.

Wasabi complements raw fish, certain cooked fish such as salmon, tuna and prawns, soy, sesame, pickled ginger, potatoes, beef and, according to Lindt, dark chocolate. I haven't tried this last combination yet.

- **Beef sandwiches** Spread a little wasabi in beef sandwiches instead of English mustard, which tastes similar to me!
- **Bloody Mary** Try wasabi in a Bloody Mary instead of regular horseradish.
- **Fishcakes** Brighten fishcakes (p114– 15) with a speck or two of wasabi.
- **Roasted nuts** Add a pinch of wasabi powder to hot, freshly roasted nuts (p176) together with salt to taste.
- **Vinaigrette** Make a powerful salad dressing by whisking a little wasabi powder or paste into vinaigrette, preferably one made with rice vinegar and a touch of fresh ginger. See vinaigrette recipe on p312.
- **Wasabi butter** Mix 1 tbsp wasabi paste into 125g of soft butter together with a crushed garlic clove and a little chopped parsley, chives or watercress. Serve with grilled fish or steak. See recipes for compound butters on p288.
- **Wasabi mayonnaise** Mix into mayonnaise to taste to serve with salmon and other seafood.

Watercress

The peppery taste of watercress is good with apples, pears, blue cheese, walnuts, smoked fish, salmon, ham, bacon, potatoes and leeks.

❄ Not being a good keeper, watercress is best stored in an open plastic bag with its stems wrapped in damp kitchen paper for a couple or days or so. It doesn't freeze well unless cooked first.

- **Fish pâté** Fold chopped or puréed watercress into smoked fish pâté (p117).
- **Locket's savoury** This classic is named after the old London restaurant whose signature dish it was. Toast white bread and, to be strictly correct, cut off the crusts. Place in a shallow baking dish and top with a layer of watercress. Add thinly sliced ripe pear and, finally, sliced or crumbled Stilton. Sprinkle with coarsely ground black pepper and pop into a preheated oven at 200°C/gas 6 for about 10 minutes until the pears are hot and the cheese has melted.
- **Mashed potatoes** Add finely chopped raw or cooked watercress.
- **Salads and sandwiches** Watercress is a good addition to both of these.
- **Soup** Add at the very last minute just before serving, thus keeping its bright colour intact.
- **Watercress dressing** Purée a few sprigs into vinaigrette (p312).
- **Watercress mayonnaise** Purée with mayonnaise for potato salad, this looks very attractive with red-skinned potatoes.
- **Watercress pesto** Substitute watercress for the basil and walnuts for the pine nuts in the basic recipe (p137).

W

Watermelon – see also Melon

'Summer's loud laugh of scarlet ice
A melon slice.' José Juan Tablada

Strawberries, citrus, ginger, mint, basil, rocket, feta, goats' cheese, sweet vinegar and salt are all good with watermelon.

❄ Store cut watermelon, well wrapped on the cut surfaces, in the fridge for two or three days only. A whole watermelon will be okay in the fridge for up to a week, if you can get it in there!

- **Fruit salad** Add diced watermelon to the basic recipe (p119).
- **Ice cubes** Purée leftover watermelon, freeze in cubes and use as pretty way to cool drinks.
- **Salsa** Dice watermelon and mix with diced red onion, chopped fresh coriander and fresh chilli to taste, stir in fresh lime juice and a little oil. Serve with grilled fish or Mexican dishes.
- **Watermelon and feta salad** Toss together diced watermelon, crumbled feta, thinly sliced red onion and a little fresh basil if you have some. Add a drizzle of olive oil, the same of balsamic vinegar and a good grind of black pepper.
- **Watermelon slush** Purée frozen watermelon cubes with a little water or fruit juice until smooth. Eat or drink it, depending on its texture! Fine additions are orange juice, rum or vodka, sparkling water, lime juice etc., all to taste.
- **Watermelon sorbet or granita**. See recipes on p299.

Whelks – see Shellfish

Wiener – see Sausages

According to the *Urban Dictionary*, wiener is 'the funniest word in the world ... for now.'

White chocolate – see Chocolate

Wine – including sweet, sparkling and fortified

'What I like to drink most is wine that belongs to others.'
Diogenes (412–323 BC), the founder of Cynicism!

As a general rule, white wine is good with chicken and seafood and red wine is good with meat, game and cheese, but you probably knew that and in any case these are by no means hard and fast rules.

- **Braising meat** Replace some or all of the liquid in braises and stews with wine at the start of cooking for depth of flavour or add a splash at the end for a bright winey taste.
- **Marinades and vinaigrettes** (p311).
- **Wine cubes** Freeze in cubes for appropriate drinks or to add a frozen splash of wine when cooking.

> **HANDY HINT**
>
> If it's not worth drinking it's not worth cooking with. If it is worth drinking, my first suggestion would be to drink it.

Wine Vinegar

As you may have noticed, wine is quite capable of turning to vinegar without any help but here are a few guidelines so as to have a better chance of success. The reason I suggest organic vinegar is that this is more likely to contain strands of vinegar 'mother' in it.

a bottle of organic vinegar
2 clean jam jars
leftover wine

1. Put 2.5cm of vinegar into each jar and allocate one for white wine and one for red.
2. Pour leftover wine into the appropriate jars and cover with cheesecloth secured with a rubber band.
3. Store at room temperature, topping up with leftover wine as necessary; the liquid in the jars will evaporate so it is important to keep adding to it.
4. After 7–8 days, test the vinegar and as soon as it tastes good to you it is ready to use. If a new vinegar mother has formed in the jar – a thick blob – use it to start a fresh batch.

W

Red wine
In addition to red meat and cheese, red wine has an affinity with stone fruit, pears, red berries, oranges and, in some cases, spicy foods and chocolate.

- **Caramelised wine vinaigrette** Whisk together 60ml red wine *gastrique* (below) and 120ml olive oil, a squeeze of lemon juice and season to taste.
- **'Chef's coffee'** Drink leftover red wine out of a mug and no-one will realise.
- **Red wine *gastrique*** Slowly heat together 60ml water and 60g sugar until the sugar has dissolved and then cook without stirring, but you can swirl a bit, for a few minutes until it is thick and syrupy and starting to caramelise. Add 225ml red wine and simmer until the mixture has reduced to 60ml. Cool, then use to enhance tomato soups and sauces, drizzle over blue cheese or fruits such as peaches or strawberries, add to pan juices or top up with sparkling water for an interesting spritzer.
- **Red wine reduction** Finely chop a small onion or shallot and cook in a little oil until tender. Add equal quantities of leftover red wine and beef stock and simmer until the mixture has reduced by half. That's it although if using immediately swirl in a knob of butter to make a glossy rich sauce.

Mulled Wine Syrup

I think this is a much better way of mulling wine than the more usual method of heating a whole bottle of wine with the flavourings; it is quicker and easier at the time of serving as all the work can be done ages in advance and is a lot less wasteful of alcohol because most of it doesn't boil off.

This makes 75ml of syrup which, as luck would have it, is sufficient to mull one bottle of wine.

1 orange
1 lemon
250g light brown sugar
60ml red wine
1 cinnamon stick
1 vanilla pod
2 slices of fresh ginger
a generous grating of nutmeg

1. Remove the zest from both fruits in long strips, making sure not to get any of the white pith involved.
2. Squeeze the juice from the orange (set the bald lemon aside to do something else with (see Lemons) into a small non-reactive pan with the zests, sugar and red wine.
3. Stir together over medium heat until the sugar has melted.
4. Add the spices, turn up the heat and cook at a gentle boil for about 5 minutes to form a light syrup.
5. Cool to room temperature then strain pressing on the debris to get out all the delicious juices.
6. Pour into a clean bottle and keep in a cool place until needed.
7. To use, warm the syrup over a low heat, add the red wine and heat through without boiling. Maybe add a spoonful of rum or brandy to the glass when serving. The syrup is also good on ice cream and strawberries.

COOK'S TREAT
To clean the pan, warm a little wine in it, stirring until the syrup has melted and you have yourself a tester.

W

White wine
White wine goes well with chicken, seafood and mushrooms.

- **Spritzer** Top up a little white wine with sparkling water for a refreshing drink.
- **White wine vinaigrette** Substitute white wine for some or all of the vinegar in the basic recipe (p312) and adjust the flavour with honey and lemon juice.

Champagne and sparkling wine
Champagne goes well with expensive things such as lobster, oysters, foie gras and caviar, as well as strawberries, peaches and nectarines.

- **Buck's fizz** (aka mimosa in America) A cocktail of chilled Champagne or sparkling wine and orange juice in whatever ratios you find pleasing, 50:50 works well. This is good for breakfast or brunch.
- **Substitute** Champagne or sparkling wine make a fine stand-in for white wine in any dish calling for such a thing.

HANDY HINT

Store open Champagne in the fridge but be aware it will probably lose at least some of its fizz. Special stoppers can be purchased for Champagne bottles or legend has it that a silver teaspoon inserted into the open bottle, handle into the neck, will help keep it sparkly.

Dessert wines – and Mead which is honey 'wine' and can be treated similarly
Naturally dessert wines are good with desserts (although not always chocolate ones) and also blue cheese, rich pâtés, foie gras, honey and fruits.

- **Fresh fruit** Pour a little over fruits especially honeydew melon, peaches and nectarines.
- **Vinaigrette** Replace 1–2 spoonfuls of vinegar with dessert wine when making vinaigrettes (p312) to go with cheese or pâté.
- **Wine-roasted pears** Peel, halve and core ripe pears and arrange cut-side down in a buttered dish. Drizzle with a little honey and pour over a glass of dessert wine. Cook at 190° C/gas 5 for 30–40 minutes until tender and starting to

caramelise on the bottom. Serve warm with cream or blue cheese.

Fortified wines
Fortified wines have had brandy (or other spirit) added during fermentation and include sherry, port, Madeira, Marsala and vermouth.

Madeira and Marsala
These two are different but similar enough to be treated the same for our purposes. They are good with chicken, veal and beef, liver, blue cheese, honey, chestnuts, figs and mushrooms.

- **Caramelised onions** Stir a spoonful into caramelised onions (p303) for the last minute or two to serve with steak.
- **Chicken livers** After sautéing chicken livers, deglaze the pan with a little Madeira or Marsala and stir in a knob of butter or a sloosh of cream.
- **Glazed winter squash** Dice a butternut squash or similar and toss with a drizzle of olive oil, coarsely chopped red onion, and seasoning. Roast in a preheated oven at 200°C/gas 6 until tender and lightly browned, then remove the squash and keep it warm. Deglaze the pan with a little Marsala or Madeira and simmer to a light glaze. Pour over the squash and toss all together.
- **Mushrooms** Stir a little into sautéed mushrooms or add a spoonful to mushroom sauces.
- **Pan sauce** Deglaze the pan after cooking chicken, veal or steak, reduce a little and swirl in a knob of butter.

Port
Port has a great affinity with cheese and is also good with duck, pigeon, venison, some dark chocolate and it used to go with lemonade but I'm not sure it does any more.

- **Cranberry sauce** Enhance cranberry sauce by stirring in a spoonful of port.
- **Marinade for game** Mix together equal quantities of port, red wine and olive oil and season with garlic, rosemary or juniper plus salt and pepper.

W

- **Pan sauce** Add to pan juices for duck or pigeon.
- **Port syrup** Stir together 60ml of port and 1 tbsp sugar over a medium heat until the sugar has dissolved. Turn up the heat and simmer for about 4 minutes until the mixture is thick and syrupy. Cool to room temperature – any colder and it will be too thick. Drizzle over cheese. I realise this is probably a no-no but if it crystallises, the crunchy pieces are gorgeous with creamy Cambozola.

Sherry
Dry sherry is great with crab and sweet sherry is good with trifle and mince pies.

- **Gravy** Finish turkey gravy with a splash of dry sherry.
- **Mirin substitute** Sweet sherry can be substituted for mirin in Japanese cooking.
- **Sake substitute** Dry sherry can be substituted for sake in Chinese cooking.
- **Soup** Stir dry sherry into butternut or turkey or especially crab soup (p237 for an easy crab soup recipe).

Vermouth
Dry vermouth is not as good a keeper as other fortified wines so keep it in the fridge and use within a few months.

- **Substitute** Dry white vermouth for white wine in cooking; it is particularly good for perking up fish dishes.

Wraps – see Tortillas

X

Even with a bit more cheating, there's not much here!

Xigua
This is the Chinese name for watermelon and is purely here to help out the letter X – if you do have leftover xigua see Watermelon.

Xmas cake – see Christmas cake and also Cake

Xmas leftovers generally – see Christmas leftovers and also Cranberry, Mincemeat, Turkey, Various and Vegetables

Xmas pudding – see Christmas pudding

Xmas stuffing – see Christmas stuffing

Y

Yam – see Sweet potatoes

These large tropical tubers are actually unrelated to sweet potatoes, with which they are often confused. Having said that, treat leftover yams like leftover sweet potatoes apart from one important proviso: **never eat yams raw as they are toxic in that state** although fine when cooked.

Yoghurt – aka yaort or yogurt

Generally speaking this entry deals with plain yoghurt, although in some cases flavoured will work well too.

❄ Store tightly closed in the fridge where it will keep well for a little after its sell-by date! After freezing, the texture will be separated and grainy so I wouldn't recommend it.

- **Cream** Use to replace cream in desserts and with fruits.
- **Lassi** This Indian yoghurt drink is served either sweet or salty and basically consists of plain yoghurt blended with enough water or milk to make a drinkable consistency. Sweeten with honey or sugar, if you like. Salted lassi often includes a pinch of ground cumin and perhaps a squeeze of lemon juice. That is not all, however – you can add fresh fruits.
- **Marinade** Yoghurt is a good medium in which to marinate fish, chicken and meat, particularly lamb. Add curry paste or roasted spices for an Indian effect; try it with lemon, oregano and garlic to be a bit Greek; or go for orange and lemon juice with yoghurt to marinate fish.
- **Smoothies** Use yoghurt as part of the liquid. See recipe on p308.

Cucumber Raita or Tzatziki

These two sauces, Indian and Greek respectively, are very similar. Although you can just use finely chopped fresh cucumber, there is a better way in which the cucumber stays crisp with more flavour and doesn't water down the yoghurt.

1 cucumber
1 tsp salt
plain yoghurt

1. Seed and chop a cucumber fairly finely.
2. Toss with the salt and leave in a nylon strainer over a bowl for 1–2 hours until it has exuded some of its juices.
3. Rinse well, pat dry and stir into plain, preferably Greek, yoghurt.
4. For Indian raita, flavour with fresh mint, chilli powder and ground cumin to taste.
5. For Greek tzatziki, add lemon juice, chopped garlic, mint or dill and a little olive oil.

Yorkshire pudding
See page 284 for how to make Yorkshire pudding.

❄ Keep leftovers in an airtight container in the fridge or freeze them.

● **Breakfast** Provided you haven't added mustard or other inappropriate ingredients, leftovers are good served hot with honey and butter, maple syrup, golden syrup, lemon and sugar or similar for breakfast.
● **Reheat** Pop into the oven at 200°C/gas 6 for a few minutes only. Microwaving is out of the question.

Z

Zest – see also individual citrus fruits

Zest is the brightly coloured skin (not including the white pith underneath, which is bitter) of citrus fruits. I expect it goes without saying to use unwaxed, washed and dried fruit but I've said it anyway; who cares about word count!

HANDY HINT

Grate the zest before squeezing the fruit, as doing it afterwards is really difficult. Even if a recipe doesn't use zest, it is useful to freeze it.

❄ Wrap small quantities of grated or shredded zest in clingfilm and freeze in an airtight container where it should retain its potency for up to a year. In most cases, the zest can be used immediately from frozen.

- **Baking** Add finely grated zest to baked goods.
- **Citrus butter** See compound butters (p288).
- **Citrus salt** Make in the same way as Citrus sugar below but use 150g lovely crunchy sea salt to the zest of one fruit.
- **Citrus sugar** Finely grate the zest from a citrus fruit and mash it into 250g caster sugar until very well combined. Spread out on a tray and leave for several hours to dry. Use to replace ordinary sugar in appropriate recipes, sweeten tea, rim a cocktail glass or sprinkle on fruits.
- **Drinks** Use a twist of fresh citrus zest to garnish drinks or freeze a little twist in ice cubes.
- **Drying** Remove strips of pith-free zest with a potato peeler and dry by spreading them out on a plate and leaving a few days.
- **Gremolata** Lemon zest is traditional in gremolata (p142).
- **Pastry** Mix finely grated zest into pastry at the breadcrumb stage (p291); orange zest pastry makes for great mince pies.
- **Stocks, stews and tea** Add zest to flavour these.

Zucchini – see Courgettes

Basic Recipes and Guidelines

This section covers all kinds of basic techniques and useful information that doesn't fit in the A to Z of Leftovers section.

Acidulated water

Acidulated water is just cold water with a small amount of an acidic ingredient, such as white vinegar, citrus juice or white wine. The approximate proportions are 1½ tbsp vinegar, 3 tbsp citrus juice or 120ml dry white wine per 1 litre of water.

The primary use of acidulated water is to stop fruits and vegetables discolouring when exposed to air. Either briefly dip the pieces of fruit or veg in the water or submerge them for a few minutes.

Fruit and vegetables can also be cooked in acidulated water, which will maintain their bright colour.

Alfredo pasta sauce

This easy recipe makes a truly luscious sauce, traditionally served on pasta but good in other dishes too and very amenable to leftovers.

Alfredo sauce

This quantity makes enough to coat 225g (raw weight) pasta which is enough for two people and is completely delicious with no further additions other than perhaps a sprinkling of more Parmesan.

SERVES 2

1 tbsp butter
200ml double cream
50g freshly grated Parmesan, plus more for sprinkling
salt and freshly ground black pepper

1. Gently heat the butter and the cream together, stirring, until

the butter has melted, then stir in the Parmesan.

2. Slowly bring to a gentle boil, turn down the heat and simmer, still stirring, for a minute or so until you have a smooth, creamy sauce.

Batters, pancakes and fritters

This section includes all kinds of batters, from thin ones for pancakes to thick ones for fritters.

Pancakes

These are not the crêpey Pancake Day-style pancakes; they are the American-style thick and fluffy pancakes which are useful for incorporating all sorts of leftovers.

- **Adding leftovers** The important thing to remember is not to add the leftover to the whole batch of batter but to sprinkle it onto each pancake as soon as you have poured it into the pan. This means that whatever you have added won't burn as the first side cooks. The second side of the pancake normally takes less time and in any case the pancake has fluffed up round the additions and protects them.
- **Delicate additions** When adding very fragile additions (chocolate, nuts, berries, etc.) drizzle a little more batter over the top to protect the second side while it cooks.
- **Variation** For an unhealthy but delicious variation put 1 tbsp oil into the middle of the pan and heat through. Pour the batter carefully into the centre of the oil and cook as above; the hot oil frazzles the edges of the pancake and makes them crispy. Turn carefully so as not to splash yourself.

Basic Pancakes

MAKES 5 X 10CM PANCAKES

125g plain flour
pinch of salt
1 tbsp sugar for sweet pancakes OR seasonings of your choice
1 heaped tsp baking powder
1 egg
150–175ml milk
a little vegetable oil

1. Stir together the first four ingredients. Make a well in the middle of the flour mixture.
2. Break the egg into the well.
3. Gently whisk the egg into the flour and gradually add the milk, still whisking, until you have a thick pourable batter. This may or may not take all the milk, or might even need a smidgen more, depending on the make and age of the flour.
4. Heat a non-stick frying pan or griddle and grease lightly.
5. Pour about 60ml of batter per pancake onto the surface and cook until pitted with burst bubble holes.
6. Turn and cook until the other side is golden.
7. Serve immediately or keep in a low oven until all the pancakes are cooked so that everyone can eat together.

Yorkshire Pudding
Firstly here are three important things you need to know about making Yorkshire Pudding.

- **Plain flour** You must use plain flour and no raising agent or it won't work – strange but true.
- **Rest the batter** The batter needs a rest before cooking so make it at least an hour before you need it.
- **Hot oil** The oil in the pan must be seriously hot when you add the batter.

Yorkshire Pudding

Although using so little in the way of ingredients this recipe makes six individual puds.

SERVES 2–3

1 heaped tbsp plain flour
¼tsp of salt
1 egg
a little milk
a little oil

1. Stir together the flour and salt.
2. Whisk in the egg until smooth, then whisk in enough milk to make a batter as runny as single cream. Cover and set aside at room temperature for an hour or more.
3. When ready to cook, preheat the oven to 220°C/gas 7.
4. Put ½ tsp of oil into each cup in a muffin pan for individual yorkies or a little more oil in one dish and put in the oven for a few minutes until hot.
5. Whisk the batter and, if it has thickened, add a little more milk to return to single cream consistency.
6. Pour the batter into the pan and immediately return to the oven.
7. Do not open the door for about 10 minutes and, even then, do so with caution.
8. They are ready when seriously puffed up and golden but sadly they do tend to go down a bit once out the oven so time them to be ready at the last minute.

HANDY HINT

I stand individual silicon muffin cups inside each hole in the muffin tin and my Yorkshires never stick.

Clafoutis

Follow the Yorkshire Pudding recipe (above) simply adding 2 tbsp sugar to the flour at the start of making the batter and using just a pinch of salt. A drop or two of vanilla extract could be a great addition. After resting, pour the batter over hot cooked fruit and cook as above.

Crêpes

Make these with exactly the same batter as the Yorkshire Pudding but with just a pinch of salt. Heat a lightly greased 24cm or similar non-stick frying pan and when hot add about 60ml batter, tipping and swirling to coat evenly. Cook over a medium heat until the edge is turning golden and the middle is fairly dry. Toss or turn with a spatula and cook the second side for half a minute or so.

Toad in the Hole

This is traditionally made with sausages but other leftovers are good too. Heat your cooked leftovers in with the oil in stage 4 of the Yorkshire pudding recipe and, when hot, pour the batter over and around it. Continue as in remainder of recipe.

Fritters

There are several ways to achieve a fritter.

- **Crisp coated fritters** Dip the item to be coated first in seasoned flour, secondly in lightly beaten egg and finally in the intended coating such as breadcrumbs, panko crumbs, cornmeal and so on. Deep-fry.
- **Tempura batter for delicate things** Beat together an egg yolk and 150ml icy cold water (still or sparkling). Whisk in 100g flour plus 1 tsp cornflour and a pinch of salt until just mixed in. Lumpy is okay but thick isn't; this should be a very runny batter so add a bit more icy water if necessary. Use this batter very cold.
- **Beer batter for fish and other robust items** This can be made with just iced or sparkling water instead of beer but is less tasty (p37).

Thick Fritter Mix

This can be used for many different leftovers.

2 tbsp flour
1 tsp baking powder
seasonings, such as salt & pepper, spices or grated cheese
1 egg
a little milk
about 100g leftovers
oil for frying

1. Mix together the flour, baking powder and seasonings.
2. Stir in the egg and enough milk to make a very thick batter.
3. Stir in the leftovers.
4. Drop spoonfuls into a little hot oil and fry until crisp and golden on both sides.
5. Drain on kitchen paper and serve.

- **Other types of fritters** Mashed potato, leftover dhal and pease pudding can all be mixed with other leftovers and fried as fritters, cakes or croquettes.

Blanching vegetables and fruits

Blanching vegetables and fruits means to plunge them quickly into boiling water then immediately put them into a bowl of ice water to stop them cooking further and to maintain their bright colour.

Bring a large pan of water to the boil over a high heat while you prepare the vegetables to be blanched. Cut them into even-sized pieces so that they will all blanch in the same amount of time. Only blanch one type of vegetable at a time. Put a large bowl of iced water next to the hob.

Add 1 tbsp salt to the boiling water, then blanch the vegetables a small batch at a time so that the water continues to boil. Different vegetables require different blanching times but as a general rule 3– 5 minutes is about right. Scoop them out with a slotted spoon (or one of those large Chinese strainers is made for the job – literally) and put into the iced water for a few minutes until cold.

Strain and drain well on kitchen paper then freeze them, or whatever you intend doing next.

There are a few good reasons to blanch vegetables:

- **Colour** To set their bright colour, rather than lose it into cooking water, blanching is the perfect cooking technique for some vegetables.
- **Crunch** The briefest of cooking helps to retain crunch for vegetables like asparagus, which you want to be just perfect, not soggy and overcooked.
- **Freezing** Blanching vegetables before freezing destroys enzymes, which could otherwise cause changes in colour, flavour and texture when the vegetables are frozen.
- **Prepare ahead** When you're nearly ready to serve your meal, you can finish off blanched vegetables with just a brief sauté in butter.
- **Salads** Part cooking vegetables for salads means they remain crunchy and colourful but also helps them to absorb the other flavours of the salad or dressing.
- **Skin** Blanching makes it easier to remove the skins of fruits such as tomatoes and peaches.

Coleslaw

Even at its most basic, just shredded cabbage, onion, carrot and mayonnaise, coleslaw is delicious. You can add all sorts of things: chopped or grated veggies, fruits, nuts, seeds, seasonings and different dressings, so coleslaw is referred to many times throughout the book for its versatility with leftovers.

SERVES 4

400g or so tightly formed cabbage, red, white, green or a mix, shredded
1 onion, red or white, thinly sliced
1 carrot, coarsely grated
enough mayonnaise to coat generously
salt and freshly ground black pepper

1.   Toss the vegetables together, add the mayonnaise and stir

until everything is coated.

2. Taste, season and keep in the fridge until needed.

Compound butters – how to make and use them

Garlic butter is probably the most ubiquitous of compound butters but the idea is good for all sorts of ingredients and can be used in myriad ways. Generally speaking, people think of a compound butter as savoury but sweetly flavoured butters are lovely too.

You'll find ideas for great flavour combinations throughout the A to Z.

How to do it

It's so simple to make compound butters that you can do it quickly with any small amount of suitable leftovers you might have. Just make sure that you keep a ready supply of butter in your fridge for the purpose.

1. Put softened butter into a small bowl and beat until smooth, either by hand or with a mixer.
2. Finely chop, mince or even purée additions and drain off any excess liquid.
3. Mix the flavourings with the butter in the rough proportions of one part additions to four parts butter and combine thoroughly.
4. Taste, add any further ingredients and seasonings and give it a final whisk.
5. Shape into a block or sausage and chill or freeze until needed.

For freezing

There's a good way of freezing the butter for use later. With a hot, sharp knife you can slice into the frozen butter to take out just as much as you need at any one time.

1. Spread a square of clingfilm or baking parchment onto the counter.
2. Scrape the soft and tasty butter into a sausage about 30mm from and parallel to one edge.
3. Lift that edge and use the film or parchment to roll and shape the butter into a cylinder.
4. When satisfied, roll the butter in the rest of the clingfilm and twist the ends to secure.
5. Chill or freeze until needed.

6.   Use a hot knife to slice cold or frozen butters.

Uses for compound butters

- **Baking** Use flavoured butter as the fat when rubbing in suitable recipes.
- **Croûtons** Spread compound butters on toast and you won't need any other topping. Use to make flavoured croûtons (p45) – sweet or savoury.
- **Garlic bread – and more** Cut a baguette or similar loaf into thick slices but not right through, leaving the bottom crust intact. Spread the butter on each slice. Re-assemble the loaf, wrap in foil and bake for a few minutes in a preheated oven at 200°C/gas 6. Alternatively, make individual portions of flavoured, buttery bread by spreading the butter on slices of bread and grilling until crisp and golden. It's easier and possibly more delicious than baking a whole baguette.
- **Garnish** Top meat, fish or chicken with a slice of flavoured butter just before serving or melt a knob over corn on the cob.
- **Potatoes** Fill jacket potatoes with flavoured butter or beat into mash.
- **Soups and sauces** Compound butters are sometimes referred to as finishing butters as they are used to enrich sauces by whisking in at the last minute. You could also float a slice on soup when serving.

Crumble, pastry and a versatile dough

The key to this section is the technique of rubbing in, which is how you break up the butter into the flour to create several alternatives, such as crumble topping, pastry, and my super-versatile dough which transforms into all kinds of dishes.

Rubbing in

In short, this is just rubbing flour with butter or margarine until the mixture resembles breadcrumbs. Use this technique for pastry and crumbles, as well as some biscuits and cakes. You can also do this in a food processor but it hardly seems worth the faff for a few scones or whatever. It is quick and easy and more controllable by hand.

1. Use cold fat, a cold bowl and cold hands.
2. If using butter, cut it into small pieces for easier rubbing in; margarine being softer doesn't need this.
3. Add the fat to the flour and, holding your hands a little above the bowl so that the flour and fat stay cool, airy and flaky, take small portions between your fingertips and rub lightly together until small crumbs are formed. Carry on doing this until the mixture is all crumbs.
4. Shaking the bowl occasionally will cause larger pieces of fat to rise to the surface ready for more rubbing in.

Basic Crumble Topping

This makes enough crumble to top about 750g fruit.

❄ Uncooked crumble mix freezes very well ready for next time and can be used directly from the freezer.

SERVES 4

240g plain flour
160g cold butter or margarine
120g sugar

1. Preheat the oven to 180° C/gas 4.
2. Rub in the flour and butter until the mixture resembles breadcrumbs (see Rubbing in, above).
3. Stir in the sugar.
4. Sprinkle the mixture over raw or cooked fruit.
5. Bake in the oven for about 25 minutes until the fruit is hot (and cooked, if using raw) and the crumble is golden.

- **Leftover crumble mix** Spread on a baking tray and bake in a preheated oven at 180°C/gas 4 until crisp and golden. Sprinkle over sweet dishes such as trifle or add to ice cream sundaes especially those using fruits.
- **Sugary additions** Ingredients such as fudge, toffee or amaretti will tend to cook faster than the rest of the crumble so to stop them burning, cover with a layer of plain crumble to protect from the direct heat.

Shortcrust Pastry

For how to rub in, when making this easy and basic pastry, see above (or pages 289– 90).

1. Rub together twice as much plain flour as cold butter.
2. Mix in icy cold water a little at a time until the dough holds together – you need 2– 3 tbsp water for 225g flour. Everything I have ever read says to use a cold knife for this but I have always used my fingers. Too little water and the dough will be too crumbly, too much and it will be hard when cooked.
3. Gently form into a ball, wrap in clingfilm and let it rest in the fridge for a quarter of an hour before using.

Dough – a simple and versatile recipe

I first focused my mind on this basic, flexible dough when I met my 'love interest', who is a Geordie lad (from Newcastle in the north-east of England). He described to me 'Singin' Hinnies', a local dish, a sort of scone, often fruited, cooked in a pan on top of the stove. Traditionally they were cooked in animal fat, preferably lamb oddly enough, and the sound of the fat melting on the griddle made a singing sound. 'Hinnie' is a Northumbrian term of endearment as, apparently, is 'fatty', 'poopants' and 'you big woofus'.

Basic Dough

This very simple dough, sometimes with a few minor additions or adjustments, can be used to make a surprisingly humungous variety of other dishes: scones, shortcakes and American biscuits, cobblers and slumps, a very short crumbly crust, dumplings and doughnuts.

225g self-raising flour or plain flour
1 tsp baking powder, if using plain flour
1–2 pinches of salt
50g cold butter or margarine
80ml milk

1. Stir together the flour, salt and baking powder, if using.
2. Rub in the fat (see Rubbing in).
3. Add the milk and mix in, by hand is easiest, to make a soft dough.
4. Add a little more milk if too dry or a little more flour if too wet – it should be soft but not sticky. Lightly knead a few times to bring it together.

Singin' Hinnies

Make a basic dough mix (above) and add a handful of dried fruit (optional)

1. Mix the dried fruit into the dough, if you wish.
2. On a floured surface, press the dough into a rough circle about 1cm thick and cut into wedges.
3. Lightly grease a frying pan with a lid and heat over a high heat.
4. Lay the hinnies in the pan, turn the heat down to moderate and cover.
5. Check after a few minutes. They should be risen and have brown spots on the bottom.
6. Gently turn them and finish cooking uncovered. This keeps the first side crisp.
7. Serve warm, split and buttered.

Sweet Scones or American Biscuits

basic dough mix (opposite)
1 tbsp caster sugar

1. Add the sugar to the dough after rubbing the fat into the flour. You could add it before; it is a little uncomfortable on the hands although it does exfoliate!
2. Preheat the oven to 200°C/gas 6.
3. On a floured surface, press or roll the dough to about 2cm thick and cut into rounds.
4. Transfer to a greased baking tray, brush the tops with a little milk and bake in the oven until risen and golden – about 20 minutes.
5. Cool on a rack for a few minutes before eating.

Cheese Scones

Add about 50g of grated cheese to the basic dough mixture and cook as you would sweet scones.

Cobblers, pie crusts and slumps

- **Cobblers** These can be sweet or savoury. Make scones as above and lay them on top of a warm pie filling. It is important that the filling is already warm, as by the time a cold filling had warmed up your cobblers would be overdone. Brush with milk, sprinkle with sugar, if appropriate, and bake in a preheated oven at 200°C/gas 6 until hot, risen and golden.
- **Pie crusts** A natural progression from cobblers is to roll the dough a little thinner and use as a crust. It is very short and crumbly so fragile when handling but if you do mess up and make a hole, just smidge a bit of dough over to mend it. Rustic!
- **Slumps** These are similar to cobblers but make the dough somewhat wetter so that it can be spooned onto the filling. Fruit slumps are the norm.

Doughnuts

Roll the dough into balls and deep-fry until golden and crunchy. Drain on kitchen paper, put a little sugar in a bowl and shake this doughnuts in this to coat.

Dumplings

These should be cooked in a delicious stew. Roll the dough into about a dozen walnut-sized balls. Drop them, spaced out a bit so they don't touch, into the already simmering stew. Turn down the heat, cover the pan and cook for about 20 minutes until the dumplings are risen and firm. Uncover and simmer for a couple more minutes to dry out their tops.

Eggs

Baked eggs – aka Oeufs en cocotte

To bake an egg, simply butter a ramekin, break in the egg, season, pour over a spoonful of cream, and bake in an oven preheated to 180°C/gas 4 for 18–20 minutes until the egg white is set and the yolk isn't. You can vary and enhance a baked egg in many ways.

- **Buttering the ramekin** Use a compound butter (p288) to grease the ramekin.
- **Hide something underneath** Put an interesting leftover into the ramekin before adding the egg: a spoonful of leftover soup or casserole, sautéed mushrooms, cooked meat or fish, a little pâté and so on and so forth. Season creatively to suit your ingredients.
- **Vary the topping** Replace the cream with crème fraîche, Alfredo or other creamy or non-creamy sauce. Sprinkle with cheese and/or buttery crumbs.

Boiled eggs

Although eggs can easily be boiled by plunging them into boiling water, I think it is easier to do them right this way.

1. Bring your eggs to room temperature. This is for two reasons: firstly they can be more accurately timed and secondly they are less likely to crack.

2. Put them in a pan of cold water to cover by about 1cm.
3. Bring to the boil, then turn down the heat and simmer for the following times:
   – Very soft boiled: 3 minutes
   – Soft boiled: 4 minutes
   – Semi-firm yolks: 5 minutes
   – Hard boiled: 8 minutes.

- **To cool boiled eggs** Submerge them immediately in cold water; any delay can result in a grey edge to the yolks.
- **To peel boiled eggs** Wait until they are completely cold then roll gently on the counter top to crack the surface and loosen the membrane. I use the handle of a teaspoon to then lift the pieces of shell from the egg.

Fried eggs

Before I worked in the Caribbean, where there is a strong American influence, I didn't realise there was a lot of choice so far as fried eggs were concerned. Simply put, you either had a fried egg or you didn't. Clever American chaps, however, have identified several grades of fried egg from sunny-side up and over-easy to basted and over-hard!

- **To fry an egg** Break it into the middle of 1 tbsp hot oil or butter. Cook over a medium heat for about a minute until the white is white and then do one of the following:
  Sunny-side up serve as soon as the white around the yolk looks cooked.
  Basted when the white looks pretty well cooked splash the hot fat over the yolk until it assumes a glazed look.
  Over-easy carefully flip the egg, yolk side down, cook for about 5 nanoseconds and then serve.
  Over-hard As above but cook that way until the yolk is firm.

Frittatas

A frittata is a substantial relative of the omelette made by first frying leftovers and then pouring over the beaten egg.

Frittata

Cut into wedges and serve hot, warm or cold.

1 tbsp oil or butter
1 onion, chopped
leftover potatoes, and/or other suitable leftovers
salt and freshly ground black pepper
5–6 eggs
about 50g cheese, grated (optional)

1. Heat the oil or butter in a frying pan and fry the onion gently until soft.
2. If adding leftover potatoes, increase the heat and add these now, crushing them slightly, and cook until they start to colour and go crisp. Add a little more oil or butter as necessary. Now add any other cooked ingredients and mix into the potatoes, taste and adjust the seasoning. Turn down the heat.
3. Whisk together the eggs and pour them over everything else.
4. Preheat the grill.
5. Cook the frittata gently for a few minutes until the bottom is set but the top still moist.
6. Sprinkle with grated cheese, if using, and slide under the grill until melted and a little golden.

Omelettes

Omelettes are not as difficult to make as we have been led to believe; in fact they are quite easy. This is how to make an omelette for one person and as you should always make an omelette for just one person, this is all the information you need. For additional people, make additional omelettes, they only take a minute or two and work out much better than trying to double up ingredients.

- **Fillings** You can add pretty well anything to the middle of an omelette, remembering to pre-warm most fillings first (not cheese) as the filled omelette will only be over the heat for a few seconds.

Omelette

SERVES 1

2–3 fresh eggs
salt and freshly ground black pepper
a knob of butter
fillings of your choice

1. Break the eggs into a bowl. Season and lightly beat together just to break the whites into the yolks, there is no need to whisk until fully amalgamated.
2. Melt the knob of butter in a 24cm or thereabouts non-stick pan. When the butter has melted and starts to foam, swirl it about the pan and pour in the eggs.
3. Allow to sit over the heat for a few seconds and when you see the edges start to solidify gently lift them with a spatula, tilt the pan and encourage the runny egg on top to flow to the side of the pan and under the cooked egg.
4. Keep doing this until the top of the omelette is merely moist.
5. Add any fillings and fold one half of the omelette over the other.
6. Slide onto a warm plate.

Poached Eggs

I don't think I have mentioned poached eggs much in the A to Z but feel it would be rude not to include them here. By the way, a poached egg is not, strictly speaking, cooked in a little cup in or above water – that is a steamed egg. For real poached eggs this is what you do.

1. Bring about 7.5cm depth of salted water to a gently rolling boil in a small pan.
2. Break your eggs into the water.
3. After 3 minutes, the eggs should be cooked with firm whites and runny yolks.
4. Lift out with a slotted spoon, allow to steam and lay them on kitchen paper to drain for a few seconds.

5. Serve on buttered toast or smoked haddock or whatever you have planned.

- **Break into a cup** If you are nervous about breaking the eggs directly into the water, break them into cups first and then slide into the water.
- **To hold poached eggs for later use** Submerge them in cold water as soon as they are cooked and leave them there until needed. Reheat briefly in simmering water.
- **Use fresh eggs** It is imperative that you use fresh eggs, the fresher the better. Older eggs will break up and disperse in the water, whereas fresh eggs with their firm whites will hold their shape.
- **Vinegar** Some people add a little vinegar to the water which helps them hold together and has a tenderising effect on the whites but I rarely bother with it.

Scrambled eggs

It is absolutely essential than any intended accompaniments to the eggs, buttered toast for instance, are ready before you start scrambling. This is how I scramble eggs.

1. Melt a generous knob of butter over a medium heat in a small pan, non-stick preferably for washing up reasons.
2. Break two or three eggs directly into the partly melted butter and immediately stir the two together.
3. Season and stir constantly over a low-ish heat.
4. As the eggs cook and solidify, fold them into the uncooked egg till you have a pan of softly cooked scrambled eggs.
5. Stir in a little more cold butter or cream simply because this will stop the eggs continuing to cook, any added deliciousness is purely incidental. Serve immediately. Sometimes I add so much butter I call these 'buttered eggs' on menus so that diners have been forewarned!

HANDY HINT

Interestingly a study by Mindlab on behalf of the British Egg Industry Council has recently revealed a relationship between one's egg preference and one's lifestyle and personality. For instance they discovered that the average poached egg eater is likely to have two children, although they did not say whether this was before or after eating the egg.

How to freeze fruit, simple syrup, sorbet and granita

Freezing Fruit
Raw fruit is best frozen with sugar and there are two ways to do this. Either way, freeze in freezer bags or airtight containers.

- **Coat with sugar** Toss the prepared fruit in about a quarter of their weight in caster sugar (but taste the fruit and vary accordingly) before freezing.
- **Make a light syrup** Dissolve sugar in about twice as much water, cool and then toss with the prepared fruit.

Simple syrup
A simple syrup is made by simply boiling together equal parts of sugar and water till the sugar has dissolved or melted or whatever it does, I'm never sure. Cool till needed.

Sorbet
Purée your chosen fruits, measure the result and mix with an equal quantity of chilled simple syrup. Freeze in an ice cream machine or pour into a pre-chilled container and put in the freezer. If using the second method, every half hour or so visit the sorbet and stir or mash the frozen edges into the middle, this is important to give a good smooth texture. If you don't this you will get a solid lump.

- **Give it a kick** If you are moved to add alcohol, such as a spot of rum with tropical fruits, remember that this will inhibit freezing and make the sorbet softer so be abstemious.
- **Pick the best of the bunch** Use only good-quality fruit; nothing bruised or starting to go over-ripe.
- **Smooth or crunchy** Strain out seeds if you wish and you'll have a smooth sorbet or leave them in for a bit of crunch.
- **Spice it up** Herbs and spices can be infused into the syrup during cooling and puréed into the fruit or they can be added to the final mix.
- **Sweet or sour** Taste before freezing bearing in mind that flavours are muted when very cold. If too sweet, add a squeeze of citrus juice such as orange with strawberry or lime with papaya.

Granita

If you are not too assiduous with stirring and mashing your sorbet during freezing the result will be larger ice crystals and you will have to call it a granita!

Fruit coulis and fools

A coulis is a simple purée of fruits, or sometimes vegetables, served as a sauce, garnish or as part of a fool. The easiest coulis to make are those of soft summer fruits such as raspberries, strawberries and mango. Other fruits such as rhubarb, peaches, gooseberries and even blueberries are better cooked first with a few spoonfuls of water then strained, sweetened and cooled.

Simply purée the fruit in whatever manner you find best (liquidiser, processor or through a sieve), strain and sweeten to taste.

Fruit Coulis

300g soft summer fruits
about 150g sugar
few drops of lemon or other citrus juice (optional)
a little liqueur (optional)

1. Wash and prepare the fruits, removing stems, stones and whatnot.
2. Crush, mash, liquidise or process with the sugar. Taste and adjust the sweetness, adding a little citrus juice or liqueur to brighten the flavour.
3. Strain out pips or seeds.

Fool

This is so easy – fold the above amount of coulis into 200g double cream, whipped until thick.

For variations, keep back a little coulis and marble through the fool for extra prettiness or use a contrasting coulis such as peach fool with raspberry ripple. Fold in a few whole fruit. Fold in crushed meringues and call it a Mess.

Hummus bi Tahini

There are numerous recipes for this Middle Eastern dip but they all contain chickpeas, garlic, tahini (sesame seed paste), olive oil and lemon juice. Common additions include cumin, black pepper and cayenne.

SERVES 4

225g cooked chickpeas
60g tahini
2 garlic cloves
60ml olive oil
juice of 1 lemon
a little warm water
salt and freshly ground black pepper to taste

1. Process together the first five ingredients to a coarse purée.
2. Gradually process in enough warm water to give a good soft dipping texture.
3. Taste and season, chill until needed; it may thicken slightly.

Muesli, granola and trail mix

Muesli and granola are very similar and yet very different. They are both made of oats mixed with nuts, seeds, and dried fruit but whereas muesli is served raw soaked in milk, yoghurt or fruit juice, granola is tossed with sugars and syrups and baked until crunchy – less healthy and more yummy. You can see that the basic 'recipes' are open to huge variation and are perfect vehicles for leftovers in the fruity, nutty, seedy department.

Muesli

300g rolled, flaked or porridge oats
200g nuts and seeds – whatever type you like
200g dried fruit – again, whatever you like, but chop larger fruits into
manageable pieces
healthy stuff – oat bran, wheat bran, wheat germ etc. at your discretion
unhealthy stuff – by which I mainly mean sugar and will depend on what
fruits are used and what liquid you intend using. I think light brown sugar
is best for muesli
salt, a pinch of which will bring out the sweetness of the dish

1. Mix everything together and store in an airtight container
where it will be fine for at least several weeks.
2. To eat, moisten with milk or yoghurt or fruit juice at bedtime,
soak overnight and eat in the morning.

Granola

For granola you need a similar selection of similar ingredients in
similar proportions to muesli above, plus:

140ml maple syrup or honey or a mixture
2 tbsp vegetable oil
1 tsp vanilla extract

1. Preheat the oven to 150°C/gas 2.
2. Mix together the above ingredients, add the oats, nuts and
seeds and toss to coat well.
3. Spread the mixture onto greased baking trays and cook for
about 30 minutes, stirring occasionally and breaking up
lumps.
4. Add the dried fruits and healthy stuff and return to the oven
for a further 15 minutes.
5. Break up any clumps and cool completely before storing in an
airtight container.

- **Trail mix** This is just any combination of nuts, dried fruits (chocolate covered or otherwise), seeds, grains and cereals that would be nice to take on a walk.

Onions and leeks – the best way to cook, in my opinion

This is the way I most often cook onions; it concentrates the flavour and makes them sweet and very tender. Use these as the basis of many dishes – from onion soup to bread sauce – or add to sandwiches, burgers, steaks or pizza.

Leeks are also good cooked this way but cook for just 20 minutes. I rarely caramelise them. Stir them into risottos, cream sauces, fishcakes, mashed potatoes or Alfredo sauce.

❄ They keep well in the fridge for a couple of days and are a useful standby so don't worry about cooking too many.

Onions and Leeks

PER ONION

15g butter OR 1 tbsp vegetable oil (healthier and still delicious)
1 onion, peeled, halved and thinly sliced (or a leek prepared as on p156)
pinch of salt

1. Heat the butter or oil in a small pan with a lid and toss and separate the sliced onions or leek in the fat to coat. Sprinkle with a little salt.
2. Press a piece of foil, baking parchment, greaseproof paper or a butter wrapper directly onto the onions to cover them completely.
3. Turn the heat down to low and put the lid on the pan. The onions should not so much fry in the butter or oil as gently steam in it.
4. Cook gently for about 20–30 minutes until they are soft enough to cut with the edge of a wooden spoon, stirring once or twice during cooking.
5. Cooked this way, the onions will be soft and delicious, and

quite sweet because the cooking has released their natural sugars. To enhance this sweetness, remove the lid when the onions are completely soft, turn up the heat and cook on high for a few minutes, stirring constantly, until they begin to caramelise and just start sticking on the bottom of the pan.

Potatoes

As I refer throughout the A to Z to mashed, scalloped and baked potatoes, I thought I might as well give a few tips.

Mashed Potatoes

Use floury potatoes such as King Edward, Maris Piper or Russet.

1. Peel and cut into similar-sized pieces. Don't make the pieces too big; there's no point in wasting time and energy waiting longer than necessary for them to cook.
2. Put the potatoes in a saucepan with enough cold lightly salted water to cover by a depth of about 1cm.
3. Bring to the boil over a high heat, then turn down the heat, partially cover with a lid and simmer until completely tender, which takes about 20 minutes or a bit more depending on the size of the pieces and the type of potato.
4. Drain thoroughly, return the potatoes to the hot pan and leave to steam, uncovered, for 1–2 minutes.
5. Add a knob of butter and a splash of milk or cream, cover and set aside for 5 minutes, which makes the potatoes mash more easily.
6. Mash the potatoes but don't go on for ages or they'll become gluey.

Scalloped Potatoes

Also known as Pommes Dauphinoise, there are numerous versions
of this classic recipe to be found but I have always made it quite
simply. You can also sprinkle the top with cheese or cheese mixed
with buttered crumbs for the last 15 minutes of cooking, although
this is not the classic style.

a generous knob of butter
1kg potatoes, peeled and thinly sliced
salt and freshly ground black pepper
400ml cream and/or milk (or a mixture of the two in any proportions but
obviously the creamier the better!)
1 garlic clove

1. Preheat the oven to 180°C/gas 4.
2. Butter a shallow ovenproof dish or roasting tin.
3. Layer up the potatoes in the dish, lightly seasoning each layer
   as you go.
4. Meanwhile, bring the milk, cream and garlic clove just to
   boiling point.
5. Discard the garlic, then pour the hot cream mixture over the
   potatoes and shake the pan to encourage it to filter down
   between the layers.
6. Cover with a piece of buttered foil and bake in the oven for
   1– 1 ½ hours until tender.
7. Remove the foil and return to the oven for further 15 minutes
   until the top is golden.

Jacket or Baked Potatoes

The first thing I want to say here is that if you wrap your potatoes in foil before baking, they are steamed potatoes, not baked, as are potatoes cooked in the microwave. Furthermore this totally ruins the skin.

The best potatoes to bake have a floury texture, such as Maris Piper, Russet or King Edward and it is usual to cook larger potatoes this way.

1. Preheat the oven to 220°C/gas 7.
2. Wash and dry the potatoes.
3. For a crisp skin, rub lightly with olive oil and then sea salt.
4. To stop them bursting, prick all over with a fork.
5. Place on a baking tray or directly onto the oven rack and bake until the skin is crisp and the potato gives slightly when squeezed. This depends on the size of the potatoes but an hour is about average.

Risotto

I loved making risotto when I cooked professionally because I could stand by the stove with a coffee (maybe even a 'chef's coffee' – see Wine) and a book and have a little 'me time' as long as I kept stirring.

- **Additions** Some ingredients, such as garlic, are best cooked in with the onion at the start of the risotto so they can soften and cook; others, spring vegetables or crispy bacon, smoked or cooked fish, for instance, are better prepared separately and stirred in at the end because they only need to be warmed through.
- **Don't wash the rice before cooking** Its starchiness is what makes the dish special.
- **Use unsalted stock** The stock will reduce and strengthen in flavour so don't use anything too salty.
- **Warm the wine** They do say that the wine should be warmed before it is added as cold wine will shock the rice and make it flaky.

Basic Risotto

1 small onion, finely chopped
2 tbsp olive oil or butter
additions such as chopped garlic, sliced mushrooms
400g risotto rice, such as Arborio or Carnaroli
1 small glass of wine, usually dry white but red works too
1.2 litres vegetable or chicken stock, which should be simmering gently
with the lid on
salt and freshly ground black pepper
additions such as crispy vegetables
Parmesan cheese, freshly grated, to taste
a knob of butter or a spoonful of cream or crème fraîche

1. Gently cook the onion in the oil or butter in a large pot until tender.
2. At this stage, add garlic or mushrooms or any other early additions.
3. Stir in the rice and continue cooking and stirring for 7–8 minutes until it looks translucent.
4. Add the wine and cook, stirring, until absorbed.
5. Add a ladleful of hot stock and continue to cook, stir, absorb, add more and so on until the rice is just tender with a little bite in the middle (*al dente*) and is coated in creamy sauce. This will take about 20 minutes.
6. Stir in any other additions until heated through and then the Parmesan and maybe a knob of butter or a little cream.

Smoothies and milkshakes

At first thought these would seem to be very similar but think again: smoothies are perceived as being good for you whereas milkshakes are not!

Smoothies

The definition of 'smoothie' seems to be open to interpretation; generally speaking, it is a blended drink made of fruits and/or vegetables together with milk, yoghurt, fruit juice or other liquid and ice so it's difficult to give a definitive recipe. The liquid could also be chocolate milk, buttermilk, coconut milk, tea, coffee or even water. Put it into the liquidiser or processor first so that the blades don't get stuck in the fruits.
Follow the below guidelines.

❄ Most leftover smoothies can be frozen for later.

- **Additions** You can choose anything you like to complement your chosen fruits: chocolate sauce, peanut butter, a shot of strong coffee, a pinch of spice. A drop of vanilla extract is often a good addition, a drop of rum a naughty one.
- **Fruit** Add about the same quantity of whatever fruit you like as the liquid, cut into manageable pieces and, if time allows, frozen for a thicker and, of course, colder smoothie. Bananas are very popular because they give a rich, creamy texture to the drink.
- **Healthy variations** Nuts, seeds, green tea or supplements can all be added to boost the goodness of a smoothie.
- **Ice** It is better by far to make your smoothie using frozen fruit as this makes for a richer drink and is easier on the blades of your liquidiser, but if you must use fresh fruit, add a couple of ice cubes to cool it down.
- **Purée** Blend everything together until smooth. You can use a stick blender, but a special smoothie maker will work faster and probably last longer, if you make a lot of smoothies.
- **Sweeteners** Depending on the fruit used, the smoothie may be sweet enough but if not add honey, maple syrup, simple syrup or sugar to taste.
- **Vegetables** Good smoothie contenders include pumpkin and avocado.

Milkshakes

A milkshake is approximately one part milk and two parts ice cream blended together. If it's too thick, add more milk; if it's too runny add more ice cream. Obviously with the plethora of ice cream flavours available and all the potential additions, the possibilities are endless. A simple but delicious milkshake could comprise vanilla (or 'plain') ice cream and milk with perhaps a drop or two of vanilla extract but anything you can add to a smoothie you can add to a milkshake.

As milkshakes are not intended to be healthy, maybe add a sweet liqueur for adult milkshakes and/or whipped cream and sprinkles.

Soup – 'normal' soup recipe for every day

Years ago, I used to make this very basic soup: just onions, potatoes and stock. Occasionally I would get all exotic and add grated carrot and courgettes. For some reason, I always called this 'normal' soup. After a while I started to experiment even beyond the carrots and courgettes – if you can imagine such a thing – and now I would say about 80 per cent of the soups I make derive from this one simple recipe. Nobody ever seems to mind or even to notice.

Normal Soup

This quantity makes enough soup for four people as an appetiser or two to three as a meal in a bowl, depending on what additions you add and how hungry you all are.

about 500g onions, thinly sliced
30g butter OR 2 tbsp olive oil
2 large floury potatoes, peeled and thinly sliced
stock or water and stock cubes, as required
salt and freshly ground black pepper

1. Cook the onions as on page 303.
2. When really tender, add the potatoes and enough water or stock just to cover the top of the potatoes. You may need more liquid to finish the soup but it's best not to use more than necessary at this point – it's less splashy when mashing.

3. Bring to the boil, then turn down the heat, cover with the lid and cook until utterly tender.
4. Taste and season and stir in crumbled stock cubes, if necessary, until delicious. I find that if I add the stock cubes before the potatoes are cooked, they don't get truly tender.
5. At this stage there are a few options:
   – Leave as it is for a chunky effect.
   – Mash the potato into the stock to achieve a rustic sort of texture.
   – Use a hand blender; this is a good choice as it doesn't make much washing up. Put through a food processor to produce a purée.
6. Put through a liquidiser for a sophisticated smooth finish.
7. In all cases, dilute to your ideal soup consistency with more water, stock, milk, cream or liquid of your choice, then taste and adjust the seasoning.

Stir-frying tips

Stir-frying is not difficult but does need to be done properly for best results.

1. **Be prepared** Have everything utterly, utterly ready before you start stir-frying. Finely chop aromatics such as garlic, chilli and ginger. Cut all the rest of the ingredients to uniform bite-sized pieces that will cook quickly and be easy to pick up with chopsticks! Raw meats should be cut into thin strips across the grain as this will make them tender. All ingredients should be at room temperature so they cook quickly. Have all your flavourings – soy sauce, chilli sauce, chopped nuts, herbs, and so on – to hand.
2. **Heat your pan** This should be a wok or a large, high-sided, well-seasoned frying pan (if using a non-stick pan, go easy on the preheating as this may damage the surface).
3. **Add the oil and meat** Add a spoonful of oil and then the raw meat and aromatics. Some people add the aromatics first but I am always scared they will burn! If cooking a lot of meat, do so in small batches otherwise it won't so much fry as steam in its own juice. Sear the meat over a high heat, then remove from the pan and set aside.

4. **Add the long-cook vegetables** Now add onions and any other long-cooking veg such as carrots. Stir over medium high heat for a 1–2 minutes.
5. **Add the tender vegetables** Add broccoli, cauliflower and green beans and carry on stir-frying for another minute.
6. **Add the final vegetables** Next add fast-cooking leafy veg and mushrooms and toss quickly until just cooked.
7. **Finish the dish** Stir in cooked meat or fish (either leftovers or set aside above) and cooked rice or noodles. Toss everything around in the pan until hot then add sauces (soy sauce, rice wine vinegar, chilli sauce etc.), nuts, seeds and herbs. Serve immediately.

Vinaigrettes and marinades

Simple, classic vinaigrette is made by mixing together three parts oil to one part vinegar and seasoning with salt and pepper, so that's easy. Quite often, a spoonful of Dijon or wholegrain mustard is added as this emulsifies the dressing, adds flavour and is quite an improvement all round. Different vinegars can be used. Balsamic is lovely, as is sherry vinegar, and citrus juices or wine are good alternatives.

Additional flavourings can include finely chopped onion, shallot or garlic, herbs, spices or cheese, although protein and vegetable additions shorten its shelf life.

The dressing can be made using a liquidiser, a whisk or by shaking in a jam jar, which is a really good idea if you have a mustard jar with just a little left in it.

Basic Vinaigrette

Unadulterated, this dressing should keep indefinitely in the fridge, but if you include perishable additions, use it fairly quickly. It may separate but a good whisk or shake will bring it all back together.

1 tsp Dijon mustard
2 tbsp vinegar
6 tbsp olive or other good vegetable oil
salt and freshly ground black pepper
pinch of sugar or drop of honey (optional)

1. Blend, whisk or shake together the mustard and vinegar.
2. Gradually, a little at a time, whisk or shake in the oil.
3. Taste and season with salt and pepper. I often add a pinch of sugar or a drop of honey to round out the flavour.

Marinades

A marinade can add flavour to meat, keep it juicy whilst cooking and, to an extent, tenderise it. The basic components are so similar to those of a vinaigrette they are pretty well interchangeable. Here are a few more guidelines.

- **Flavourings** Once you have the basic oil and acid mixture you can add flavourings to complement the meat, poultry or fish to be marinated and the style of dish: for example, fresh coriander, chilli, a pinch of cumin and lime juice for a Mexican-ish marinade; or perhaps mint and garlic for lamb; or add a little brown sugar to beef marinades. Be creative.
- **Freezer bags** A sealable freezer bag is just about the best container in which to marinate things; squeeze out the air and the marinade will be pressed up against the meat, it will take up less space in the fridge and you can, if you like, throw the bag away afterwards rather than wash up! Any sealable non-reactive container, however, will suffice.
- **Marinating time** Obviously, the longer you marinate something, the stronger the flavour will be, within reason, but there's more to it than that! Another no-brainer is that thicker pieces of meat will take longer than thinner. Meats can take

the longest of all to marinate, poultry somewhat less but is quite robust too. The most important thing to remember is that fish should only be marinated for a short while – 30 minutes or so – or the acid will 'cook' the flesh and it will fall apart. Of course, this can be put to advantage when making Ceviche which, as it should not be made from leftovers, is not mentioned in this book.

- **Overnight** It is often said to marinate overnight but overday is just as good. Prepare the meat and marinade at breakfast time and then the meat is ready to cook at dinner time.
- **Throw it away** Never re-use marinade as it will have been contaminated by the raw meat or fish.

Your Storecupboard

I keep a very well stocked storecupboard, although I admit that some of it is pure indulgence on my part – I realise it is not essential to have maple sugar, truffle salt and balsamic jelly! I shall try here to be more realistic. These are my suggestions but you know your own habits and preferences. It may that you eat a lot of fish and chips at home so that malt vinegar is an essential or perhaps you love cream teas and always have clotted cream to hand. So these are just my opinions for you to personalise however it suits you. Under each category, ingredients are listed as being, in my opinion: essential, very useful, nice to have extras, personal peccadilloes.

Throughout the book I make frequent reference to alcohol. Whilst I cannot claim to be a full-on dipsomaniac having always worked in licensed premises with ready access to liquor, I always consider it as another useful ingredient. Out of the vast choice available domestically I have red and medium dry white wine and brandy or rum. It is not, however, worth keeping wine for cooking unless you are prepared to drink it too because it doesn't keep well.

Baking

Essential
- Baking powder
- Flour, plain
- Flour, self-raising – if you do a lot of baking but alternatively add 1 tsp baking powder to each 200g plain flour

Very useful
- Cocoa powder
- Yeast, dried active yeast

Nice to have extras
- Bicarbonate of soda – but I rarely use it
- Cornflour – and I rarely use this too
- Flours, wholewheat and other speciality

Canned goods and alternatives

Essential
- Anchovies in oil or salt
- Ginger, garlic, chilli pastes or purées if not storing fresh
- Beans – a good multi-purpose bean such as cannellini
- Chickpeas – canned or in a carton
- Coconut milk
- Diced or chopped tomatoes – these sometimes come in a carton
- Tomato paste – actually I prefer this in a tube
- Tuna fish in oil

Cheese

Essential
- Mature Cheddar
- Parmesan or Gran Padano

Very useful
- Hard blue – maybe keep a piece in the freezer

Condiments, tracklements and sauces

Essential
- Creamed coconut
- Mayonnaise – you know the brand I mean, or something similar. I use Light and can tell little difference
- Dijon mustard
- Soy sauce

Very useful
- Cranberry sauce
- Curry paste – easier to use than curry powder, choose one that you like, obviously!
- Hot sauce or Tabasco

Nice to have extras

- Gherkins
- Olives
- Horseradish sauce
- Whole grain mustard
- Sweet chilli sauce
- Tomato ketchup
- Tomato pasta sauce – I always keep a jar of ready-made pasta sauce (in my case with chilli in it) which I use for many things from brightening up a sandwich to a quick pizza sauce, mixing into dips and dressings, stirring into soups and so on
- Worcestershire sauce

My personal peccadilloes

- *Balsamic glaze – I use this as a kind of glorified ketchup to enhance cheeses, pâtés, salads and dips*
- *Black garlic – I only mention this because it is wonderful. Like a dried fruit version of garlic; sweet, soft and caramelly, it can be eaten straight out the packet and goes marvellously well with blue cheese plus other things too*
- *Caramelised red onion marmalade – for cheese and also good stirred into gravies*
- *Chilli pickle – which I use in all sorts of dishes*

Fats and oils

Essential

- Butter – I know this is unorthodox advice but I only buy salted butter because a bit of salt goes well in most things, including sweet dishes. Just remember to season accordingly
- Unsalted butter – if you do a lot of baking or things with anchovies!
- Vegetable cooking oil – I use light olive oil

Very useful

- Salad oil – for instance, extra virgin olive oil

Nice to have extras

- Goose fat – for roasting potatoes
- Lard
- Margarine
- Nut oils
- Sesame oil – don't fry in it, just add a drop to dishes

Milk and eggs

Essential
- Eggs
- Milk – your choice of full fat, semi skimmed or skimmed – or even goat or soy

Very useful
- Double cream
- Yoghurt, plain

Nice to have extras
- Clotted cream
- Crème fraîche
- Soured cream

Frozen foods

Essential
- Collections of bread, beef, game and fish scraps
- Ice cubes
- Peas
- Puff pastry
- Vanilla ice cream

Fruit and vegetables

Essential
- Lemons
- Large floury potatoes

- Onions
- Tomatoes

Very useful
- Carrots
- Celery
- Chillies – fresh, frozen or lazy paste
- Dried herbs – I don't approve of many dried herbs but the following are okay – whole bay leaves, oregano, sage
- Fresh herbs, growing if possible – basil, chives, coriander, mint, parsley, rosemary
- Garlic – fresh or lazy paste
- Ginger root – fresh, frozen or lazy paste
- Red onions

Meats

Essential
- Bacon
- Ham – air dried not only for flavour but it has a good shelf life

My personal peccadillo
- *Chorizo*

Miscellaneous

Essential
- Coffee
- Tea

Preserves and spreads
Very useful

- Bovril or Marmite – these are good for adding flavour and can be substituted for beef stock cubes
- Jam – a good all-purpose fruit such as strawberry

- Peanut butter – not organic or homemade as these are not good for cooking purposes

Nice to have extras
- Marmalade

My personal peccadillo

- *Black treacle or molasses*

Pulses, nuts, dried fruit and seeds

Essential
- Dates
- Mixed dried fruit

Very useful
- Dried cranberries, cherries and other fancy stuff
- Split red lentils or split peas
- Nuts – whichever would be most useful to you; I always keep pecans and salted cashews
- Panko crumbs
- Seeds

Nice to have extras
- Desiccated coconut
- Cornmeal

Rice, pasta and grains

Essential
- Dried pasta – I keep a robust pasta (usually penne) and a fine one (tagliatelle) and if I want a tiny one I break up the tagliatelle. I don't recommend quick cook pasta as it goes too soft too quickly
- Rice – basmati and risotto rice

Very useful
- Noodles
- Oats

Nice to have extras
- Barley
- Couscous
- Quinoa
- Brown rice
- Wild rice

Seasonings and spices

Essential
- Bouillon cubes – I usually keep beef and veg, I don't bother with chicken as a) it is easy to make and b) veg stock works well for me instead
- Capers
- Chilli flakes
- Whole black peppercorns – in a grinder
- Crunchy sea salt
- Table salt
- Vanilla extract – the real thing, **not** vanilla essence which may contain vanilla extract but will be partially or entirely synthetic

Very useful
- Cardamom
- Cinnamon sticks
- Ground cinnamon
- Cloves
- Ground coriander
- Ground cumin
- Ground ginger
- Mustard powder
- Paprika and/or Smoked paprika
- Vanilla pods

Sugars and syrups

Essential
- Clear honey
- Brown sugar – for this I would recommend soft light brown as the most flexible
- White sugar – I usually just buy caster sugar as it stands in fine for granulated

Very useful
- Golden syrup
- Icing sugar – if you will be doing a lot of cake icing
- Maple syrup
- Soft dark brown sugar – this is necessary for Sticky Toffee Sauce (p56)

Vinegars

Essential
- Balsamic vinegar
- Cider vinegar – which doubles up as white wine vinegar
- Red wine vinegar

Very useful
- Sherry vinegar

Nice to have extras
- Malt vinegar

Wine and Spirits

Essential
- Red wine
- Medium or dry white wine
- Brandy and/or rum

Storage tips

- **Chilling leftovers** Cool leftovers as quickly as possible before chilling.
- **Empty tins** Don't leave unused tinned food in its tin – once opened put it in a covered container in the fridge.
- **Freeze in ice cube trays** It is useful to freeze liquids and sauces in ice cube trays so that you can take just what you need, in small quantities.
- **Fridge temperature** Keep the fridge at below 5°C.
- **Raw meat** Store raw meat and fish at the bottom of the fridge where it is coolest and where they can't drip on other things.
- **Seal** Always re-seal open packets with clips or clothes pegs or transfer the contents to airtight containers to keep them fresh.
- **Separate ripe fruit** When ripe, many fresh fruits give out a gas called ethylene which hastens the ripening of other fruits so either avoid this effect by keeping them separate or utilise it by putting unripe fruit in a paper bag with ripe fruit.

Best-before dates – a short rant

I really don't want to encourage anyone to take risks with their food but would nevertheless like to moan on a bit about 'best-before' dates. Whilst I am, of course, as delighted as the next person by a bargain, I am also often irritated.

Fruits and vegetables have sometimes not reached their 'best after' date when being offered as past their prime. I have bought out of date 'ripen at home' avocadoes that weren't soft for weeks, I once lost a bargain white cabbage in the car when bringing in the shopping and it was still okay when I found it there ten days later (it was cold out) and I even snapped up a healthy growing basil plant with roots for 10p because it was 'past its best-before date'!

Cheese is another case in point. Bearing in mind that it was developed as a way to preserve milk and that many cheeses improve over time, I was surprised last Christmas to see small gift Cheddars, coated in wax, which were supposedly out of date by 9 January. Why? What would happen then? And don't get me started on honey!

'Are best-before dates a cunning ruse to make nervous people throw food away and buy more?' I ask myself cynically. According to the UK Department of Fishing and Rural Affairs, these dates indicate how long a food can be expected to retain its optimal condition, and yet in my own experience many bargains have not even reached optimal condition by that date. May I therefore suggest that you rely on your own brain and your senses of smell and taste?

Use-by dates

'Use-by' dates are an entirely different matter as they concern food spoilage and safety and I don't recommend you mess with them.

Index